Naming Grace

Naming Grace

*Preaching and the
Sacramental Imagination*

Mary Catherine Hilkert

CONTINUUM · NEW YORK

1998

The Continuum Publishing Company
370 Lexington Avenue, New York, NY 10017

Printed in the United States of America

Library of Congress Cataloging-in-Publication Data

Hilkert, Mary Catherine.
   Naming grace : preaching and the sacramental imagination / Mary Catherine Hilkert.
     p.   cm.
   Includes bibliographical references (p.) and index.
   ISBN 0-8264-1060-X (alk. paper)
   1. Preaching. 2. Catholic preaching. 3. Grace (Theology)
4. Sacraments. 5. Sacraments—Catholic Church. 6. Imagination—Religious aspects—Christianity. 7. Catholic Church—Doctrines.
8. Feminist theology.   I. Title.
BV4211.2.H47   1996
251—dc20   96–8907

To

my family,
especially my parents,
Mary Louise and William Albert Hilkert,

and to

the Order of Preachers,
sisters and brothers of Dominic, *praedicator gratiae,*
especially William J. Hill, O.P.

Contents

Preface

Theology, like preaching, emerges from the wisdom of many communities and conversations. While it is not possible to name all the individuals or groups who contributed to the insights in this book, I do want to express my appreciation to the Association of Theological Schools for the grant that supported the initial stages of research for the project and to the Katholieke Universiteit Leuven for hospitality during the fall semester, 1988. Key ideas for several chapters developed in the dialogue that followed lectures I was invited to deliver at the Atlantic School of Theology, Halifax, Nova Scotia; Saint John Seminary, Brighton, Massachusetts; the Center for Pastoral Leadership, Cleveland, Ohio; St. Paul Seminary School of Divinity, College of St. Thomas, St. Paul, Minnesota; Eden Theological Seminary, St. Louis; St. Meinrad School of Theology, St. Meinrad, Indiana; the Missouri Liturgical Conference; the annual meetings of the Midwest Association of Theological Schools, the Catholic Association of Teachers of Homiletics, and the St. Louis Theology Group; the opening conference of the Catholic Coalition on Preaching; the program for continuing education for priests and pastoral ministers in Adelaide, Australia; and the National Formation Ministry Programme in Pietermaritzburg, South Africa. I am grateful to all who participated in those sessions.

The chapters in this book were enriched considerably by years of collaboration and dialogue with faculty, students, administration, and staff at Aquinas Institute of Theology in St. Louis. Thanks to all my colleagues and students there from 1984 to 1995: "Great was the company of the preachers." For critique and suggestions on specific chapters, I am grateful to Joan Delaplane, Gregory Heille, Mary Margaret Pazdan, Edward Ruane, Frank Quinn, Catherine Vincie, Diane Kennedy, Charles Bouchard, Carla Mae Streeter, Marygrace Peters, Will Soll, Samuel Torvend, Thomas Brodie, Harry Byrne, Joseph Gillespie, Michael Demkovich, and Regina Siegfried.

I am also grateful for my new colleagues at the University of Notre Dame. Special thanks to those who read individual chapters and offered very helpful suggestions during the final stages of writing: Thomas O'Meara, Kathleen Cannon, Paul Philibert, James White, and Nathan Mitchell.

For their own creative theological work, their interest in and encouragement of this project, and critical reading of selected chapters, my deep gratitude goes to Kate Dooley, David Power, and especially Elizabeth Johnson. For their careful reading of portions of the manuscript, stimulating conversations about preaching, and many rich insights, I thank Colette Ackerman, Donald Cozzens, Thomas McKenna, Mary Maher, Ellen Murray, Mary Ann Nelson, and Jude Siciliano.

Both my experience of preaching and my interest in theological questions related to preaching took root in and have been consistently supported by the Order of Preachers. My special thanks to my religious congregation, the Dominican Sisters of Akron, Ohio, in particular, Janet Schlichting, Mary Ann Wiesemann, Diana Culbertson, Loretta Petit, Rosemarie Robinson, Elizabeth Ann Schaefer, and Bernadine Baltrinic. Thanks to the Dominican Leadership Conference, Siena Spirituality Center in Water Mill, New York, the promoters of preaching, and all those groups who have invited me to preach or to reflect with them on the charism of preaching and on women's role in the preaching ministry. Another group of "preachers," the members of St. Teresa of Avila parish in St. Louis, taught me in new ways what it means to believe in the God who "makes a way where there is no way."

My sincere appreciation to Justus George Lawler for his careful editing of the manuscript, his wise suggestions, and his patience with an author "in transition." Thanks, too, to Hank Schlau for attention to all the details of copyediting, and to Evander Lomke and Ulla Schnell and the staff at Continuum for their assistance in the publication process. Diane Steele and Elizabeth Dively, my graduate assistants, and the research librarians at the University of Notre Dame provided invaluable help in the final stages of preparing the manuscript.

William J. Hill, mentor, friend, and colleague, was the first to encourage my work on a theology of preaching, and his work in that area remains a source of learning and inspiration. My family has been another source of inspiration and a different kind of school for learning that concrete human experience is where we discover the mystery of grace. This book is dedicated to them with gratitude and affection.

July 22, 1996
Feast of Mary Magdalene

Grateful acknowledgment is given for permission to reprint material from the following journal articles of mine:

"Naming Grace: A Theology of Proclamation," *Worship* 60 (1986) 434–48.

"Retelling the Gospel Story: Preaching and Narrative," *Église et Théologie* 21 (1990) 147–67; copyright *Église et Théologie,* 1990; used with permission.

"Revelation and Proclamation: Shifting Paradigms," *Journal of Ecumenical Studies* 29, no. 1 (winter 1992) 1–23; copyright 1993.

"Women Preaching the Gospel," *Theology Digest* 33 (1986) 423–40.

"Words from the Future," *Liturgy* 11, no. 1 (1993) 17–27; copyright, the Liturgical Conference, 8750 Georgia Avenue, Suite 123, Silver Spring, Maryland 20910; all rights reserved; used with permission.

Introduction

On the whole, I do not find Christians, outside of the cata-
combs, sufficiently sensible of conditions. Does anyone have the
foggiest idea of what sort of power we so blithely invoke? Or,
as I suspect, does no one believe a word of it? The churches are
children playing on the floor with their chemistry sets, mixing
up a batch of TNT to kill a Sunday morning. It is madness to
wear ladies' straw hats and velvet hats to church; we should
all be wearing crash helmets. Ushers should issue life preservers
and signal flares; they should lash us to our pews. For the sleep-
ing god may wake someday and take offense, or the waking god
may draw us out to where we can never return.[1]

While that charge by Annie Dillard was directed to the entire mystery
of Christian worship, it applies equally well to the preaching event.
Almost twenty years ago *Time* magazine featured an article entitled
"American Preaching: A Dying Art?" The author's analysis of the
state of preaching in the United States at that time began as follows:

The Word became flesh, says John's Gospel of the incarnate
Christ of Bethlehem. In Christmas sermons before some 75 million Americans this week, words about Christ will become flesh
in the person of the preacher. Through their strange and marvelous craft, Christianity has been transmitted and reshaped for
every age since Christ himself went "preaching the Gospel of
the kingdom."

For many American churchgoers, though, a Sunday sermon
is something merely to be endured. Many preachers and parish-
ioners alike think that passionate and skillful preaching has
grown rarer and rarer in individual congregations in postwar
years. The chilling of the word is a major contribution to the
evident malaise in many large Protestant denominations these
days. For Roman Catholics, the sermon has not been as important, but rather a kind of spiritual hors d'oeuvre before the
Eucharist.[2]

The article then identified "seven star preachers" — none of them women, none of them operating in a team ministry, none of them indicating that they discover the word of God in the midst of their communities; all identified by the media as individual "stars."

In many ways the situation has not changed significantly since 1979. Even if Catholics in the post–Vatican II church might validly protest the caricature of preaching as a mere "hors d'oeuvre before the Eucharist," the concern about the "chilling of the word" is shared by all Christian denominations. Almost twenty-five years ago Paul VI identified the problem: "In our day, what has happened to that hidden energy of the good news which is able to have such a powerful effect on the human conscience? To what extent and in what way is that evangelical force capable of really transforming people of this century?"[3]

When preachers, pastors, or sociologists of religion gather to identify why there is not more energy surrounding the preaching of the church, questions of the theology and spirituality of preaching rarely are the focus of the discussion. Even the homiletic literature to date is very limited in those areas.[4] With all the pressing pastoral and social issues of our day, a book on the theology and spirituality of preaching may seem to be of only academic interest. Yet a 1988 sociological survey conducted among lay church members in four denominations in the United States — Episcopal, Lutheran, Methodist, and Roman Catholic — suggested otherwise.[5] In the survey, parishes or congregations were asked to list in order of priority their highest hopes and expectations from their church and then to rate those same items according to how successfully their expectations were met. All four denominations listed "preaching" as their first priority and the broad category of "spiritual life" as their second. When asked how successfully their church met their expectations, a significant number indicated their disappointment in both areas. The wager of this book is that one factor contributing to the blocking of the power of the gospel in our day is precisely our misunderstanding of where the word of God is located and who are the preachers of good news.

Most theologies of preaching to date have been developed from the perspective of the Reformation traditions, usually in neoorthodox categories that have highlighted the utter transcendence of God's word, the sinfulness of the human situation, and some form of law-gospel paradigm for preaching. When adopted by those from other religious traditions, the underlying theological assumptions often remain unexamined. Yet even when implicit, the preacher's fundamental theology, anthropology, christology, and ecclesiology are operative in the preaching event.

In an age of ecumenical dialogue and significant diversity within specific religious traditions, it becomes difficult to identify clear distinctions between Protestants and Catholics. David Tracy has suggested that the most significant differences may occur at the level of "imagination."[6] We might speak of two distinct Christian spiritualities that cannot be identified simply as Protestant and Catholic. The dialectical imagination stresses the distance between God and humanity, the hiddenness and absence of God, the sinfulness of human beings, the paradox of the cross, the need for grace as redemption and reconciliation, the limits and necessity for critique of any human project or institution including the church, and the not-yet character of the promised reign of God. The sacramental imagination (or what Tracy calls the analogical imagination) emphasizes the presence of the God who is self-communicating love, the creation of human beings in the image of God (restless hearts seeking the divine), the mystery of the incarnation, grace as divinizing as well as forgiving, the mediating role of the church as sacrament of salvation in the world, and the "foretaste" of the reign of God that is present in human community wherever God's reign of justice, peace, and love is fostered.

Proclaiming the good news of salvation is the mission shared by all Christian churches. Ecumenical divisions remain a scandal in our day precisely because in our divisions and disputes we fail to witness to the power of the Spirit to bring about reconciliation and unity. While our divisions are a genuine stumbling block to contemporary faith, the diversity of our religious traditions can be mutually enriching. To date, Catholics have not made many significant contributions to a theology of preaching, but the sacramental heritage can offer a number of rich resources and alternative perspectives in the contemporary ecumenical search for a more vital preaching of the gospel.[7]

Some of the more central theological convictions within the sacramental imagination that have distinct implications for the preaching ministry include: the goodness and redemption of creation, an incarnational christology, the presence and action of the Holy Spirit in the community of the church, the transformation of humanity by grace, the role of human cooperation in the process of salvation, and the relationship between word and sacrament. The significance of each of these accents for preaching becomes apparent in the chapters that follow.

The first two chapters contrast the theologies of revelation and proclamation of major figures who represent in classic ways the two distinct imaginations. Of particular interest to preachers are the focal questions: Is there a point of contact in human experience for the preaching of the gospel? Where does the preacher discover the word of God?

The theology of preaching proposed in chapter 3 begins not with the power of the divine word but with the presence of the Spirit mediated through creation and human experience. Nevertheless, if preachers are to announce the gospel of Jesus Christ and not "some other gospel," they must listen to human experience with an ear for "an echo of the gospel." Drawing on the human experience of "depth words," chapter 4 develops a sacramental theology of the word. Tempered by the critique of the dialectical imagination, however, the chapter describes the fundamental stories and symbols of the Christian faith as "words from the future" — God's promise, not human accomplishment.

Like the sacramental imagination's claim that the assembly is formed by liturgy, the dialectical imagination's conviction that the Christian assembly gathers to be shaped by the text can be dangerous. This is particularly true when dealing with passages that function as "texts of terror" for women, Jews, gays and lesbians, or whoever functions as the subordinated, rejected, or demonized "other." Chapter 5 calls for a hermeneutic of suspicion and a communal process of interpreting biblical texts that requires the discerning exercise of imagination that Sandra Schneiders calls "paschal" and Walter Brueggemann names "prophetic."[8]

The dialectical and sacramental imaginations diverge most dramatically on questions of theological anthropology. Can the human story or narratives drawn from other world religions be used to proclaim the Christian gospel, or is the good news of salvation to be discovered only in *the* story of Jesus Christ? Chapter 6 explores the theological grounds for narrative preaching from the perspective of the sacramental imagination's stress on the role of grace in human experience and an inclusivist incarnational christology.

The sacramental imagination's wager that grace is to be found in human experience reaches its limits when faced with the reality of suffering and evil. Chapter 7 maintains that preachers can "name grace" in human experience and history only if the sacramental imagination incorporates the central concerns of the dialectical imagination: the reality of sin, the hiddenness and even absence of God, the folly of the cross, and an eschatological hope that is truly radical.

If, as the sacramental imagination maintains, the word of God is entrusted to human communities of believers, there is always the danger of distortion of the gospel. From the earliest Christian era concerns have arisen regarding the authentic interpretation of the tradition. Two thousand years later in a variety of cultures many continue to question whether preachers are handing on "the essentials of the Christian faith." Chapter 8 suggests that liturgical preaching provides the paradigm for preaching that is at once biblical and doctrinal.

Here a contemporary stumbling block to the preaching of the gospel must be faced squarely. Can preaching remain biblical, liturgical, and doctrinal and at the same time be genuinely inclusive of the experience of women? Chapter 9 calls for attention to the biases — both traditional and contemporary — against women's preaching and leadership in the Christian assembly. The chapter further raises significant questions for all the Christian churches regarding the charism of preaching, the source of the authority to preach, and the relationship between ordination and preaching. The question of what is meant by "women's experience" is addressed in chapter 10 and leads into a fuller discussion of the way social location shapes the human experience of both preachers and hearers of the gospel.

The concluding chapter examines the vocation of those within the community who are given a specific charism and mission to preach and shows how the insights of both the dialectical imagination and the sacramental imagination are essential for a contemporary theology of preaching.

Chapter 1

The Dialectical Imagination: The Power of the Word

The profound "shaking of the foundations"[1] that has been occurring in both Catholic and Protestant theology in the twentieth century has crucial importance for an understanding of what is going on in the preaching event. Like all those engaged in ministry, preachers and professors of homiletics are searching for new and more effective modes of communication. For those in the preaching ministry that quest includes the search for "some new theoretical basis for homiletics in philosophical theology" according to David Buttrick, professor of homiletics at Vanderbilt Divinity School.[2] In his assessment, the field of homiletics is being radically affected not only by paradigm shifts in biblical criticism and the rise of hermeneutics and critical theory in foundational theology but also by major shifts in systematic theologies of revelation. Contemporary scholars, he notes, are "clearly breaking with the ruling neo-orthodoxy that has been with us for half a century."[3] The "aftershocks" of these major tremors are reshaping the terrain of contemporary preaching and promise even further upheaval in the future.

The field of homiletics has been particularly dependent on the "ruling neo-orthodoxy" because of the latter's rich theology of the word of God. Because of the lack of emphasis in their own tradition on a theology of the word and the ministry of preaching, Catholic preachers and teachers of homiletics who were searching to ground their preaching in the scriptures frequently turned to biblical theologies of the word developed by theologians in the neoorthodox tradition. This ecumenical influence has made a major contribution to the rebirth of vital biblical preaching in the Catholic tradition where, prior to the liturgical renewal of Vatican II, sacraments were emphasized as the locus of the encounter with God but preaching was often omitted from sacramental celebrations. However, there are fundamental differences in the theologies and spiritualities of the two traditions that can affect not only one's understanding of preaching but even the process of preparation of the homily and the dynamics of the actual preaching event.

Karl Barth

Because the neoorthodoxy that Buttrick describes as ruling (Protestant) theology for half a century is identified largely with Karl Barth, his theological and homiletic writings provide a helpful starting point for exploring the dialectical imagination.[4] Barth's criticism of anthropocentric liberal theology was directly related to his responsibility to preach the gospel in the pastoral ministry of the Swiss Reformed Church. His experience in ministry led Barth to reject the liberal view that located revelation within religious experience and history, a perspective in which he himself had been formed during his years of theological study at Berlin, Tübingen, and Marburg.

The main goal of the liberal tradition, whether associated with the German theologians with whom Barth was familiar, including Friedrich Schleiermacher, Albrecht Ritschl, Wilhelm Hermann, and Adolph von Harnack, or the American tradition of theological liberalism as represented by such figures as William Adams Brown, Horace Bushnell, and Walter Rauschenbusch, was, in the words of the famous American preacher Harry Emerson Fosdick, to make it possible to be both "an intelligent modern and a serious Christian."[5] The major historical and cultural shifts of the nineteenth century had resulted in religious alienation and a real inability to hear the proclamation of the gospel in the terms of either traditional Protestant orthodoxy or pietism/revivalism.[6] From Schleiermacher's *Speeches on Religion to Its Cultured Despisers* to Ralph Waldo Emerson's Harvard Divinity School address in 1838 or the preaching of Harry Emerson Fosdick at Riverside Church a century later, the concern of the liberal tradition of preachers was to find a point of contact in contemporary human experience and culture for the hearing of the Christian gospel.[7] For that reason liberal Protestant preaching would have more affinity with what is described in this book as the sacramental imagination than with the neoorthodox dialectical imagination.

David Jenkins has written that Barth's fundamental critique of Protestant liberal preaching was that when these "preachers spoke about God it sounded as though they were doing little more than speaking about humanity in a loud voice."[8] Barth's 1922 commentary on the Letter to the Romans has been described as "a bombshell" that divided the German theological world into "advocates and bitter detractors."[9] From Barth's perspective, the liberal failure to take seriously the extent to which sin has destroyed the image of God in humanity resulted in a fundamental misreading of the tragedy, terror, and despair of human existence and a related inability to perceive the radical "good news" of the "strange new world of the Bible" where God — not humankind — is at the center of reality. Barth writes:

The Bible tells us not how we should talk with God but what he says to us; not how we find the way to him, but how he has sought and found the way to us.... We have found in the Bible a new world, God, God's sovereignty, God's glory, God's incomprehensible love.[10]

Turning to the Protestant Reformers' touchstone, the Letter to the Romans, Barth rediscovered the wholly other, living God and the infinite qualitative difference between God and human beings. There can be no continuity between revelation and creation since creation as destroyed by sin reveals only God's "no." The hidden God (*Deus absconditus*) of Christian revelation can never be discovered directly in human history or experience, both of which are deeply scarred by sin.

Nevertheless, "while we were still sinners" God chose to be revealed in the paradox of the humanity of Jesus and the scandal of the cross. While there is no way from humanity to God, the way from God to humanity has been revealed in Jesus Christ, who came to deliver self-contradictory human beings from their slavery to sin. Yet God's self-revelation in Jesus remains indirect and veiled. In a world where sin continues to rule, the paradox of revelation remains always "in spite of." Barth writes:

That the promises of the faithfulness of God have been fulfilled in Jesus the Christ is not, and never will be, self-evident truth, since in Him it appears in its final hiddenness and its most profound secrecy.... In Jesus the communication of God begins with a rebuff, with the exposure of a vast chasm, with the clear revelation of a great stumbling-block.[11]

God's "triumph of grace" in freely turning toward humankind in reconciliation in and through Jesus Christ is the specific focus of Barth's later theological writings. In spite of the incarnational emphasis of this phase of Barth's writings, it remains clear that revelation is not to be sought or discovered directly within human history or creation. Rather, "the conception of an indirect revelation in nature, in history, and in our self-consciousness is destroyed by the recognition of grace, by the recognition of Jesus Christ as the eternal Word who was made flesh."[12]

For Barth, the "Word of God" refers strictly speaking to Jesus Christ, the incarnate Word, the sheer grace of God's reconciliation with us. Scripture, the written word of God, witnesses to the incarnate Word, since it is the record of salvation history that culminates in Jesus Christ. Barth admits that the Bible is the word of human beings and is historically and culturally conditioned. Nevertheless, he asserts that by the miracle of grace it is both human word and word of God when the Holy Spirit reveals the true meaning of a passage in terms of Jesus Christ. Barth cautions against the claim that the Bible *is* God's word; he prefers to emphasize that we have heard God's word and we hope to hear it again. Specifically the Bible becomes God's word when it is proclaimed and heard in the church in the power of the Spirit. When the word is the commission, theme, and judgment in preaching, in such a way that the Holy Spirit seizes the heart of the believer and summons the decision of conversion, then the words of the preacher become the word of God as well.

The implications of this neoorthodox theology, also known as "theology of the word of God," for a theology of proclamation are clearly drawn out by Barth in his classic *The Preaching of the Gospel* as well as in a number of essays, including "The Need and Promise of Christian Preaching."[13] In contrast to the liberal model, Barth is quite clear in his conviction that the proclamation of the gospel is not a matter of interpreting human experience (whether the preacher's or the congregation's) or human history religiously. Rather, the preacher's task is to announce what God has made known to us in Jesus Christ. As Barth insists: "Not general reflections on man and the cosmos, but Revelation is the only legitimate ground for preaching."[14] Revelation is totally God's action; the preacher is not to be seen even as mediator:

> It is not the function of the preacher to reveal God or to act as his intermediary. When the Gospel is preached, God speaks: there is no question of the preacher revealing anything or of a revelation being conveyed through him.... Revelation is a closed system in which God is the subject, the object, and the middle term.[15]

The preacher is the herald who bears witness to God's sovereign power and grace in Jesus Christ. When the proclamation of the word is true to revelation, the Spirit of God effects reconciliation and enables the human response of obedience to the word. Barth reminds us, however, that the relationship between humanity and God is "effected from on high by a divine miracle. [We are] not naturally disposed to hear the Word of God: we are children of wrath" (Eph 2:3).[16]

Rudolf Bultmann

Although his emphasis is significantly more anthropological than Barth's christological approach, Rudolf Bultmann is often grouped with Karl Barth and Emil Brunner in the paradigm of "dialectical theology" or "crisis theology" because of their common emphasis on divine transcendence and human sinfulness. Like Barth, Bultmann viewed revelation as the salvific encounter with the living God in the reconciling event of the cross and resurrection of Jesus Christ as made available to believers in and through the proclamation of the word of God. Through the preaching of the gospel in the power of the Spirit, hearers of the word are revealed to themselves as sinners and called to the conversion of authentic self-understanding through faith. Bultmann preferred to talk of *Heilsereignis* or *Heilsgeschehen* (salvation event) rather than what he perceived to be the mythological language of *Heilsgeschichte* (salvation history) in order to emphasize that God's saving grace breaks into human history in the preaching event. Underlining that revelation occurs precisely in and through the word, he remarked that "God encounters us at all times and in all places, but he cannot be seen everywhere unless his Word comes as well and makes the moment of revelation intelligible to us in its own light."[17]

Influenced by Martin Heidegger's existential philosophy, Bultmann disagreed with Barth on the crucial question of whether there is a "point of contact" in human experience for the preaching of the gospel. Convinced that there is no presuppositionless exegesis, Bultmann argued that the ultimate existential questions of human existence constitute the preunderstanding necessary for hearing and interpreting the gospel as a call to radical obedience, freedom, and trust. Nevertheless, he remained convinced that the cross and resurrection of Jesus provide the only ultimate answer to the questions of human existence. Thus the biblical texts continue to "call us up short" and challenge, expand, and even dismantle our limited human preunderstandings.

Bultmann's well-known concern for the demythologization of the biblical text and its remythologization in the categories of existential philosophy was at root a concern for the effective proclamation of the gospel. He feared that mythological language would become a false stumbling block preventing twentieth-century secular thinkers from attending to the true challenge of the "word of the cross" calling hearers to authentic existence. The revelatory event of preaching is intended to confront the hearer with a crisis not of understanding but of decision.

New Hermeneutic Theologians

The insights of dialectical theologians Karl Barth and Rudolf Bultmann, with their profound appreciation of the power of the word, were taken a step further by the group of theologians identified as post-Bultmannians or "the new hermeneutic theologians," notably Ernst Fuchs and Gerhard Ebeling. While Bultmann admitted that the word of God challenged and dismantled all human presuppositions, the new hermeneutic theologians stressed that "*the Word of God interprets and judges us* in delivering us from the grip of inauthenticity 'like a flash of lightning that strikes.' "[18] Building on dialectical theology's emphasis on the character of revelation as event, the new hermeneutic theologians developed a more philosophical approach to language, meaning, and the functioning of words.

Emphasizing the linguisticality of human existence, the post-Bultmannians focused on the language of a text and viewed the proclamation of the word not only as a salvation event, but precisely as a language event. Jesus, the Word made flesh, was described as the language event (Fuchs) or word event (Ebeling) that creates new possibilities of what it means to be human. The shift of the post-Bultmannians to the singular "hermeneutic" rather than the traditional "hermeneutics" was intended to signal their conviction that human interpreters do not use hermeneutical method to "figure out" a biblical text; rather, "The word interprets us." Rather than our "questioning of the text," the word of God calls our understanding of existence into question through the medium of the biblical text.

Influenced by Heidegger's later writings and the work of Hans-Georg Gadamer, the new hermeneutic theologians opposed philosophical efforts to explain being or ultimate reality. In contrast to the modern attempts to grasp, manipulate, and ultimately master reality, Heidegger and Gadamer encouraged a more contemplative stance of trusting that being reveals itself through language. The new hermeneutic theologians translated this philosophical conviction into theological terms: God expresses self through word. Stressing that revelation as the unveiling of mystery is sheer gift, the new hermeneutic theologians described the hermeneutical task as that of "dwelling in the word," "letting truth happen," "letting the word emerge," "waiting in trusting silence for a word that will be given." The role of the interpreter of the word is openness and submission to the self-disclosure of the word and obedience to its demands. Playing on the German expression for response or answer (*Ant-wort*) to the word (*Wort*), Fuchs emphasized that faith's response to the word is the result of the word having come to birth in us, making us responsible, creating us as witnesses.[19]

The theology of the new hermeneutic theologians offers a strong linguistic foundation for proclamatory preaching in which the text becomes a word event once again in and through the power of the Spirit. The christological focus on the power of the word to radically convert the human hearers of the gospel is the strength of this approach. However, the implicit anthropology in this perspective raises questions concerning the role of the preacher (we do not interpret the word; the word interprets us) and makes clear that grace is not to be viewed as a radical transformation of the human person or society.

Robert Funk underlines the dialectical approach to grace, sin, and anthropology that undergirds the new hermeneutical stance by contrasting the way the Pharisee and the publican respond to parables of grace. Sinners, says Funk, hear and understand parables of grace — grace interprets the sinner. Pharisees, however, insist on interpreting the word of grace rather than letting themselves be interpreted by the word. Two of Funk's five theses regarding the deeds and parables of grace reveal clearly the classic Reformation foundation of the new hermeneutic approach: (1) "Grace always wounds from behind — where we feel most vulnerable," and (2) "Grace is not something man can have at all."[20] P. J. Burns has summarized the relationship between grace and preaching in the new hermeneutic approach, highlighting the classic Reformation view of the human person as *simul justus et peccator*:

> Salvation comes to man — existing in his distorted relationship to a guilty past and a threatening future not as a liberated witness but as a crumpled-up question mark — through the concrete proclamation of the Word of God summoning him to faith. Faith is thus authentic human existence, healed linguisticality grounded in God.[21]

The theology of preaching that emerges from the Reformation traditions is classically described as a law-gospel hermeneutic. The preacher first diagnoses the human situation under the burden of God's law that we have not the power on our own to observe. The "first word" to be said about the human condition, Richard Lischer reminds us, is the "bad news" of our failure to live in fidelity to God's covenant, resulting in the condition of enmity with God. We are "children of wrath."[22] The primary task of the preacher, however, is to announce the good news that in and through the death and resurrection of Jesus Christ we are no longer "under the law"; rather we live in the freedom of the children of God. The dialectic of both judgment and grace (*simul justus et peccator*) remains the fundamental truth of the human situation. The final victory of God's grace over the sin of the world in the life, death, and resurrection of Jesus Christ, however, gives the final word to grace: "We preach life and death — with the advantage to life."[23]

Paul Tillich: A Bridge between the Dialectical and Sacramental Imaginations

Before contrasting the Catholic tradition's sacramental heritage with the dialectical Protestant emphasis on the word, one important Protestant theologian and preacher who drew from the resources of both traditions deserves mention: Paul Tillich. Tillich shared the neoorthodox critique of what he called "the bourgeois synthesis of liberal theology"[24] and emphasized the power of sin in his description of humanity's radical existential estrangement from our essential being. His theological method of correlation, however, was developed in explicit rejection of the Barthian kerygmatic approach that denied a point of contact in the human situation for the hearing of the gospel. As Tillich critically assessed this approach: "The message must be thrown at those in the situation — thrown like a stone."[25]

By way of contrast, Tillich's apologetic theology took seriously the need for theology to be in dialogue with its historical and cultural situation and urged that mediation between religion and culture need not involve uncritical adaptation. Convinced that religion is the depth dimension that reveals what is of "ultimate concern" or gives unconditional meaning to human life, Tillich asserted that both theology and preaching should begin with an analysis of the human situation. Although human beings are estranged from God in the concrete existential situation, the divine and the human can never be separated because God is the very ground of being. Existential analysis of the human situation, Tillich suggested, reveals structures of anxiety, conflict, doubt, and guilt and discloses the ultimate human question to which the gospel responds: "the question of a reality in which the self-estrangement of our existence is overcome, a reality of reconciliation and reunion, of creativity and meaning and hope."[26] Yet while philosophical and/or psychological analysis can bring to light ultimate human questions and the fundamental human need for grace, only the power of New Being in Jesus the Christ can reconcile the fundamental estrangement and alienation in human existence.

Tillich's apologetic method of communicating the Christian message, whether in theology or preaching, begins with an analysis of the predicament of human beings that highlights both the estrangement from our own deepest truth ("the old eon") and the potential latent in the present crisis, a potential that Tillich describes in one of his sermons as openness for "the creative moment which may appear in the midst of what seemed to be waste."[27] The "eternal now" of God's reconciling grace, the healing of our fundamental alienation, is offered paradoxically, Tillich reminds us, in the present moment of existence "while we are still sinners." Thus an existential crisis is also a moment of grace in which the challenge to radical courage in the face of doubt, despair, death, or even nonbeing is extended to believers in and through the symbols of Christian faith.

If the good news of salvation is to be heard today, however, contemporary reinterpretation of those symbols in a way that highlights their revelatory possibility to evoke an awareness of God's offer of courage and hope in the present moment is crucial. Like Bultmann, Tillich remained convinced that the apparent crisis of faith for many contemporary believers was rather a crisis of culture and language. Thus he argued:

> Many of those who reject the Word of God reject it because the way we say it is utterly meaningless to them. They know the dimension of the eternal but they cannot accept our names for it. If we cling to their words, we may doubt whether they have received a word from the Lord. If we meet them as persons, we know they have.[28]

The task of the preacher, the theologian, or any minister of the word is first to help people to recognize their human situation in its depth dimensions — to "open up an empty space in the soul"[29] — and then to interpret the biblical symbols and Christian message in a way that reveals the religious response to that empty space, the real power of New Being available in and through Jesus the Christ.[30] Revelation occurs when the dialogical relationship between the preacher and listeners evokes an awareness of God's presence for those who embrace the challenge of "the courage to be."[31] Tillich concurred with Bultmann's judgment that the categories of existential psychology are the most productive for creative contemporary reappropriation of the biblical message. Thus in his preaching he consistently reinterpreted the central Christian symbols in existential terms, speaking of sin as separation, estrangement, or sickness and of grace as reunion, reconciliation, and health.

In his emphasis on the negative moment within any description of the relationship between the divine and the human, in his insistence on the paradox of "the abounding of sin and the greater abounding of grace" as "the two all-determining facts of life,"[32] as well as in his underscoring of the ambiguous, estranged, and broken dimensions of human existence, Tillich remained rooted in the dialectical imagination. Yet in identifying the possibility that the gracious presence of God is disclosed within the created and the human[33] and in his method of apologetic theology and preaching that searches for a point of contact in the human situation for the revelation of God, Tillich revealed dimensions of the sacramental imagination more frequently associated with the Catholic theologians to whom we now turn.

Chapter 2

The Sacramental Imagination: Grace Enfleshed in Word and Action

It is in terms of anthropology that the dialectical and sacramental imaginations diverge most dramatically. The 1983 ecumenical break-through statement from the U.S. Lutheran–Roman Catholic dialogue on justification by faith highlights the theological differences in this area:

> The Lutheran hermeneutical understanding of justification by faith in some ways heightens the tension with Catholic positions. It does so by excluding from the gospel proclamation all reference to the freedom and goodness of fallen human beings on the ground that this would undermine the unconditionality of God's promises in Christ.... Theological disagreement about the structure of thought in relation to proclamation of the gospel, though serious, need not be church-dividing.[1]

While contrasting emphases in theological anthropology need not be church-dividing, disputes about the relationship between sacraments and preaching as well as scripture and tradition were central to differences between the Reformers and the Roman Catholic Church at the time of the Reformation. The belief that God, rather than the human interpreter, was the source of grace in the preaching event had been accepted throughout the Christian tradition. In scholastic language, Thomas Aquinas described God as the principal cause, while the apostles and preachers were the instrumental cause, of preaching.[2] In the polemical context of the Reformation, however, in order to defend the validity and necessity of the sacraments against the Reformers, who emphasized the power of the preached word, most scholastic theologians began to make a new distinction: the principal cause of preaching was a human cause, while the principal cause in the sacraments was God; therefore, only the sacraments could be said to "confer grace." Disputes about the efficacy of the proclaimed word and the relationship between sacraments and preaching dominated Catholic theological writings about preaching well into the twentieth century. Various authors proposed that preaching brings about faith, but not sanctifying grace, and argued that preaching cannot be considered an eighth sacrament.

Further, the Catholic emphasis on tradition (usually understood prior to Vatican II as church teaching) resulted in an implicit propositional and doctrinal understanding of revelation. From the time of the Roman catechism commissioned by the Council of Trent, a systematic presentation of Catholic doctrine was presumed to provide the best guide to preaching. Bishops and priests, who were the only official preachers, were encouraged to explain the church's doctrines in a pastoral way that would draw believers more deeply into the whole mystery of faith. Nevertheless, by the twentieth century preaching had become merely "the vulgarization of theological tracts" in the estimation of Josef Jungmann.[3] The major Catholic theologian to address that situation through rethinking the theology of revelation, and specifically the relationship between word and sacrament, was Karl Rahner.

Karl Rahner

Rahner's influence on Vatican II's Dogmatic Constitution on Revelation was considerable. Titled *Dei Verbum* (The word of God), that document shifted Catholic theology beyond a post-Tridentine and Vatican I propositional approach to revelation as a body of authoritative doctrines toward a relational, incarnational, sacramental, and trinitarian perspective rooted in the biblical conviction that "God is love." If God, in God's very being, *is* self-communicating love, and if God has freely chosen to extend to humanity the possibility of divine friendship, then, Rahner suggests, humanity must be structured as openness or desire to receive that offer of love. The explicit social and historical mediation of that love (grace) is necessary precisely because human beings are constituted as body-spirit. As spirit-in-the-world, the human person can experience an invitation at the spiritual depth dimension of existence (transcendental pole) only insofar as that offer is mediated or made known in and through the social, tangible, and concrete manifestations of one's body, one's relationships, the events that constitute one's history, and the world in which one lives (categorical pole). Like all free personal self-communication, God's proffer of grace requires the word to reveal (unveil) definitively the offer of relationship. Thus Rahner argues that God's self-offer, which has remained anonymous or ambiguous throughout human history and creation, came to the explicitness of word in the Hebrew prophets and to the definitive and irrevocable pledge of God's love for humanity in the Word-made-flesh, Jesus.

Using the incarnation as the key with which to interpret all of reality, Rahner proposes that all reality is structured symbolically — signs of grace are to be found everywhere if one has "eyes to see." Here Rahner opposes the emphasis of a word-event theology by insisting that the word of proclamation or the sacramental word is not an event breaking into one's "guilty past and threatening future." Rather, he argues that "grace is *here*. It is present wherever we are. It can always indeed be seen by the eye of faith and be expressed by the word of the message."[4]

In his approach to the once-neglected theology of the word in the Catholic tradition, Rahner, like the new hermeneutic theologians, draws on the resources of the later Heidegger, but from an anthropological foundation that views creation and human existence as fundamentally graced. Granting that sin has profoundly altered human life, Rahner nonetheless remains convinced of the Pauline claim that "where sin abounds, grace abounds still more" (Rom 5:20). The significance of this very different anthropological foundation for Rahner's approach to the word-as-symbol and the event-character of "grace come to word" is underscored in his essay "Priest and Poet." There he writes:

> Only a Protestant and a theologian of the most extreme dialectical obscurity could maintain that the divine, grace, redemption, and our new freedom, light and the love of God remain so much in the beyond that one can experience nothing at all of them in this world; that on the contrary all human discourse witnesses to the word and to the reality of God only by its character of absolute paradox.[5]

In contrast, Rahner, speaking from a sacramental perspective, emphasized the continuity between creation and redemption and the openness of humanity to the divine. Human beings are structured from creation as "hearers of the Word"; while sin has affected, it has not destroyed, the image of God within humanity. Thus Rahner could make a claim that contrasts sharply with the dialectical perspective: "Preaching is the awakening and making explicit of what is already there in the depths of [the person], not by nature but by grace."[6] Ultimately Rahner's theology of revelation and his theological anthropology are inseparable, and both contribute to his conviction that the word announces the grace that is already there in the depths of the person and in the midst of human history and creation.

The close connection between anthropology and grace in Rahner's thought allowed him to locate the word of God within the primordial words that emerge from the depth of the human heart. Reflecting on the connections between the vocation of the poet and that of the priest (and by extension, the preacher), Rahner contrasted human words that simply convey information (technical or utility words) with "depth words," which he calls "living words" or "gifts of God." "They bring light to us, not we to them," Rahner remarked.[7] While citing explicitly the influence of the later Heidegger here, Rahner parted company with the word-event theology of the new hermeneutic theologians in claiming that these primordial words "spring up out of our hearts" precisely because of the call to grace located at the depths of the human heart from the first moment of existence (the supernatural existential). With that understanding of the human as graced, Rahner could assert that "the primordial words of human beings transmuted by the Spirit of God are allowed to become words of God."[8] Human words have the potential to become sacraments of divine love.

Human words spoken from the center of ourselves (words like "I love you"; "I have a dream"; or "Here I stand; I can do no other") are in a profound sense revelatory — they allow a deeper dimension of reality to emerge. These kind of "depth words" are not merely signs that point to a reality that exists independently of the naming. Rather, in a public, conscious, historical way, these words "embody" the deeper spiritual reality from which they emerge. Primordial words become sacraments — they function as symbols that allow a deeper mystery, the offer of grace, to become more concretely present and available in human life.

Rahner's understanding of the roles of scripture and explicit preaching as words of the church's faith and identity becomes clear only within the larger context of his treatment of the church as sacrament in his vast schema of "a world of grace."[9] The self-communication of God in love has an intrinsically incarnational structure — it is oriented toward the fullness of its expression in embodied word. God has spoken throughout creation and history "in varied and fragmentary ways," as the Letter to the Hebrews states, but only in Jesus, the Word of God incarnate, has God spoken God's own self-expression. Jesus, the Word made flesh, became the primordial sacrament of God in the midst of human history. As the ongoing body of Christ in the world, the church participates in the abiding sacrament of Christ to the extent that the church embodies, speaks, and acts upon the grace and truth of Jesus Christ. Preaching and the sacraments, preeminently the eucharist, function as the church's self-expression through naming, proclaiming, and celebrating the mystery of God's salvific self-offering of love in the life, death, and resurrection of Jesus.[10]

While he never worked out a fully developed theology of preaching, it is clear that for Rahner, the preaching of the gospel must necessarily connect people's ordinary experience with the presence of God in their lives. The mystery of grace has been revealed both throughout the history of salvation culminating in Christ (as recorded in the scriptures) and within the depths of the human heart (in and through the power of the Spirit). The role of the preacher is to bring the depth dimension of the mystery of human existence as God's self-offer of love to explicit expression through interpreting that experience in light of the scriptures, the liturgy, and the whole of the Christian tradition. Thus preaching draws the hearers of the word into a deeper relationship with God that is at the same time a deeper experience of their everyday human life and relationships as graced.[11]

Edward Schillebeeckx

Edward Schillebeeckx, who shares Rahner's concern for the proclamation of the gospel in the contemporary world, has, like Rahner, located revelation within human experience. In pointing to experience as the locus of revelation, however, Schillebeeckx locates revelation not in the transcendental depths of the human person but rather in history. *Human* history, he notes, always involves interpreted experience. The very structure of human experience might be described as revelatory according to Schillebeeckx, since human beings learn by a process of discovery. We are born into a world of language and culture that provides us with frameworks for interpreting our experience. Yet new experiences can and do expand, revise, and even break down our previous frameworks for perceiving the world. New experience frequently challenges the former horizons of our world and adds new dimensions to our living tradition of experience.

Expanding on this idea, Schillebeeckx observes that experience has a narrative structure. Here he stresses that experience is shared; meaning is communicated through words and stories. Traditions, formed from collective experience, become the social framework for understanding. We are born into multiple traditions of shared meaning — our family, ethnic, and racial traditions; the values and stories of our religions (or the "religion" of secular humanism); the myths, symbols, and values of our nation; and so on. Further, when we want to share an experience of great significance, we ordinarily "tell the story" of what happened to us. Through narrative, we are able to offer others the possibility of interpreting their own past history in such a radically new way that they truly experience themselves and their lives differently.

In the midst of our ordinary daily lives, certain events or experiences provide a kind of "gestalt shift" in the way in which we live and understand ourselves and the world. Whether suddenly or gradually, something unexpected happens in which, upon reflection, we recognize deeper dimensions of ourselves and reality. We reach the boundaries and limits of human experience in moments of love or joy or insight that seem so profound that secular language is no longer adequate to express the depths of meaning we have experienced. We also reach the limits of human language and understanding in the negative experiences of human suffering, injustice, and death when we know the "pain of contrast" with our hopes for salvation or for "fullness of life." Human life then appears ultimately absurd or cruel, and reality itself random, if not malicious.

Forged consciously in the face of immense global suffering, Schillebeeckx's conviction that revelation occurs within, yet transcends, human experience focuses particularly on negative experiences of injustice or apparent meaninglessness, raising the question of God's presence in apparent absence or even in the midst of evil. Here

Schillebeeckx argues that God is to be encountered not directly (in unmediated presence or as willing or even permitting evil) but rather "on the underside" or "in contrast." God is present to the majority of the world's population in the way God was present to Jesus in the crucifixion — as the source of endurance and hope in the darkness and apparent abandonment and as the promise to be the faithful "God of the living" that was realized in the resurrection's final defeat of the forces of evil.

While Schillebeeckx has not developed his own contemporary theology of preaching, implications for proclamation flow directly from both his theology of revelation and his christological writings. In *Jesus: An Experiment in Christology* and *Christ: The Experience of Jesus as Lord,* Schillebeeckx insists that in our day christology needs to adopt a narrative-practical approach — a retelling of the story of Jesus that moves its hearers to "go and do likewise."[12] In speaking the word of faith of the community, even or perhaps especially in the midst of suffering, persecution, or the experienced absence of God, the preacher names the creative presence of God to be found in "fragments of salvation" and in "hidden revelation." The "fragments" that the preacher identifies as salvation experiences are to be found in the hope that emerges in the most hopeless of situations, the protest that rebels in the name of all that is human, and the persevering trust that clings to God even when God seems distant or absent. The community's hope proclaimed by the preacher is grounded in the resurrection of Jesus. There Jesus' own trust in God in the face of the ultimate rejection of the crucifixion was confirmed and vindicated as God brought life and a new future even out of death. Living in the spirit of the risen Jesus, the Christian community proclaims the hope of new possibilities even in the most hopeless of human situations. In continuity with the biblical experience, the preacher announces that "in our human experiences we can *experience* something that transcends our experience and proclaims itself in that experience as unexpected grace."[13] The preacher speaks the word of God in naming the community's experience in faith of that unexpected grace in ordinary human history.

In a unique blending of the sacramental imagination's insight that grace is to be discovered in human history and experience with the dialectical caution that sin and suffering abound and God remains a "hidden God," Schillebeeckx returns to the shared conviction that only "the eyes of faith" enable us to see God's presence in a world that often stands "in contrast" to the promise that God is "God of the living." The conviction that, despite all the evidence to the contrary, the compassion of God is at the center of reality is ultimately an experience available only within the language of faith.[14] Thus Schillebeeckx rejects as a false dichotomy the question of whether "faith comes from hearing" (Rom 10:17) or faith begins with experience. The Christian story that is now recorded in the scriptures, he notes, began with an interpreted experience — the experience of salvation from God in Jesus. Further, that story can be passed on to others only if it remains the living experience of a community of believers who continue to hand on the story in a vital way that addresses the experience of others. As Schillebeeckx reminds us: "Christianity is not a message which has to be believed but an experience of faith which becomes a message. Then, as an explicit message, it seeks to offer a new possibility of life experience to others who hear it within their own experience of life."[15] Again this would suggest for preachers that "announcing the good news of salvation" means not only proclaiming "God's wonderful deeds" in the past history of salvation but also performing the prophetic task of pointing to the continued workings of the Spirit of God in our present day. The preacher is called to tell the Christian story in such a way that people can recognize the experience of grace — God's presence — in their everyday lives. Another way of approaching the role of preaching then is that the preacher interprets the human story in light of the story of Jesus and the story of Israel.[16]

As Schillebeeckx's book *Jesus* makes clear, however, the preaching of the gospel can never be done only in words. Jesus announced the reign of God not only in his teaching and preaching but also by inviting sinners and outcasts to the shared intimacy of table. He proclaimed mercy and healing in touching lepers and entering the homes and the lives of the sick and grieving. He spoke of justice and of God's revisioning of the social order in his relationships with women and Samaritans and the poor. The story of hope in human history is a narrative that must be told ultimately with human lives if it is to be heard as credible. Precisely because the Christian message is a living tradition of grace — the mystery of God-among-us — it must be handed on through the lived experience of the community as well as through word. Proclamation interprets the life of discipleship, but the community's shared discipleship embodies the proclamation. In fact, Schillebeeckx remarks that

Christians should have the right to use the word God only
where they find their identity through their identification with
life which is still unreconciled and in their actual attempts at
reconciliation. What is promised to us in the story which the
church tells us about Jesus is disclosed precisely in this praxis
in conformity to the message of Jesus.[17]

Further, precisely because we claim the gospel is universal salvation — good news for every time and culture — the gospel must be
proclaimed authentically in the uniqueness of every time and culture.
New dimensions of the story that Schillebeeckx calls "new memories
of Jesus" emerge as the proclamation of the gospel is heard in the
voices of women and children, from the context of South Africa and
Asia, in the life-stories of African-American, Native American, and
Hispanic communities, in the struggles of refugees and those who offer sanctuary and resist structural injustice. In every new situation
Christian communities are called to proclaim the "fifth gospel" with
their lives.

Liberation Perspectives

Schillebeeckx's emphasis on the role of the community's praxis in
handing on the Christian tradition and on inculturation as the major
hermeneutical challenge for those who would announce the gospel
in the twentieth century reflects the way his own theological perspective has been affected by the voices emerging from the third world[18]
and particularly from liberation theologians. In the Catholic context,
liberation theology emerged in the late 1960s in Latin America. In
1968, the year Gustavo Gutiérrez published his first article using the
term "liberation theology," the Latin American Episcopal Conference met in Medellín, Colombia, and issued a prophetic message that
affirmed the core of any theology of liberation. The bishops called
for an understanding of the good news of Jesus Christ as a call for
consistent commitment to the poor, the hungry, and the oppressed,
who constitute the nameless majority of the Latin American population. The Medellín documents go on to describe the institutional
violence and the exploitative relations of dependency in the Latin
American social situation and to point to the need for cultural and
economic liberation. Several years later, in his now-classic book, *A*

Theology of Liberation, Gutiérrez described the project of liberation theology as

> an attempt at reflection, based on the Gospel, and the experiences of men and women committed to the process of liberation in the oppressed and exploited land of Latin America. It is a theological reflection born of the experience of shared efforts to abolish the current unjust situation and to build a different society, freer and more human.[19]

Given that context, Latin American liberation theologians underline the 1971 statement by the Synod of Bishops that "action on behalf of justice and participation in the transformation of the world fully appear to us as a constitutive part of preaching the gospel."[20] Liberating praxis, rather than reflection on existential questions, becomes the preunderstanding necessary for both the hearing and the proclaiming of the gospel. The liberating word of the gospel cannot be separated from liberating praxis; rather, it is precisely commitment to, and involvement in, action on behalf of justice and peace that enables one to hear the good news in all its power and truth.

This new hearing of the gospel from the experience of the powerless[21] makes clear that identification with Jesus' preaching of the reign of God, his respect for the dignity of every human person, and his particular compassion for the marginalized of his society has very real political and social consequences for those who would preach the "good news of salvation" in our day. Catechists and other ministers of the word who foster base communities centered on the word of God in politically repressive situations are profoundly aware of the connection of Jesus' death with his prophetic preaching and liberating lifestyle. The scriptures cannot be faithfully proclaimed if conversion of heart is separated from commitment to transformation of concrete political, social, and ecclesiastical structures that continue to impoverish, oppress, or marginalize God's people. Just as Jesus' preaching caused conflict and met rejection, so will the preaching of a church that is faithful to the vision of the reign of God that he preached. Yet as Oscar Romero, the archbishop from El Salvador who was assassinated by government soldiers during the celebration of the eucharist, once preached:

> A church that doesn't provoke any crisis, a gospel that doesn't unsettle, a word of God that doesn't get under anyone's skin,

a word of God that doesn't touch the real sin of the society in which it is being proclaimed, what gospel is that? Very nice, pious considerations that don't bother anyone, that is the way many would like preaching to be. Those preachers who avoid every thorny matter so as not to be harassed, so as not to have conflicts and difficulties, do not light up the world they live in.... The gospel is courageous; it's the good news of him who came to take away the world's sins.[22]

Highlighting this prophetic dimension of preaching and the transformative power of grace from a liberation perspective, Leonardo Boff remarks that

[i]n its prophecy the Church is judge, in the light of the revealed Word, of the sociohistorical reality into which it is inserted. The Church proclaims God's design, and denounces anything that opposes that design. In its pastoral ministry the Church animates the Christian life, coordinates the various tasks incumbent on the Christian, creates the vital synthesis between Gospel and life, and joyfully celebrates the presence of the grace that sets men and women free.[23]

While many liberation theologians describe the liberating word as transformative of sinful social structures, that perspective can overlook the complexity that comes with the claim of the sacramental imagination that revelation can be discovered also in human experience and culture. More representative of that perspective is the assertion of Brazilian Carlos Mesters that it is impossible to separate the Bible, the life of the community, and the sociopolitical realities of the surrounding world. In a brief article entitled "Life Is the Word— Brazilian Poor Interpret Life," Mesters avoids locating the word of God only or primarily within the scriptures. Rather, he cites the central conviction of basic Christian communities: "[T]he Word of God is within reality and it can be discovered there with the help of the Bible."[24] Precisely because of the conviction that God's word is spoken also in the experience of people's lives, liberation theologians remark that preaching is most effective when members of the community are encouraged to tell their own stories. The focus is on the word of God heard in community reflection on daily life and political struggles in light of the scriptures, rather than on the proclamation of an individual preacher or priest.

Liberation theologies are not to be limited, of course, to either Latin America or the Catholic tradition. In fact the emphasis on the sinful social situation and the transforming word of God is more characteristic of the dialectical imagination than of the sacramental perspective. However, characteristic threads of the Catholic perspective that have implications for a theology of preaching are evident in liberation theology's stress on grace operative in and through the human, the role of human praxis as cooperation in God's transformation of the world, hearing the word of God in community, and the location of God's word of revelation in the life struggles of the community as well as in the scriptures.

A difficulty with the focus on the scriptures as the liberating word of God, however, comes from third world women doing theology. They note that while "the poor find that the Word reaffirms in a clear and direct way that God is with them in their fight for life,... women find clear, explicit cases of the marginalization or segregation of women in... both Old and New Testaments."[25] As the word of God in human words, the scriptures contain sinful human perspectives as well as the revelatory word of God, and all too frequently the two have been identified. In the Catholic tradition and beyond, feminist liberation theologians are calling for an expansion of the fundamentally critical perspective of liberation theology: the "good news of salvation" can be heard and proclaimed only by communities actively committed to overcoming all forms of sin that block the reign of God — including patriarchy.[26]

Feminist liberation theologies, while plural and diverse,[27] find common ground in the concern for justice and specifically in opposition to whatever diminishes the dignity of women and children as well as of men and to whatever destroys the flourishing of all creation. The critique of patriarchy includes critical analysis not only of the dynamics of sexism but also of the interrelated dynamics of racism, classism, heterosexism, and anthropocentrism. While emphasizing that women as well as men are created in the "image of God" and that all baptized Christians, whether female or male, are baptized into "the image of Christ," recent feminist theology explicitly includes all living creatures and the earth in its circle of concern.[28] Extending the focus of liberation theology on the poor and the marginalized, ecofeminist Christian theology includes the suffering of all creatures and the wounded earth within the scope of salvation. Further, if "the footprints of the Trinity" are to be discovered throughout creation (Augustine), the "mysteries of the universe" offer abundant resources for preachers to recover the doctrine of creation and discover ways to preach the "good news of salvation" that go beyond the human story.[29]

Beyond their critical work, feminist and ecological theologians are embracing the most fundamental theological task: exploring and articulating the interconnectedness of all of creation in relation to the mystery of God. From a variety of perspectives, they are rediscovering that relationality is at the heart not only of human life and of the creation story but of the very mystery of God.[30] A number of feminist theologians, including some who identify more clearly with dialectical thought,[31] find real affinities with the sacramental imagination's emphasis on the goodness of creation and the body;[32] the location of revelation in creation, history, and human experience;[33] the creation of human beings in the "image of God";[34] the importance of incarnation and divinization as well as redemption; the mediation of grace through human persons and communities;[35] the central role of ritual and symbols in human and Christian life;[36] and the essential connections between liturgy and life.

Suffering, injustice, and the "groaning of all creation" are stark realities, indeed the starting point, for liberation theologians, including feminist and ecological liberation theologies.[37] In that sense the dialectical imagination always critiques and tempers the sacramental vision. But together with Hispanic/Latino,[38] African-American,[39] and other forms of liberation theology, feminist and ecological theologies broaden as well as concretize the basic focus of the sacramental imagination on "liberating grace."[40] From diverse social locations, voices of suffering and hope challenge preachers to grapple with the concrete cultural situation in which they preach. The mystery of God is to be found in human experience, but human experience never occurs in the abstract. No two stories of human suffering are alike. So, too, every story of the triumph of hope or courage is unique. Preachers are called to listen to both and to analyze the situations that give rise to those stories, if they are to discover Paul's claim enfleshed: "[W]here sin increased, grace abounded all the more" (Rom 5:20).

Thus, as we have seen from a variety of perspectives, both the dialectical imagination and the sacramental imagination have a contribution to make in the contemporary ecumenical search for a more adequate understanding of the preaching event. The word of God does indeed create a new context for human life and bring about radical conversion, but it is also true that "the Holy Spirit runs ahead of the preacher" (Rahner) and dwells within creation and human history, "renewing the face of the earth." The next three chapters propose a theology of preaching (chapter 3) and a theology of the word (chapters 4 and 5) that are rooted in the sacramental imagination but that also recognize the essential contribution of dialectical theology to the proclamation of the gospel.

Chapter 3

Preaching as the Art of Naming Grace

Peter's preaching following the cure of the crippled beggar in Acts 3 is often cited as a classic example of early Christian preaching.[1] When the model sermon in Acts 3:12–26 is relocated in the broader context of the chapter, new dimensions of the mystery of preaching emerge from the perspective of the sacramental imagination. Rather than beginning with emphasis on the power of the proclaimed word to transform sinful humanity, we might reflect on preaching as the art of naming grace found in the depths of human experience.

Within the larger context of Acts 3, some essential dimensions of preaching and preparation for preaching come into focus even before Peter speaks a word. As the passage opens, two disciples are going to the temple to pray. They stop and give their attention to a crippled beggar who has been relegated to the margins of their social and religious world. The hearer of the word calls out to them and expects to get something. The preachers recognize their own poverty: they have nothing of value to offer except the name of Jesus. Trusting the power of that name, not only does Peter speak a word of healing, but also he acts with compassion: he "took him by the right hand and raised him up, and immediately his feet and ankles were made strong" (Acts 3:7). The salvation that the preacher announces in word has already been made tangible and visible in deed. Before a word is spoken, the disciples of Jesus have already proclaimed the power of the resurrection in healing touch and in the community's attention to the needs of the world, especially to those whose well-being is most threatened. The result of this "preaching in praxis" is the very kind of conversion that is the goal of all preaching: freedom, wholeness, reconciliation, and human flourishing that overflows in joy and praise.

Only after preaching through concrete action does Peter deliver his formal sermon. He starts with the concrete event the community has just witnessed: "People of Israel, why do you wonder at this? Why do you stare at us as though by our own power or piety we had made him walk?" (Acts 3:12). First, Peter describes the experience of salvation that has happened in their midst, and only then does he speak of the power of God. That is the art of any ministry of the word: to speak the name of God neither too soon nor too late. As preacher, Peter interprets what has been operative in the depths of the community's human experience; he points to the power and presence of God. He names grace.

Yet the word of truth is also a word of judgment — a point the dialectical imagination urges upon all those who would speak of "cheap grace." The human heart and the human community give evidence not only of the call to grace but also of "the invitation to betray."[2] Yielding to the power of evil, human beings can live not as a community of grace but as "people of the lie."[3] A consistent pattern in all the preaching events in the Acts of the Apostles is evident in this passage: the preacher announces God's constant offer of life in the face of human rejection. Thus Acts 3:13–15 states: "[T]he God of our ancestors has glorified his servant Jesus, whom you handed over and rejected in the presence of Pilate, though he had decided to release him. But you rejected the Holy and Righteous One and asked to have a murderer given to you, and you killed the Author of Life, whom God raised from the dead."

Preaching announces that God has defeated the power of sin and death in the resurrection, but this good news is also a call to repentance and conversion. Christian conversion always involves a twofold movement: the turn toward God (which is also a turn toward the human community, toward all of creation, and toward one's own deepest truth) and the turn away from sin (from living as "people of the lie," as less than fully human).[4] The final word of the preaching event is not a word of judgment, however; nor does the preacher leave the community in a state of temporary awe and amazement. Rather, preaching is an invitation to follow; it is a word of hope rooted in God's promise. Preachers announce a word of life that empowers the conversion it demands.

The passage from Acts also reveals the most fundamental identity of preachers as witnesses to the resurrection giving testimony with their lives, not only with their words. Preachers do not simply retell a

word & deed must match = dabar
full or empty
not wrong or right

story from the past, not even the story of the death and resurrection of Jesus. Rather, preachers point to the power of the resurrection here and now in concrete human lives: "[The name of Jesus] itself has made this man strong, *whom you see and know;* and the faith that is through Jesus has given him this perfect health *in the presence of all of you*" (Acts 3:16). Or as the opening prayer for the liturgy of Christmas Day announces: "*This* day a Savior is born in your midst." The sacramental imagination celebrates the mystery of God's presence here and now, summoning creation to a new future.

Incarnation and the Sacramental Imagination

Rarely do either preachers or hearers of the word experience the kinds of dramatic preaching or conversions described in the Acts of the Apostles. Contemporary assemblies of believers seldom are moved to exclaim like the disciples at Emmaus: "Were not our hearts burning within us?" (Luke 24:32). One factor contributing to the blocking of the power of the good news may be a lack of understanding on the part of both preachers and hearers of what is really going on in the preaching event.

As noted in chapter 1, most fully developed theologies of preaching have been constructed either in terms of a biblical theology of the word or in terms that highlight the transcendence of God's word and the radical effect of sin on the human condition. Many would agree with Richard Lischer's analysis: "Any theology that takes the Word of God seriously must reckon with its greatest source of embarrassment: the Word must be spoken and received by sinful human beings."[5] But as chapter 2 suggested, it is precisely at this point that a contribution to the growing ecumenical discussion of the theology of preaching might be made from a Catholic perspective that views grace as active in and through humanity and describes revelation in sacramental terms. Grounded in the conviction that sin never completely destroyed the created goodness of humanity, the sacramental tradition responds affirmatively to the debate initiated by Emil Brunner as to whether there is a "point of contact" in human experience for preaching the gospel of grace. The Catholic tradition has stressed that grace effects a real inner transformation of the human person. Karl Rahner has taken the insight even further in his claim that human beings always stand within the call to grace, God's offer of friendship. Human persons are constituted as "hearers of the word."

Because human beings are essentially embodied and social, however, grace as the spiritual mystery at the heart of reality has to be manifested in concrete, historical, visible ways. God's presence is mediated in and through creation and human history, but that mystery remains hidden and untapped unless it is brought to word. The proclamation of the word and the celebration of the sacraments (Augustine's "visible words") bring the depth dimension of reality — grace — to recognition and thus effective power.

Some would argue that this naming of grace that is already present in human life does not do justice to the power of the word to bring about salvation, rather than simply to identify it.[6] But because human persons live according to the meanings they perceive and construct, naming grace is no small matter. Bringing a deeper dimension of human life to awareness and conscious responsibility has serious implications. A change of perception or worldview is essential to a radical change of life. A friendship forms before it is fully recognized and claimed, but when friends or partners explicitly claim the bond of love between them, they also deepen their commitment to one another and make decisions that will affect future choices. Communities and individuals respond in outrage when the innocent are violated, but "naming" the structural evils that perpetuate individual crimes focuses the anger of those who protest and strengthens their commitment to justice. Multiple examples could be drawn from personal, interpersonal, or social life to illustrate the power of words as symbols to bring about or to deepen what they signify. (The next chapter returns to this understanding of the sacramental power of the human word.)

A related fundamental question that reemerges throughout this book has crucial significance for a theology of preaching: What is the relationship between the explicit word of the gospel and the word of grace spoken in human history and experience?[7] Preachers are convinced that there is a dynamic power in the biblical *dabar* YHWH, that God's word cannot be separated from God's actions, that the word of God is creative, bringing about what it declares. Preachers also declare that the word of God has the power to touch hearts and to convert lives: "[T]he word of God is living and active, sharper than any two-edged sword, piercing until it divides soul from spirit, joints from marrow; it is able to judge the thoughts and intentions of the heart" (Heb 4:12). But what are the implications of believing that *that* word has become flesh in Jesus of Nazareth, that God is to be discovered enfleshed in human history?

Any Christian theology of preaching will center on Jesus Christ as Word of God. Most frequently theologies of preaching emphasize the uniqueness of Jesus and the Christian gospel. A significant shift takes place, however, when the focus moves to another aspect of the incarnation: the mystery that God's fullest word has been spoken in history, in a human being, in human experience. Because of the incarnation and redemption, nothing created can be considered profane. That shift affects both the theology and the practice of preaching.

Preaching: Theory and Operative Belief

Every preacher has a theology of preaching even if that theology remains implicit. Underlying convictions about where God's word is to be heard and by whom and how it is meant to be proclaimed will affect very practical decisions regarding homily preparation, communal faith-sharing, team preaching, dialogic modes of preaching, and the creation of opportunities for response to preaching. Reflection on how one goes about creating and proclaiming a homily can disclose one's operative beliefs about the locus of revelation and the goal of preaching.[8]

Specifically, one's understanding of the relationship between the word of God and human experience emerges in the process of homily preparation. Often preachers operate as if the word of God is to be discovered only in the biblical passage, in prayer, and in study of the commentaries by scripture scholars. If the preacher understands the goal of the sermon or homily to be application of the word of God to people's daily lives, she or he will attend to congregational analysis and potential connections with culture and the world situation as ways of searching for clues as to where the revealed word of God might touch a chord in "secular" human experience. The implicit underlying assumption here is that preaching somehow bridges the sacred and the profane.[9]

The sacramental imagination claims a different foundational perspective, asserting that God's word of salvation, hope, healing, and liberation is being spoken in new ways today in people's daily lives. According to this vision of revelation, the same creative Spirit of

God who was active in the history of Israel, in the life, ministry, death, and resurrection of Jesus, in the church of the past, in the lives of the saints, is still active today. Therefore reflection on culture, people's lives, and human experience is necessary not merely to make a homily relevant but to hear God's word *today*. From the sacramental perspective, preachers listen with attentiveness to human experience because they are convinced that revelation is located in human history, in the depths of human experience — a mystery that should not come as such a surprise to those who profess a belief in the incarnation.

Contemporary christology confirms this new starting point for a theology of proclamation. Traditionally christology began with the mystery of the incarnation "from above," from the mystery of the divine Word, the second person of the Trinity, becoming human. While "from above" and "from below" cannot be distinguished too sharply precisely because of the mystery of the incarnation, most contemporary christologies take the history and humanity of Jesus as the starting point of a "low ascending" christology that concludes with, rather than begins with, the mystery of divinity and incarnation. In a similar way, a theology of preaching can begin with the power of God's word not as something totally other and beyond our experience but rather as that which is to be discovered in the depths of what is authentically human. The mystery of preaching is at once the proclamation of God's word and the naming of grace in human experience.

To describe preaching as "naming grace" requires, however, three qualifications: (1) the experience to be named is human experience in its depth dimension; (2) in the contemporary world situation, most people's experience of God is in the face of, and in spite of, human suffering; and (3) the interpretative keys to identifying grace in human experience are located in the biblical story and the basic symbols of the Christian tradition.

Human Experience in Its Depths

Naming the presence of God in human experience requires pressing to the limits of human existence where both the threat of radical human finitude and the experience of overwhelming meaning and joy raise the fundamentally religious question of the "ground of our being." At the boundaries of human life "signals of transcendence" emerge within human experience. "Secular" language reaches its limits in trying to express "the other dimension" or the "surplus of meaning" disclosed from the depths of human experience.[10] While revelation takes place in human experience, it cannot be identified with human experience. Rather, as Edward Schillebeeckx has noted,

> Revelation takes place *in* historical human experience in this world, but at the same time it summons us *from* what we take for granted in our limited world. It is therefore not to be found in any *direct* appeal to our so-called self-evident experiences within the world. As experience, it is the crossing of a boundary within the dimensions of human experience.[11]

At this boundary of human experience, human beings either speak in religious language or remain silent.[12]

Thus one of the contemplative tasks of the preacher or preaching community is to reflect on human experience in order to identify the ultimate foundation of the mystery of human life — the God who often remains hidden. The ability to make that connection presumes that preachers are in touch with the human struggle — their own and that of others. Both the prophets in the history of Israel such as Hosea, Ezekiel, and Jeremiah and authentic early Christian preachers like Mary Magdalene, Peter, and Paul were formed for their preaching through their own human experience of conversion. So too those who hope to become ministers of the word in our day are asking to be baptized in the experience from which that word emerged. Whether it is experienced in the preacher's own life or through attending to the stories of others, nothing that is human should remain foreign to preachers if they are to grasp what it means to proclaim that all of humanity has been taken into God and redeemed in Christ.

The poet Rainer Maria Rilke knew well that the authentic word can flow only from the depths of life experience. As he once described the source of the poetic word:

> For the sake of a single verse, one must see many cities, people and things. One must know the animals, one must feel how the birds fly and know the gesture with which the small flowers open in the morning. One must be able to think back to roads in unknown regions, to unexpected meetings and to partings one had long seen coming; to days of childhood that are

still unexplained,...to days in rooms withdrawn and quiet, and to mornings by the sea, to the sea itself, to seas, to nights of travel..., and it is not yet enough if one may think of all this. One must have memories of many nights of love,...of the screams of women in labor....But one must also have been beside the dying, must have sat beside the dead in the room with the open window and the fitful noises. And still it is not yet enough to have memories. One must be able to forget them when they are many, and one must have the great patience to wait until they come again. For it is not yet the memories themselves. Not until they have turned to blood within us, to glance and gesture, nameless and no longer to be distinguished from ourselves — not until then can it happen that in a most rare hour the first word of a verse arises in their midst and goes forth from them.[13]

The contemplative embrace of life that Rilke describes as essential to the creative writer is all the more necessary for the preacher who is called to enflesh the word of God.

Naming Grace in the Midst of Suffering

One of the fundamental challenges to any preacher of the good news of God's abiding presence is all the evidence to the contrary. Whether one turns to Haiti, Rwanda, Bosnia, U.S. city streets, battered women's shelters, AIDS hospices, unemployment lines, centers for abused children, or the more daily struggles of families and individuals, stories of suffering abound. Is it really possible that grace abounds still more? Can contemporary believers proclaim with conviction that the Spirit of God continues to raise the dead to life? The media's daily examples of suffering on a global scale confirm that not everyone's experience overflows with a surplus of meaning that can be described only in religious language. On the contrary, for the majority of humanity, the basic experience of life is suffering or struggling for survival. How then can preachers talk of God as revealed at the depths of human experience?

Here Schillebeeckx has made a valuable contribution to a theology of revelation with the notion of "contrast experience," which was alluded to in chapter 2.[14] He suggests that, while the immediate experience of two-thirds of humanity is that of suffering and the apparent absence of God, a still deeper mystery is revealed in their response to that suffering — responses of protest, hope, and sheer endurance. Human beings are able to cling to life against all odds, to cling to God in the face of God's silence. That kind of human resistance and hope can be sustained only by a deeper spirit of life — the very Spirit of God within humanity. It is the Spirit who creates life out of nothingness, who raises the dead to life. Because the suffering people of this world share in a daily way in the experience of crucifixion and in the hope and protest that are rooted in God's final word — the resurrection — they have a unique experience of the mystery of God at the limits of their human experience. This is at the heart of what it means to claim that the poor or the crucified of this world have a privileged hearing of the word.[15]

Preachers need to stand in solidarity with the poor and outcast of this world if they are to share the good news that Jesus promised would be heard by the poor. The preacher is sent to the poor not to announce good news they have not heard but rather to be among the poor to hear the good news they experience when they listen to the scriptures from the context of their lives and struggles. As Gustavo Gutiérrez remarked, the liberating power and truth of the gospel will not be proclaimed effectively until the poor are among those who proclaim the gospel. But he also warned, "[T]hen we shall have a gospel that is no longer 'presentable' in society. It will not sound nice and it will not smell good."[16] As communities gather to listen to human stories in all their grace and disgrace, preachers are called to name the "echoes of the gospel" that can be heard there.

Listening for an Echo of the Gospel

Finally, one cannot talk of revelation occurring in human experience without recalling that human life is interpreted, and therefore experienced, through a variety of filters. Human persons do not have experience apart from some framework for understanding or perceiving. Human life is always interpreted in the context of the multiple traditions within which one stands, including personal history, family stories, ethnic roots, and culture. New experiences may call for modification, change, or even rejection of previous horizons, but initially all human experience occurs within some framework of meaning that has been handed on. Children are born into systems of language and cultural symbols; they do not create them.

To speak of recognizing grace at the depths or limits of human experience is to operate within the framework of a faith tradition that identifies a depth dimension in human experience and provides a language to name that dimension. The living tradition of the Christian community hands on the stories of both Jewish and Christian ancestors in faith. At the center of the Christian pattern for understanding and living human life is the story of Jesus as recounted in the scriptures, as remembered, lived, and celebrated in the community, and as retold uniquely in every age and culture.

In the story of Jesus, Christians discover that in its depths, and even in radical suffering, humanity has been united with God. The word that Jesus preached, the word that Jesus is, discloses both the mystery of human existence and the mystery of God. Thus when preachers listen to human experience they are listening from a perspective; they are listening for an echo of the gospel. To tell the story of Jesus is to tell the final truth about the human story, and to tell the human story in its depth, as Jesus did, is to point to the mystery of God at the heart of human existence, to "name grace." In offering the good news of the Christian story, preachers offer not an interpretation of human life but rather an invitation to "come and see" and to "go and do likewise," to make Jesus' story one's own, and in doing so, to experience ordinary human life as graced:

> This is what we proclaim to you:
> what was from the beginning,
> what we have heard,
> what we have seen with our own eyes,
> what we have looked upon
> and our hands have touched —
> we speak of the word of life. (1 John 1:1)

Proclaiming Grace in Word and Deed

In the broadest sense, preaching is the retelling of the story of Jesus in word and deed. Retelling the story requires that the Christian community both make grace or salvation more of a reality in this moment of history and name the power that makes that possible. Proclamation *in word* forms, but also is formed by, proclamation

in deed. That is the point of the claim of the 1971 Synod of Bishops: "Activity on behalf of justice is a constitutive part of preaching
the gospel."[17]

Jesus' own preaching reveals the sacramental paradigm: his words
were enfleshed in his actions and in his very person. He announced
the reign of God in word and deed. He forgave sins not only by
words of forgiveness but by eating with sinners. He announced
the healing mercy of God by touching lepers. He taught community by celebrating with his disciples. He challenged preconceived
social roles by talking with and loving Samaritans, tax collec-
tors, prostitutes. Jesus told the story of God by sharing ordinary
human experience and transforming it through his presence, words,
and actions.[18]

So, too, contemporary preachers can announce compassion, healing, mercy, and hope only if the community and the preacher are
involved in making those words concrete realities. This living of the
gospel life in fidelity to the gifts of the Spirit bestowed in baptism
and confirmation becomes the source and the power and authority
to preach the gospel.[19] The Spirit active in the life of those who live
the gospel impels communities of disciples to speak of the source
and power of that gospel life.

If the story of Jesus is a living tradition, a universal story true
for every age and culture, it has to be retold anew in every period
of history. Never before has the gospel been proclaimed or heard in
the way we will announce it from our own unique moment in history and culture. What new dimensions of the story of Jesus unfold
when it is retold by women, by children, by Nicaraguan peasants,
by prisoners, by refugees or communities that have declared sanctuary? How is the word of God heard and proclaimed in South Africa,
in the experience of African-American or Hispanic communities, in
Asian contexts, or by Native Americans? How is the story retold in a
world of ecological devastation? The life experience of the preacher
affects what she or he will hear in the text. The Spirit is active in new
experience, stirring up what Schillebeeckx referred to as "new memories of Jesus,"[20] opening new possibilities of the meaning of his life,
his words, his death and resurrection. If contemporary communities
of believers do not hand on the tradition by telling the story of salvation from the context of their unique and diverse experiences, no
one else can or will.

Handing on a Living Tradition

This chapter has accented an incarnational theme that has been underdeveloped or ignored in traditional theologies of preaching: contemporary human experience can disclose new dimensions in the story of Jesus. At the same time, that claim has to be held in balance with the classic emphasis of the dialectical imagination: the story of Jesus as preserved in the biblical texts also challenges and confronts contemporary experience. The Spirit who calls forth new memories in the community is the Spirit of Jesus, the crucified and risen one. In the face of the perennial danger that every age will try to refashion the story of Jesus in its own image, the Gospels and the history of Jesus limit and focus the contemporary retelling of the story. The Christian community in every context is confronted by the text and by the life and words of Jesus. Here is the truth of Paul's concern that we preach God's word and not a mere human word; it is the gospel of Jesus Christ that has been handed on, not "some other gospel."

Communities of faith, as well as preachers, are called not only to be rooted in the scriptures but to participate in the process of the transmission of a living tradition of faith that produced the written scriptures. The Hebrew scriptures, for example, emerged from the faith experience of the Jewish people. God's word, they claimed, had been "spoken" in their concrete human history. They announced that God was active in their liberation from slavery, in desert wanderings, in the conquest of a foreign land, in wars and exiles, in political struggles. Very human and political events were interpreted, and thus experienced, as the action of God. It was YHWH who "smote the firstborn in Egypt," who led the people through the wilderness, who made their land a heritage, who freed them from all their foes, who brought them out of exile. Israel's ongoing history of faith was handed on from generation to generation in the shared memories and stories of the Jewish tradition. The framework of their ancestors' faith provided a key by which later generations could interpret their own experience. Remembering God's fidelity in the past opened up the hope that God would again be faithful in this new moment in the tradition and in the future. In claiming their ancestors' history and faith as their own tradition, the tribes of Israel experienced their own history as another moment in the ongoing covenant relationship. The same process was at work in the Gospels and the Christian scriptures as a whole. The meaning of Jesus' life was reinterpreted in light of the resurrection and the concrete contexts of diverse communities of faith.

Preaching requires the contemplative and prophetic gift of making connections between the story of God's fidelity in the past, God's continuing fidelity in the present, and God's promise of "a future full of hope" (Jer 29:11). Preaching is not a matter of retelling the story of the past, no matter how creatively. The story continues — as our story. Hence the challenge of Isaiah is one that preachers and communities of the word need to take to heart: "See, I am doing something new! Now it springs forth, do you not perceive it?" (Isa 43:19).

The "new thing" God is doing, however, is being done in and through the community. The experience of salvation is a communal event. Hence the word of faith that the preacher proclaims is the community's word. The preacher speaks in the name of the community and proclaims the deepest convictions of the entire church, to whom the word has been entrusted. Naming the grace that is to be found in the faith experience of the community obviously involves listening to and learning from the members of the community. Prophetic preaching will involve difficult words of challenge, but those words will come from the stumbling block that the gospel is for the preacher as well as for the rest of the community.

In the African-American community, the ultimate criterion for acceptance of a new pastor has been expressed in the question: "Can the reverend tell the story?"[21] No one asks whether it is the story of Jesus or the people's story; the community knows that in the end it is the same story. Preaching is the retelling of the story of Jesus in word and deed. But one might also say that the preacher interprets the human story in light of the story of Jesus in such a way that people can recognize and respond to the mystery of God in their lives and world. The hearers of the word are drawn to "follow Jesus" and empowered to "go and do likewise."

Preachers called to relate the story of grace active in and through creation and human history might learn the art of storytelling from the paralyzed grandfather in Martin Buber's Hasidic tale:

> My grandfather was paralyzed. One day he was asked to tell about something that happened with his teacher — the great

Baalschem. Then he told how the saintly Baalschem used to leap about and dance while he was at prayers. As he went on with the story my grandfather stood up; he was so carried away that he had to show how the master had done it, and started to caper about and dance. From that moment on he was cured. That is how stories should be told.[22]

Chapter 4

Words from the Future

The sacramental imagination's emphasis on the pervasiveness of grace can result in serious concerns about the power of the word and the importance of preaching the Christian gospel. Further, some fear that the claim that the preached word culminates in sacramental celebration does not do justice to the power of the proclaimed word to effect conversion. Yet more than twenty-five years ago French theologian Yves Congar, who is noted for his contributions to liturgical and sacramental theology as well as to ecumenical dialogue, challenged a false dichotomy between word and sacrament. Speaking at a point in the Roman Catholic tradition when the renewal of preaching was still fairly recent, Congar made the startling claim that "[i]f in one country Mass were celebrated for 30 years without preaching and in another there was preaching for 30 years without the Mass, the people would be more Christian in the country where there was preaching."[1] In exploring the power of the proclaimed word to form a community of faith, we might begin with what we know from human experience about the power of the word.

The Power of Human Words

Some words simply convey information: "This commission will meet on the first Monday of every month." But other words carry a deeper power. Words can betray a human trust, manipulate people, or reinforce structures of injustice. For example, the system of apartheid in South Africa was, until a few years ago, justified in the name of the Bible and God's will. In the contemporary society of the United States, many have become suspicious of the promises of government leaders, of the persuasion of advertising and the mass media, and of the careless way in which people take oaths and make vows or commitments. In many ways the culture is surrounded by speech that lacks truth. All too frequently people are willing to follow the advice of Thomas More's daughter Margaret when he was facing death for refusing to sign an oath with which he vehemently disagreed. She urged him: "[S]ay the words of the oath and in your heart think otherwise." More reminded his daughter that we lose our very selves when our words aren't consistent with our hearts: "What is an oath but words we say to God? . . . [W]hen a man takes an oath, Meg, he's holding his own self in his own hands. Like water. And if he opens his fingers *then* — he needn't hope to find himself again."[2]

More spoke of the kind of words that come from the center of our being. They are the kind of depth words with which we define ourselves and give shape to our lives.[3] Words that change the future course of human lives are words like:

I love you.

This relationship is over. I want a divorce.

You are extremely gifted. Have you ever considered that you might be called to the vocation of artist, or scholar, or musician, or minister?

I'm sorry to have to tell you: your cancer is inoperable.

Here I stand; I can do no other.

You are hereby sentenced to life imprisonment.

I, Maria, take you, Juan, to be my husband.

No more war. War never again.

I'm sorry your services won't be needed any longer.

Those kinds of words open up new futures — or cut off the future. They are not "just words"; they are symbols that evoke a deeper mystery — whether of love, possibility, belief, commitment, or death. The relationship of love was there before the words were spoken; the problems in the relationship were there before any mention of divorce; but somehow with the words the reality of the relationship or commitment is deepened or changed. The words bring a new awareness to the experience and therefore a new level of responsibility. In a real sense those kinds of words have the power to create a new experience. One's world is not the same before and after words like that are spoken. Those words are revelatory because they disclose levels of the mystery of human life that are too deep for words.

Words are connected with the depths of human freedom. We have the power to keep our inner self hidden or to reveal ourselves to one another, to share who we are in vulnerability and truth. We develop relationships by gradually allowing what is hidden to be seen — by sharing our secrets, our fears, our hopes, our failures, and our joys, by telling the story that is uniquely ours. Most of us are cautious about sharing our deepest truth. To an extent, we speak beyond our explicit words — our behavior speaks; body language speaks; even silence speaks. But words spoken in truth make explicit the secret intentions of the human heart. With our words we commit ourselves and our futures.

Many parents, teachers, or friends have had the experience of interpreting another's behavior or apparent attitude in one way only to discover later that something very different was going on inside the person. The other person couldn't share the deeper truth — or chose not to. Depth words express the fundamental freedom that is at the core of the human person — a freedom that only God knows fully because God has spoken the Word in whose image human beings are created.[4]

Reflection on human experience highlights key aspects of the mystery of the power of the word. Words create new possibilities. Words preserve memories. Words change relationships and worlds. Words break hearts and mend them. Words cause grief and give hope. Words move us to action. If all that is true of human words, what about the words Christians proclaim as the word of God in every liturgy?

The Word of God

The human words that Christians call "the word of God" came ultimately from the experience of their ancestors in the Jewish and Christian communities of faith. Those ancestors experienced the power of God in their concrete human lives, and thus they proclaimed in faith that it was their God who brought them out of the land of slavery, that God was with them in their desert wanderings, in their conquest of a foreign land, in their choice to be ruled by a king, and even in exile. Their words of faith shaped their experience in such a way that they were able to announce with conviction that the same God who had created the heavens and the earth was at work in their history and had promised to be with them in the future.

That story of faith was handed on from generation to generation and provided the lens through which later generations could view their own new experiences. Remembering the stories of God's fidelity in the desert opened up the possibility of hoping that God would also be faithful in a later time of exile. Remembering the impossible things God had done for Abraham and Sarah or for the slaves led by Moses and Miriam meant that God could work wonders again in a new time. In the minds of the biblical authors God's mighty actions and God's word were so closely connected that they had only one word for both — *dabhar*. That word carried a sense of energy, of dynamism, like something that pushes or drives one forward. The word of God carried the power of God. It was creative; it brought forth what it promised. Thus the first chapter of Genesis tells of creation being accomplished by the power of the word. God said, "Let there be light," and so it happened. The prophet Jeremiah describes the word of God as a "fire burning in [his] heart" that had to be spoken — the energy was too much to contain (Jer 20:9). Once God's promise to liberate Israel from slavery was spoken, the Exodus had to happen. God's promise of freedom — God's own freedom — was the liberating energy enabling Israel's escape. The prophet Isaiah describes Israel's conviction that God's word is the power behind human history:

> For just as from the heavens
> the rain and snow come down
> and do not return there
> till they have watered the earth,
> making it fertile and fruitful,
> giving seed to [the one] who sows
> and bread to [the one] who eats,
> so shall my word be
> that goes forth from my mouth;
> it shall not return to me void,
> but shall do my will,
> achieving the end for which I sent it.
> (Isa 55:10–11)

God's word carries God's power, God's authority, God's energy. That is why the writer of the Book of Deuteronomy saw all of history as "the unfolding of God's word." From that perspective the key to deciding how to live was to "choose life," that is, to choose fidelity to the covenant rather than to choose death through resisting the new future God was holding open. The difficult challenge in life, however, is to try to discern where God's Spirit is addressing the community in the present.

The prophets became the interpreters of where God was to be found in the history of the Jewish people; they are often described as the Jewish preachers par excellence.[5] Their task was to call to memory God's fidelity in Israel's past and present, which was at the same time to call forth hope rooted in God's promise to be with them always. The prophets were called to speak "words from the future" in a very real way since they were called to envision God's dream for Israel and for humanity, a promise that always exceeds any human imagination. Announcing the word of God meant proclaiming a new and different future in spite of dashed hopes, the destruction of the temple, or exile. The prophet stirred up hope in the promise of a future when wounds would be bound up, enemies reconciled, prisoners set free, and the land restored, precisely by recalling the memories of the past when God was always faithful, even if in unexpected ways. The prophet Isaiah described the future reign of God in words that the Gospel of Luke presents as the text for the preaching event in which Jesus claims his own mission:

> The Spirit of the Lord God is upon me,
> because the Lord has anointed me, . . .
> sent me to bring glad tidings to the lowly,
> to heal the brokenhearted,
> to proclaim liberty to the captives
> and release to the prisoners;
> to announce a year of favor from the Lord
> and a day of vindication by our God,
> to comfort all who mourn;
> to place on those who mourn in Zion
> a diadem instead of ashes;
> to give them oil of gladness in place of mourning,
> a glorious mantle instead of a listless spirit.
> They will be called oaks of justice,

planted by the Lord to show his glory.
They shall rebuild the ancient ruins;
the former wastes they shall raise up,
and restore the ruined cities,
desolate now for generations.
                    (Isa 61:1–4; see Luke 4:16–21)

Christians see Jesus in the long line of Jewish prophets who announced the good news of the reign of God, opening up a new and
different future, a future full of hope. But the Christian community
also believes that Jesus was more than a prophet. He not only proclaimed the future reign of God — he embodied it. In his person and
his actions as well as in his words he announced the good news of
salvation. He proclaimed God's reconciling mercy not only by words
of forgiveness but by sharing a table with sinners. He announced
God's healing power by touching lepers. He challenged the limited
social roles and restrictions of his culture and religion by talking with
Samaritans, entering into friendships with women, choosing a tax
collector as a disciple, curing the sick on the Sabbath. He was a faithful Jew always searching for God's will, but he came to understand
the tradition in which he was rooted in a radical way. His whole life
announced that God willed well-being and happiness not only for the
Jews but for all people — universal salvation. Christians believe that
he not only spoke God's word of compassion but *was* God's compassion enfleshed. In the words of the Gospel of John: "The Word
was with God and the Word was God.... The Word became flesh
and pitched a tent among us." In the life, death, and resurrection
of Jesus, God spoke a word from the future, God's final word for
humanity and for the future of the earth.

The Liturgical Word

In every liturgy the assembly of the baptized proclaims that the future has already begun. The gathered body of Christ celebrates God's
victory over sin and death and God's promise of a future full of hope
as they gather around the table of the Lord, welcome new members
into the community, celebrate the mystery of reconciliation, and entrust the sick or dying members of the community to God's healing
mercy. In each liturgical celebration, the assembly can announce its

faith in God's power and its commitment to work for that future only after first calling to memory God's fidelity in the past. One of Marty Haugen's hymns phrases it this way:

> We remember how you loved us to your death and still we cel-
> ebrate for you are with us here. And we believe that we will
> see you when you come in your glory, Lord. We remember. We
> celebrate. We believe.[6]

That hymn summarizes the basic structure of worship: remember-ing God's fidelity makes that faithfulness present again here and now and enables the community to enter more deeply into the celebra-tion. Memory leads to celebration, and both strengthen the baptized to go forth with a living faith to make the gospel more of a reality in the world and church. The words of the scriptures and the symbols of the liturgy are ways of deepening hope in, and dedication to, the future "city of God" that does not yet exist in either world or church.

The word of God forms the assembly of believers into a com-munity of forgiveness as they hear the story of the prodigal son, fashions them into a eucharistic people dedicated to responding to the hungers of our world when they hear again of the multiplica-tion of the loaves, shapes them into a people of compassion when they hear of the cure of the leper or the son of the widow of Naim. Believers become more deeply grateful for their heritage of freedom and more committed to the liberation of all people as they hear again the story of the Exodus. The word of God breaks down the limits the community would place on where God is to be found and who speaks God's word as the assembly listens to the testimony of the shepherd Amos, the youth Jeremiah, the Samaritan woman, or Mary Magdalene. The word of God challenges limited understandings of ministry and social roles as Jesus' washing of feet is proclaimed as the gospel narrative on Holy Thursday.

"We remember, we celebrate...." The proclamation of those words from the future moves the assembly to action: first, to the rit-ual actions of the liturgy; and, finally, to the "liturgy of the world."[7] The word of God gathers the community around a common table where the poor are welcomed and resources are shared, empowering members to offer signs of reconciliation and peace, and drawing all to reach out to the sick, the dying, and the newly initiated. These symbols of the future, like the word of God they flow from, form the assembly more deeply into the body of Christ so that, in the words of Augustine, Christians might truly "become what we eat."[8]

"We remember, we celebrate, we believe." The action that the word of God empowers extends beyond the liturgical celebration to the biblical understanding of believing as obeying and therefore embracing a life of discipleship. As members leave the eucharistic assembly, they commit themselves to building "the city of God" amid the everyday struggles of family and community life, the workplace and the political arena, parishes and neighborhoods. Christians are both challenged and enabled by the liturgy to reform their lives, their society, and their church so that they might more deeply reflect the gospel of Jesus.

This pattern of remembering in order to celebrate and to live as true disciples of Jesus lies at the heart of the eucharistic celebration. The introductory rites that precede the reading of the scriptures and the homily are already focused on the word to be proclaimed since the whole purpose of those rites is to gather a praying community that is open to, and even expectantly waiting to hear, the word of God. By its very structure the liturgy suggests that it is the word of God that prepares the community to celebrate eucharist and strengthens the baptized to live the Christian life.

But the word of God is not just a collection of stories of what happened in Jewish history and in the time of Jesus. Rather, as the Letter to the Hebrews says, the word of God is living and active. Contemporary believers remember the stories from the past precisely so that they might claim them as their own stories. This gathered assembly also wanders in its own deserts. These believers, too, are faced with storms at sea when they are not at all sure whether Jesus is in their midst. This community also stands in need of forgiveness and mercy and waits beside empty tombs weeping. Contemporary Christians continue to question whether God speaks and acts in their lives — and if so, where? They come to the eucharist and wonder: Is there any word from our God? Is there good news that speaks to sudden unemployment? to widows and widowers? to children who feel alone and confused? to teenagers who wonder whether religion is only for grandparents and children? to international politics? to the violence in our cities? to the internal tensions and struggles within the church? Is there any word?

That is the question all believers bring to liturgy. Perhaps not consciously, but at some deep level, the community turns to the family story, their people's history, the memory of the church, for clues from the past that might indicate where God is in the present and what they can hope for in the future. It is the task of the preacher, of course, to try to make those connections, but as important as the preaching ministry is, hearers of the word miss the point if they focus on the preacher instead of the living word of God. The story the preacher retells is the community's story — not some foreign word they have never heard.

The entire community has been entrusted with handing on the family story. Passing on the story from the past means handing on "words from the future" — testifying to a dream that stands ahead of us. Hebrews 11 reminds those who would walk in the footsteps of their ancestors that to journey in faith is to travel an unknown road:

> By faith Abraham obeyed when he was called, and went forth to the place he was to receive as a heritage; he went forth, moreover not knowing where he was going.
>
> By faith he sojourned in the promised land as in a foreign country, dwelling in tents with [the heirs] of the same promise, for he was looking forward to the city with foundations, whose designer and maker is God.
>
> By faith Sarah received power to conceive though she was past the age, for she thought that the One who had made the promise was worthy of trust....
>
> All of these died in faith.
>
> They did not obtain what had been promised but saw and saluted it from afar. (Heb 11:8–11, 13)

At every liturgy the Christian community gathers to hear words from the past, but the kind of words that open up the future. Having heard the story of their ancestors in the Jewish tradition of faith, Christians turn to the story of one who enfleshed the good news he announced, the Word and the Wisdom of God. The Sunday readings have been selected for the lectionary precisely so that a symbolic connection is made between the first reading and the Gospel.[9] In the Christian way of reading the scriptures, telling the story of Jesus becomes a retelling of the tradition of faith in a way that deepens our understanding and shows that God's promise of an anointed one, a new land, a future time of peace, a just ruler, the reconciliation of enemies, reached a new and deeper fulfillment in Jesus. The interweaving of the stories of Israel and of the Christian communities keeps revealing new dimensions of God's promise and God's fidelity, but the assembly only retells those stories because they believe the same God is active today.

It would be interesting to ask believers who have listened for years to Christian preaching about their understanding of the preacher's task. Even those who have been formed by good preaching might say that the preacher is supposed to explain the scriptures. But as the United States Bishops Conference's document on preaching, *Fulfilled in Your Hearing,* states, that is not enough. Rather the bishops claim:

> Since the purpose of the homily is to enable the gathered congregation to celebrate the liturgy with faith, the preacher does not so much attempt to explain the Scriptures as to interpret the human situation through the Scriptures. In other words, the goal of the liturgical preacher is not to interpret a text of the Bible (as would be the case in teaching a Scripture class) as much as to draw on the texts of the Bible as they are presented in the lectionary to interpret people's lives. To be even more precise, the preacher's purpose will be to turn to these Scriptures to interpret people's lives in such a way that they will be able to celebrate Eucharist — or be reconciled with God and one another, or be baptized into the Body of Christ, depending on the particular liturgy that is being celebrated.[10]

Or as William Skudlarek, a professor of liturgy and homiletics, has remarked: "If people have come together to make eucharist, the word addressed to them should have something to do with the 'why' and 'how' of giving thanks."[11] What would happen on Sunday if the presider addressed the congregation with the words: "Lift up your hearts to the Lord," and the assembly responded: "Why?" or "Let us give thanks and praise...," and the community replied: "How?" The homily is intended to make some of those connections.

Ideally, the words of the preacher will break open the word of God by bringing out the connections between the scriptures, the liturgy, and the lives of those gathered to celebrate. Even if the preacher fails to do that, however, and even before the preacher speaks, the word has been proclaimed in the very reading of the scriptures. The first reader and the cantor who leads the responsorial psalm are also ministers of the word — their faith in the good news of salvation is communicated in the very way they proclaim the reading. Further, studies in communication theory suggest that active listening is essential for a message to be communicated. The desire to hear the good news and prayerful listening to the proclamation of the word as well as participation in proclaiming the Christian story through singing or speaking the words of the psalmist — regardless of the quality of the preaching — are never in vain. Again the prophet Isaiah recalls God's promise: "[My word] shall not return to me void, but shall do my will, achieving the end for which I sent it" (Isa 55:11).

But the mystery of the incarnation means that God's word will be accomplished in and through human words and human lives. The biblical understanding of remembering calls the gathered assembly to become more actively involved in making credible in our day the claims that God can be trusted and that the community will be there for one another. As a form of response to the proclamation of the word of God, the intercessions reflect the breadth of the community's love and concern. As the community prays that the God of the incarnation will remember the poor, the homeless, the lonely, and the sick, it also pledges itself as the body of Christ to feed the hungry and visit the sick and the homebound, as well as to work to change economic structures and systems of housing and health care.

In a similar way the creed and the eucharistic prayer the presider prays in the name of the gathered community are in a very real sense the words of the assembly. They are the kinds of words with which human beings take their lives into their hands. These words speak the deepest identity of Christians, their greatest hopes for the future, their most profound expression of how they intend to live. To proclaim these words is to follow the one who "on the night be was betrayed . . . took bread and gave thanks and praise" (Eucharistic Prayer III).

The Promise Is Not Yet Realized

If the word of God awakens the assembly, part of what will come to consciousness is the pain that comes from the fact that the future is "not yet." The words and rituals of the Christian community do not yet embody the promise of God's reign where ministers wash feet, the poor are welcomed, there is neither male nor female, racial and ethnic differences do not divide, and the resources and responsibilities of the community are shared.

As communities of believers attend more deeply to the word of God and the symbols of the liturgy, they will grow more uncomfort-

able with all the ways the church is not yet the body of Christ —
all the divisions of clerical and lay, of race and gender, of neighborhoods and social classes — and with all the ways those differences are
reinforced in liturgical celebrations. The same questions of liturgical
roles and practice will keep emerging: Who is invited to receive from
the cup? Is concelebration appropriate? Which parts of the scriptures
do we use at liturgy and what translation? Who preaches on them?
How do we name God in public prayer? Who sits where in the assembly? Why can't women preside at eucharist or serve as pastors or
bishops? Where is the collection distributed, and who decides that?
Who is welcome at the eucharistic table?[12]

Behind each of those questions are memories of stories the community has heard from the scriptures: memories of bread broken and
a cup shared, memories of a Lord who washes feet, memories of a
God who is imaged as a strong and loving mother as well as "our father," memories of sinners and the poor finding dignity and a place
at the table, memories of a woman told to preach the good news to
the disciples, memories of the racial outcast as neighbor who res-
cues the one in need, and memories of the last being first in this
assembly. As the words form the imaginations and consciences of
the community, the assembly will not be able to hear of the feeding
of the multitudes and think it has nothing to do with an unjust distribution of wealth. Communities formed by the word of God will
not be able to say "Praise to you Lord Jesus Christ" after the gospel and refuse to forgive a family member or a friend — even one
who has betrayed. Local churches will not be able to profess faith
in one Lord, one faith, one baptism, and not grieve over the lack of
eucharistic sharing with other Christians.

The church that hears the word of God and recognizes the symbols of the liturgy will be called to its own conversion. But that
word is not always welcome. When Jesus was asked about why
people didn't see the signs he worked and didn't hear the parables
he preached, he reminded his disciples of the prophet Isaiah's words:

> Sluggish indeed is this people's heart.
> They have scarcely heard with their ears;
> they have firmly closed their eyes;
> otherwise they might see with their eyes,
> and hear with their ears,
> and understand with their hearts,

and turn back to me,
and I should heal them. (Matt 13:15)

This chapter opened with Congar's conviction that the word of God has the power to form a genuine Christian community. Perhaps the real question is whether the assembly is willing to embrace the transformation that is the cost of discipleship.

Chapter 5

Trust the Text or
Preach the Gospel?

"Be careful with words, they're dangerous," warned Elie Wiesel.
"Be wary of them. They beget either demons or angels."[1] Preachers,
like poets and prophets, spend their lives in the dangerous company
of words precisely because they are convinced of their power. Yet
preachers claim more than a human craft. From the time of the apostle Paul, Christian preachers, like the Hebrew prophets before them,
have insisted that the power of their preaching is the power of God
(Rom 1:16; 1 Cor 1:18); the word they speak, God's own. As Karl
Barth asserts in his classic *The Preaching of the Gospel:* "Preaching is
'God's own word.' That is to say, through the activity of preaching,
God himself speaks."[2]

That claim presumes, of course, that preaching is rooted in the
Bible, the one book that Christians maintain not only witnesses to or
transmits the word of God but in some sense *is* the word of God.[3]
Walter Vogels further connects this classic Christian claim with the
role of the preacher: "The preacher goes to the text because he trusts
the text. He accepts it as a part of the canon as normative for the
community. He believes that the text still has something to say to
the listener."[4] Walter Brueggemann describes the power of the text
to form the Christian community and its values: "The community
gathers to be shaped by a text that addresses us, an articulation of
reality that lies outside of us, that we cannot conjure and need not
defend.... They [the community of the baptized] are prepared to ac-
cept in a general way, that this text is their text, the voice of life
addressed to them."[5]

Whether referring to God's activity in the history of Israel, in
the person, words, and deeds of Jesus, in the biblical text, or in
the proclamation event, preaching texts often refer to the word of
God as creative, effective, and prophetic. Preachers are exhorted to

take courage from the biblical promise that God's word does not return void but always achieves the purpose for which it was sent (Isa 55:11) and are challenged by the claim that "the Word of God is living and effective, sharper than any two-edged sword" (Heb 4:12). Emphasizing the prophetic dimension of the scriptures, Leander Keck maintains that the Bible remains always the church's greatest critic and that biblical preaching is the most dangerous form of preaching the church can hear.[6]

Some of those who would agree with Keck that biblical preaching is dangerous, however, have quite a different perspective in mind. Feminist biblical scholar Elisabeth Schüssler Fiorenza suggests that a critical hermeneutics of suspicion should place the following warning label on all biblical texts: "Caution! Could be dangerous to your health and survival."[7] The "four unpreached stories of faith" identified by Phyllis Trible ("Hagar, the slave used, abused, and rejected; Tamar, the princess raped and discarded; an unnamed woman, the concubine raped, murdered, and dismembered; and the daughter of Jephthah, a virgin slain and sacrificed") present a far from exhaustive list of what Trible has called "texts of terror" to be found within the scriptures believers call sacred.[8] The psalmist's call to dash the heads of the infant children of Israel's enemies against the rocks, the Pauline exhortations of slaves to be obedient to their masters and of wives to be submissive to their husbands, the passages from John's Gospel used within the Good Friday liturgy that attribute the death of Jesus to the Jews, and the insistence of the Letter to the Romans that "all authority that exists is established by God.... [Civil] magistrates [are] God's ministers" (Rom 13:1, 6) provide some of the most obvious additional examples of texts that prove problematic when proclaimed with the liturgical refrain: "The word of the Lord."

That preaching has contributed to the use of these texts to reinforce situations of injustice is evident from the recent use of Romans 13 in South Africa (as well as its earlier exercise by Emil Brunner in Nazi Germany or by Luther in the sixteenth-century German Peasants' Revolt);[9] white preachers' uses of the Bible to legitimate, perpetuate, and sacralize slavery in the United States;[10] and the use of biblical texts to legitimate the dominance of men over women and even domestic violence.[11] One of the most chilling testimonies to the power of the word was Hitler's claim made before two German bishops that his policies toward the Jews were "simply completing what

Christian preaching and teaching had been saying about Jews for the better part of 1900 years."[12]

Even these few examples highlight a growing conviction that the power of the word is indeed "two-edged." In what sense can contemporary preachers "trust the text" when in fact many biblical texts constitute "texts of terror"? Is it sufficient to claim that the text shapes the community or that the Bible critiques the church without also asserting that the community's context shapes the contemporary interpretation and meaning of the text and that the interpreting church needs to critique the ideology within the Bible? Is every text appropriate for use in the liturgical context? If not, why not, and who decides?

Beneath these thorny issues for the preacher lie fundamental concerns regarding the nature and authority of the biblical text and the lectionary, as well as questions about critical hermeneutics. Exploration of these underlying issues can clarify theologically what is at stake in very practical decisions the preacher is called to make such as whether and how to preach a specific text on a given Sunday (e.g., Col 3:12–21 on Holy Family Sunday).

Is the Biblical Text "the Word of God"?

Disputes about the authority of the biblical text and the advisability of changing the translation or choosing not to proclaim specific texts often center around claims that we are dealing with the inspired word of God or divine revelation.[13] In an age of critical biblical scholarship, however, scholars consistently note that the very expression "word of God" is metaphorical;[14] strictly speaking, there is no "divine speech"; rather, there are human words that claim to be rooted in an experience of God. The expression "word of God" is a metaphor that refers to the entire mystery of revelation — God's self-communication to all of creation and offer of friendship with humankind that takes place through a history that reaches its definitive expression in Jesus Christ.

The Bible constitutes the church's privileged witness to the history of the Jewish and Christian communities' foundational religious experiences. But the Bible is more than a record of revelation. Sandra Schneiders notes that since the written word has the power to effect further revelatory experiences for later generations by illuminating their present experience and assuring God's fidelity in the future, the scriptures function not only as a record but also as a "sacrament of the word of God."[15] From the perspective of the sacramental imagination we might further emphasize that this quality of the scriptures as sacrament or "word event" is most fully actualized when the scriptures are proclaimed and heard in faith in and through the power of the Spirit in the context of the assembly gathered for worship. But sacraments are not fully disclosive of the reality they embody and can be manipulated or distorted. Thus when speaking of the biblical text as revelatory or sacramental, a corresponding critical reminder of the distinction between the text and the word of God is needed. As Letty Russell so clearly states:

> [The biblical text] is not considered to function as the Word of God, evoking consent of faith, if it contributes to the continuation of racism, sexism, and classism. . . . The story of these texts is experienced as God's Word when it is heard in communities of faith and struggle as a witness to God's love for the world. This hearing is a gift of the Holy Spirit, which empowers the words so that they may transform lives.[16]

Russell's analysis underscores the fundamental reality: the word of God is available only in and through the limits — including the sinful limits — of human words. Both the construction of the texts themselves and the process of selection of texts to be included in the canon of books the church names as "sacred scripture" involved human and political judgments and biases.[17] The same is also true of the choice and editing of lectionary texts that in effect constitute "no less than a new canon."[18]

As biblical and liturgical scholars continue to identify patriarchal, racial, ethnic, class, and other forms of bias within the scriptures and the lectionary,[19] the critical question for preachers is whether all of the scriptures may be proclaimed in the liturgical assembly as "the word of God." Elisabeth Schüssler Fiorenza, for example, insists that patriarchal texts should not be allowed to remain in the lectionary but should be replaced by texts affirming the discipleship of equals. Further, an inclusive translation is to be made only of those texts that articulate a liberating vision for women struggling for self-affirmation and wholeness.[20] Marjorie Procter-Smith agrees that not every biblical text is appropriate for liturgical proclamation since the lectionary is designed for the purpose of building up the community of faith. She proposes that the present canon be supplemented with noncanonical texts and feminist amplifications of canonical texts.[21] According to Procter-Smith, the "hostile texts" can and should be used liturgically, but specifically as the focus of liturgies of lament, exorcism, or repentance.[22]

Within the context of Jewish-Christian dialogue, similar concerns have been raised about the regular use of passages that cast the Pharisees in a derogatory light (e.g., the "woes" of Matthew 23); the use of the entire passion narratives, especially the reading of the Johannine narrative on Good Friday; the repeated use of the unedited speeches from Acts for the Sundays of Easter; and the whole prophecy-fulfillment approach that underlies the choice of Hebrew scripture readings in the Christian liturgy. While Raymond Brown and others have argued that every biblical text can and should be read without omission and then preached upon in a way that directly addresses the issue at stake (e.g., anti-Semitism),[23] not all biblical or liturgical scholars are convinced. As Eileen Schuller has remarked: "[B]etter translations and homilies are not the whole answer; we still come down to the question: are there not some texts or verses which must simply be omitted as 'pastorally unsuitable'?"[24]

The lectionary process itself reflects just such a judgment in the selection of some texts and omission of others as well as in the decisions as to where to begin and end a passage and which verses to omit. Further questions need to be raised, however, as to who makes those selections and on what principles.[25] As noted above, not all those who identify morally offensive passages in the lectionary would agree that selective omission of those texts is the most helpful pastoral solution. Those "hostile texts" remain in the scriptures and in the community's imagination. Some would argue, therefore, that the texts should be proclaimed, but then it is the preacher's responsibility to "oppose the text in the name of the gospel."[26] In traditions where a lectionary is not used, some would even advocate choosing one of the "texts of terror" with the explicit intent of addressing issues of racism, sexism, violence against gays and lesbians, or ecological irresponsibility.

Whether the lectionary selection presents a problematic text or one chooses a difficult text precisely to address the ethical issue that the text poses, the preacher's task is always to announce the good news of salvation. In terms of historical-critical biblical scholarship, this means that one of the preacher's tasks is to distinguish the historical-cultural bias inherent in the text from the word of God one is called to proclaim. This brings us back to the original challenge: Can the word of God be found in every text? The question itself is problematic in several ways.

First, we have already established that the word of God cannot be identified with a text, nor even with the canonical scriptures taken as a whole. Further, the history of salvation contained in the Bible includes a history of sin as well as a history of redemption. Some of that sin is recognized and named as such within the text itself. Other aspects of sin (e.g., slavery, ethnic exclusion, anti-Semitism) have been recognized and named by the church only from a later cultural perspective. Therefore, a text that was once seen to embody the "divine will" can be perceived later as a legitimation of sinful social structures ("Slaves be subject to your master"; "All civil authority is from God"; "Wives be submissive to your husbands"). The community's understanding of the word of God to be announced in a contemporary context may in fact reverse what was perceived to be the revelatory message in an earlier era or a different culture.

A second problem emerges, however, in that all language is historically and culturally conditioned. The "word of God" is not some "essential core" that can be easily distinguished from the biases of its original culture. Further, any contemporary proclamation involves yet another limited inculturation of the gospel. There is no noninculturated gospel nor any inculturation that is without its own biases.

Third, what constitutes the meaning of a text? The original intention of the author? The meaning "received" by the readers or hearers in interaction with the text? Complex issues of literary criticism and hermeneutics that apply to interpretation of any text arise here. Does a poem by Emily Dickinson or Robert Frost mean what the author intended, or does a text take on a life of its own once it is committed to writing? Any product of the creative imagination that becomes a classic contain layers of meaning often unrecognized and perhaps unintended by the original author.

Further, any theory of hermeneutics grants that a text can be interpreted only in light of its larger context. But how broadly does one define the literary, historical, and social context of a text? Can the meaning of Col 3:12–21 be determined apart from the larger context of the household code and the epistle?[27] from the sociopolitical setting of the time? from the larger Pauline and deutero-Pauline corpus? from the Christian scriptures or the Bible as a whole? What about the larger context of the ongoing Christian tradition and the effective history of the text? What about the present ecclesial and liturgical context? Even those who argue that the Bible interprets itself (Luther) make selections as to what passages or books are closer to the heart of the Christian gospel (the Letter to the Romans) and therefore provide the hermeneutical key for interpreting other passages (the Letter of James).

If the biblical text cannot be identified with the word of God, how does the preacher or a local community determine the "good news" to be announced to a particular congregation at a specific time? That decision involves the exercise of imagination and discernment on the part of both preachers and hearers of the word. The entire process is rooted in the Spirit's activity in the community and can be considered an extension of the dynamic of inspiration that was involved in both the original preaching of the gospel and the writing, editing, and canonical compilation of the written text.

Relocating the Good News: The Role of the Paschal Imagination

Feminist biblical scholar Sandra Schneiders has addressed both the foundational issues raised here and the art of interpreting difficult texts through the lens of what she calls the "paschal imagination." She directly addresses the concern of how a biblical text that expresses a position that is morally objectionable in light of the radical ethics of the gospel can function normatively as "sacred scripture" in a Christian community of faith. Focusing her attention on the androcentric character of the scriptures, Schneiders acknowledges that the Bible is "pervasively patriarchal" and "frequently enough patently sexist."[28]

Nevertheless, she remains convinced that the biblical text has a privileged position in the community of faith since the Bible is the normative witness in the Christian community to the Christ-event in Jesus of Nazareth and the living mooring of the present community of believers to its foundational past.[29] Schneiders remains convinced that through a hermeneutics of transformation, the real referent of the Christian scriptures is always good news: the world of Christian discipleship structured toward the final liberating reign of God.

Explicitly indebted to the hermeneutical theory of Paul Ricoeur, Schneiders argues for an interdisciplinary approach to the text that recognizes that meaning lies not behind the text in either the historical situation or the intention of the author but rather "ahead of the text" in the "world in front of the text." Given that conviction, Schneiders asserts that a patriarchal text can and should be interpreted in ways that in fact subvert "the patriarchal world which produced it and whose biases it expresses and promotes."[30]

Challenging the historical-critical mainstream of biblical interpretation in the Catholic tradition, Schneiders has argued consistently in her writings that the "literal sense" (or "textual meaning") of the scriptures cannot be reduced to the meaning intended by the original author and understood by the original audience ("the world behind the text"). Rather, the ecclesial interpretative task involves a truly "theological exegesis" whose goal is not only what the original author meant but also the contemporary meaning of the text as "word of God" for the present-day community of believers.[31]

Drawing upon the hermeneutical insights of Hans-Georg Gadamer as well as Ricoeur, Schneiders approaches the biblical text as a classic that is characterized by a "surplus of meaning." The meaning of a classic text is mediated through its interpreters in much the same way that the meaning of a piece of music is mediated by the interpretation of a musician rather than merely by notes on a page. A living tradition connects the text and the interpreter and enables a "fusion of horizons" between the world of the text and the world of the contemporary interpreter. In that "conversation" between two worlds, new dimensions of meaning appear. While Gadamer uses that image of a conversation in describing this emergence of meaning through a "fusion of horizons," Ricoeur introduces the important distinction between oral and written discourse. A text is not simply a record of oral discourse; hence the model of dialogue between text and interpreter (or scripture and preacher) is not entirely appropriate. Rather, as Schneiders summarizes Ricoeur's insight: "Writing creates a new kind of being, a being which originated in an event, the act of composition, but which perdures as ideal meaning, that is as meaning liberated from its originating event and capable of being reactualized in new ways in subsequent events of understanding."[32]

Ricoeur's theory of text interpretation carries several significant implications for the discussion here of whether texts that emerged out of patriarchal, racist, or otherwise oppressive cultural contexts can ever be interpreted in a liberating mode. According to Ricoeur's theory, a text becomes semantically independent of the intention of its original author and its originating circumstances as well as the understanding of its original audience. The referent of the text is not the "world behind the text" from which it emerged but rather the world disclosed by the text, the meaning projected "in front of the text."

Schneiders notes, however, that interpretation of the Christian scriptures has a particular complexity since "the reference of the New Testament is in a real sense to a world 'behind the text' ": the events of the life, preaching, and paschal mystery of Jesus of Nazareth. Yet at the same time the text discloses a "world in front of the text": the reign of God. The two "worlds" are in reality the same vision, however, since the life, death, and resurrection of Jesus are the inauguration (the "already") of the reign of God that awaits final fulfillment (the "not yet"). Further, as Schneiders notes, "It is the historical reality of Jesus which actually creates and founds the existential possibility of discipleship which the text projects before it."[33] In terms of the discussion at hand, what this means is that both the history of Jesus, insofar as that is available in and through the faith-witness texts of the Gospels, and the vision of the reign of God that the New Testament texts disclose are clearly in opposition to sexism, racism, or any other form of oppression. Thus the meaning disclosed by a text that emerges from a biased cultural framework that distorts the vision of the reign of God cannot be identified with that bias.

When explicit texts (e.g., patriarchal ones) appear to contradict Jesus' own style of relationship and ministry and the deeper vision of Christian discipleship disclosed by the scriptures, the image of Jacob wrestling with the angel for a blessing becomes an apt description of the biblical exegete's or the preacher's task.[34] Here the significance of Schneiders's insistence (following Ricoeur) that "meaning emerges in the dialectic between what the text says (sense) and what the text is about or its truth claims (reference)"[35] becomes apparent. Schneiders uses the familiar example of how the American Declaration of Independence's claim that "all men are created equal" has been progressively interpreted. In later cultural contexts, the true meaning of the text was understood to include precisely those who were not envisioned by its original authors — children, nonwhites, the landless, slaves, and females. In parallel fashion, she argues that the Second Testament has produced a people who are beginning to understand that the patriarchy its authors took for granted and affirmed is incompatible with the world of discipleship and liberation that the Second Testament projects. From our standpoint in the effective history of Christianity, the ideology of patriarchy which was exposed first of all as false consciousness in ourselves is now exposed as infidelity of the text to its own referent.[36]

In other words, Schneiders argues that the text as symbolic structure mediates the Christ-event in a way that offers the impulse and possibility of liberation even from the patriarchy and ideology clearly present in the text.[37] Other biblical and liturgical scholars make the same claim although they frame their arguments somewhat differently. Liturgical theologian David Power, for example, draws on another aspect of Ricoeur's thought that suggests that literary genres are revelatory in themselves. Power proposes that the word of God is located not so much in propositional content as in the use of forms of language that free us by disorienting our accepted worlds, opening up our imaginations, and engendering hope for a different future.

Even the narrative form, which is usually presumed to establish and legitimate order and continuity in the community, can be approached as "extended metaphor" that subverts traditional expectations of order precisely through bringing together unexpected elements.[38] Power urges that a more creative listening to biblical narrative is necessary if we are to grasp the subversive twist in many stories that has rarely been heard or proclaimed. A second hearing may unearth a meaning that seems to reverse the surface meaning and reveal instead the "Word beneath the words" that is the call of the Spirit to freedom and new possibilities. He detects examples of these subversive twists in

> the locating of victory over death in the death of the innocent, in the convergence of God's judgment on humankind with the judgment of the courts on Jesus, in the sending of a woman as apostle to those who, by reason of intimacy with Jesus and by reason of cultural supposition, thought of themselves as apostles, or in the way in which Jesus' judgments of people differ so evidently from the judgments made in virtue of the Law.[39]

Granting that narratives can contain their own twists of meaning, Power nonetheless concedes that, in general, narrative as form
favors, and is used in the service of, continuity and the established
order. Thus he argues for attention to the interaction of multiple
forms of discourse as the key to unlocking the liberating word of
the Spirit within and beneath the explicit words of the biblical texts.
In particular he highlights the genres of parables and eschatological sayings and the songs of lamentation as forms of discourse that
disrupt and disorient the presumed world of order.[40]

The critical hermeneutical proposals of both Schneiders and Power
point to the limitations of the insights that the biblical text shapes
the community or that the Bible critiques the church. More precisely
we might say: the word of God shapes the community; the reign
of God disclosed by Jesus in the Christian scriptures critiques the
church. The good news to be announced is the "world in front of
the text" — the reign of God. Individual biblical texts are then to
be critically appropriated from the perspective of the new creation
into which Christians have been baptized. In every culture and new
situation, the Christian community and the preacher are called to
grapple with what the symbols of baptism, eucharist, and reconciliation mean. In a similar way, formed by the sacramental imagination,
communities of believers are called to wrestle with the biblical text of
the day in light of where the gospel has not yet been heard or where
what has been heard or preached is less than the liberating gospel of
Jesus Christ. For both preachers and hearers of the word this means
relocating the good news not in the text but in the community in
dialogue with the text. Since that dialogue takes place not only in
the power of Spirit but also in the context of a specific culture and
sociopolitical context, the formation of the sacramental imagination
necessarily implies the cultivation of a "prophetic imagination."[41]

Prophetic Imagination: Remembering the Future

In a broad sense the vocation of the prophets was to speak God's
truth in the midst of their own culture and moment in history. While
Jesus and all the prophets who went before him were firmly rooted in
their tradition, they were called precisely from that context to radically reinterpret what God is asking of people here and now. For
members of communities to attend to "the word of God" in the

midst of the cacophony of competing voices in any dominant culture requires the cultivation of an imagination rooted in and formed
by their religious tradition. Walter Brueggemann suggests that it is
precisely the role of the prophet or anyone involved in prophetic
ministry "to nurture, nourish, and evoke a consciousness and perception alternative to the consciousness and perception of the dominant
culture around us."[42]

The fundamental conversion that this "shift in imagination" demands is part of the life/death/new-life dynamic that Christians
identify as the paschal mystery in everyday living. Brueggemann
traces a similar dynamic in the Hebrew scriptures. He describes the
fundamental trajectory within Israel's experience of faith as reflected
in the Psalms as a pattern of orientation, disorientation, and new orientation. The move from a place of settled orientation in which one
can celebrate with confidence "God's good creation" into a "season
of disorientation" is reflected particularly in the psalms of lament.
As Brueggemann describes it, the lament is "a candid, even if un-
willing, embrace of a new situation of chaos, now devoid of the
coherence that marks God's good creation. The sphere of disorientation may be quite personal and intimate, or it may be massive and
public."[43] Brueggemann explicitly connects this Jewish experience of
radical absence and anguish with the central Christian symbol of the
crucifixion of Jesus. Similarly, he connects the fundamental Christian
hope in the resurrection with a second dynamic in Jewish spirituality: "a move from a context of disorientation to a new orientation,
surprised by a new gift from God, a new coherence made present
to us just when we thought all was lost."[44] That experience of surprising new life, redemption, and healing is celebrated in songs of
thanksgiving and hymns of joy and deliverance.

Brueggemann's correlation of the dynamics of suffering and hope
as central to both Jewish piety and the Christian paschal mystery is
particularly crucial in a culture that denies suffering and grief and
grows increasingly numb through diverse forms of escape and avoid-
ance. The development of a "prophetic imagination" is critical for
preachers and for Christian communities who wrestle with the meaning of the word of God in the midst of the death-denying culture of
the first world. Yet in the tradition of all the prophets and the one
who was more than a prophet, preachers who announce radical hope
and name causes for repentance and grief will meet with resistance.
Nonetheless, the role of the preacher and of prophetic communities,

like that of the prophet and poet, is precisely to evoke and nurture an alternative perception of reality.

The prophetic imagination remains focused on the promise of the future reign of God. The absence or violation of that reign calls for lament; the memory of the vision preached by the prophets, embodied by Jesus, and promised as the future fulfillment of the cosmos elicits hope and energy for discipleship. In this alternative community of the gospel the first will be last and the last first; differences of race, ethnic origins, sex, class, or social position can no longer serve as the basis for separation or subordination; leaders wash feet; the hungry are fed; and servants and masters become friends. Wherever that vision has not yet taken hold, the preacher's task is the difficult mission of speaking the truth, naming the dis-grace in the community, and calling for a return to the covenant of the gospel. Thus Brueggemann reminds us that part of the "ministry of imagination" involves offering people a language for their pain and grief. Whether on the level of the individual or the community, the ability to articulate anguish is a necessary stage in the process of healing and transformation.[45] The embrace of pain through the process of lament is possible, however, only because one has hope that the future can indeed be different. Grief that is not despair is rooted in a memory of a past that has been lost or changed, but also in a future that can be imagined if not remembered. The hope of the paschal imagination is that death, injustice, and loss do not have the final word; the future lies in the hands of the living God.

Thus the task of the prophetic preacher and prophetic communities is not only to give language to grief but also to rekindle hope. By retelling the gospel story in light of present conflicts, the prophetic preacher invites the community to reembrace the power and freedom of their baptism. If we are a culture that denies death, we are even more reluctant to believe in the power of resurrection: the power of God to bring life out of death. If the resurrection is possible, then all of reality holds a possibility beyond human control or imagination — God's possibility.

The preacher is called to narrate the community's familiar story, but from a new vantage point — from the perspective of the new and different future that God has promised and that the resurrection has inaugurated. In remembering God's surprising but steadfast faithfulness in the past, the community hears the promise spoken again in their midst and has the courage to "hope against hope" that God can and will be faithful in this new moment and in the unknown future that lies ahead.

Prophetic Hearing: Spirit Active in the Community

Prophetic preaching is difficult because it entails, for both preacher and hearers, conversion — change of heart and life. The prophetic preacher has to be able to distinguish the kind of resistance to the genuine stumbling block of the gospel that calls for courage and perseverance from the negative response of the assembly that is a sign that the "word entrusted to the church" has not yet been proclaimed. This presumes that the preaching dynamic involves not only prophetic speaking but also prophetic hearing.

Like the transformation from death to life, the transformation that opens up new possibilities in the imagination of both preacher and community is ultimately the work of the Holy Spirit. The same creative Spirit who was active throughout the history of salvation and the process of the formation of the scriptures remains the animating source of all life in the contemporary Christian community. Hence it is important to move beyond a focus on the preacher to the "paschal imagination" or "prophetic imagination" located within the community. When texts are preached in a way that does not capture the authentic freedom of the gospel, the Spirit of God can and does empower resistance and an "alternate hearing" within the community of faith. Convinced of that possibility, David Power maintains that "whatever power the patterns or paradigms of speech adopted from dominative cultures have to silence or misrepresent what is experienced in God's Spirit, this same Spirit gives the power and freedom to hear an alternative word."[46] Renita Weems confirms that insight from the perspective of African-American women. After tracing the impact of racist and sexist interpretations of biblical texts on African-American women, Weems nevertheless observes that "African American women have continued to read the Bible in most instances because of its vision and promise of a world where the humanity of everyone will be fully valued. They have accomplished this reading in spite of the voices from within and without that have tried to equivocate on that vision and promise."[47]

The claim that the Spirit enables a hearing of the gospel sometimes in spite of preaching, rather than because of it, presumes a broad understanding of who constitutes the church to whom the word has been entrusted. Vatican II's claim that the word of God has been entrusted to the entire community has significant implications for the preaching and hearing of the gospel. If consulting the experience of the faithful (the *sensus fidelium*) is vital for the authentic doctrinal development of the church, it is all the more essential for the credible preaching of the gospel.

The sacramental imagination offers a foundational explanation of how profoundly the word of God has been entrusted to the community: human beings are structured as "hearers of the word." From the beginning humanity has been fashioned in the image of the Word and destined for freedom and love in and through the Spirit. The full realization of the reign of God that Jesus preached and embodied remains always a promised future in our limited and sinful world, but nevertheless that promised destiny remains our deepest truth and only home. We cannot fully name that mystery that lies ahead of us, but we do know when it has been violated or distorted. When living in fidelity to its baptismal vocation, the Christian assembly knows when it has not heard the word of God, when the proclamation of the reign of God is absent, manipulated, or distorted. The "anointing of the Spirit" that is necessary to hear the word includes a desire to hear and be challenged by the gospel. The Christian community knows when that has not happened precisely because the Spirit of God stirs up resistance and creates expectations that have not been fulfilled.

David Power has suggested that the Spirit is at work both in the interplay of diverse forms of discourse that are found in the scriptures and in the desire for authentic freedom operative in the Christian community and that the two are intimately linked. The language of freedom and hope has the power to retrieve the originating power of the events of creation and redemption and thus to reshape reality by disorienting and questioning all patterns of human control and domination and gifting humanity with the imagination of possibility that exceeds and escapes all human achievement.

Rooted in the experience of the mystery of the redemptive word, this paradoxical speech emerges most clearly from the experience of those who participate in the mystery of Christ's suffering and hope. Power reminds us that those who are united with Christ's passion through the power of the Spirit often, in spite of all the evidence to the contrary, hear a word of liberation and hope in listening to the scriptures or celebrating the liturgy. The paschal imagination is the community's imagination enlivened by the Holy Spirit. When the gospel is not preached in a liberating way, the Spirit of God will be active in the hearers of the word, keeping open their resistance and empowering their imaginations to continue to envision the alternative vision of the reign of God.

The subversive power of the symbols of scripture and liturgy, as the power of God, can never be domesticated or controlled by human structures or misrepresentations. Locating the "power of the word" in the "speech over which in the long run the church can claim no control," Power reminds us that no matter how distorted or limited the perspective of the biblical writers or preachers, the word of God (and the liturgical symbols) shares in the power of the same liberating Spirit of God who remains active in the community to whom these symbols have been entrusted and who are called to appropriate them in freedom and love. Thus he exhorts the hearers of the word:

> Similarly, in attending to what is written in the Bible, or what is celebrated in liturgy, or what is avowed in tradition, the church has to listen keenly for a Word that speaks from a deeper experience of redemption than do the paradigmatic patterns of speech adopted from patriarchal, hierarchical, or technological cultures.[48]

In the end, the central notion of the scriptures functioning as authoritative word for the community cannot be separated from the workings of the Spirit active within the community. We can "trust the word" only if we do not identify the word of God with either the surface meaning of the text or distorted interpretations of the gospel even when they issue from the pulpit. Rather, through the exercise of the "paschal imagination" the community can locate "the Word beneath the words" that is always mediated by the Spirit of God, who "brings all things to remembrance" in freedom and truth.

Preaching and the Ongoing Process of Inspiration

Disputes over whether the Bible is to be understood as the "church's book" or whether the Bible critically norms and forms the church raise echoes of Reformation polemics. In the wake of critical biblical scholarship, however, it has become evident that the two positions are not mutually exclusive. Both are true. From the perspective of the sacramental imagination, the question of whether and how to preach specific problematic texts finally can be resolved only in and through a process of discernment that is not unlike the process through which the scriptures were originally composed or later compiled into a canon. As Paul Achtemeier has suggested, the much disputed term "inspiration" might most appropriately describe the dynamic interaction of the tradition of a community, a prophetic interpreter, and a new situation in the community's history.[49] Inspiration is located in neither the text itself (inspired word of God) nor the author (prophet, evangelist, or preacher), but in the dynamic action of the Spirit in the community's living history. So, too, the word of God to be announced is located neither in a specific text nor in the preacher's insights or biases, but in the dynamic interaction between text, preacher, and community.

The biblical word often will challenge both preacher and community to deeper fidelity; the issue may not be one of interpretation but one of the difficulty of living the radical demands of the gospel. Preacher and community may struggle together over what a particular text means for their concrete lives. On other occasions, the prophetic preacher may be called to "preach against the text" in a way that initially meets resistance because the preaching of the gospel involves a "hard word" that the community would rather not hear. At times, however, it may be the community's resistance to a text or the way that text has been interpreted that is the Spirit's prompting, calling both preacher and community to a fuller vision of the gospel.

What does all this mean for the question raised at the beginning of this chapter about whether every text can and should be used in the liturgical context? In some sense specific communities will have to "live the questions," as the poet Rilke once suggested.[50] Further, some opportunity for response from the assembly is essential for both preacher and hearers not only because preaching is a communication event but also because the Spirit does not cease to speak when the preacher does. To return to the concrete example of the use of Col 3:12–21 on Holy Family Sunday or the use of Romans 13 in South Africa, I agree with Sandra Schneiders that we should avoid the public proclamation of oppressive texts unless the preacher intends to preach "against the text" in the name of the gospel.[51]

Judgments of what constitutes an "oppressive text" in a specific situation or what is an authentic interpretation of a disputed text are part of the pastoral responsibilities of those called to preach the gospel. But who makes those decisions? In the liturgical setting, most often the decision rests with the pastor or ordained preacher. At times a liturgist or lector or member of the pastoral team may raise the concern. But even in situations where the cultural or political bias of the text is ignored or reinforced in the preaching, the baptized are not passive recipients of whatever message is proclaimed.

If the word of God is entrusted to the community, then whether the preacher is prophetic or not, it remains crucial that members of the community reflect on their experience and voice the word they have heard in the scriptures and the preaching as well as in the entire liturgy. This communal reflection on the word of God can occur in a variety of settings, including the home. Adult education gatherings might make a priority of studying and reflecting on the scriptures. Catechists, religious educators, and pastoral ministers in a variety of contexts could invite those they meet with to respond to the gospel and the preaching of the season. Any parish group or meeting could begin with a response to the gospel of the week. Increasingly, groups of believers are meeting in homes for faith-sharing and reflection on their lives in light of the gospel.[52] In any of those contexts the prophetic vocation of all the baptized summons us to listen especially for the voices we often miss. In an attempt to facilitate that kind of attending to the forgotten word, Kenneth Untener, bishop of the Roman Catholic diocese of Saginaw, Michigan, instituted the following policy in his diocese in 1991: "[E]very meeting held under the auspices of the Church, at the diocesan or parish level, no matter what its purpose, no matter how few or many people are there, must have as its first agenda item: How shall what we do here affect or involve the poor?"[53]

If the Spirit resides in the community of the baptized, then the word of God can be discovered only gradually as the community wrestles with its own living tradition, including the scriptures it calls sacred. But then, "wrestling for a blessing" is hardly a new idea in the biblical tradition, nor is it without consequences.

Chapter 6

The Human Story and
the Story of Jesus

Preaching on Luke 1:26–38 on the Feast of the Annunciation at a eucharist for high school students, a woman related the following story:

> During World War II not only the Jews, but also other groups were persecuted by the Nazis including homosexuals, disabled persons, and gypsies. The story is told of a gypsy family who was part of a traveling circus in Poland. During one of their acts, the teenage daughter would jump from a high wire with no net below and her father would catch her. One morning the father had gone out early and the young girl was alone in the apartment building where they were staying. A stranger came to the door and said that he had a message from her father. The message was that the Nazis had come into the town and they had to escape. It was too dangerous for the father to return by daylight, but that night at 2:00 in the morning he would stand at the northwest corner of the apartment building. His daughter should jump and he would be there to catch her so that they could escape. The young girl was confused. She didn't know the messenger. She wasn't sure these were the words of her father. She wasn't even sure which was the northwest corner of the building. But as the day went on, her father did not return and she heard word that the Nazis had indeed come into the town. Having only the word of her father's promise, she went to what she thought was the northwest corner of the building at the time she had been told and whispered into the darkness: "Father, are you there?" There was no answer. She jumped.

The preacher paused for a long moment before concluding the story with the words: "And he caught her."[1]

In a subsequent preaching workshop the preacher explained how she had used that story to introduce the homily but then continued with an explanation: "The young girl was like Mary...." One of the directors of the workshop suggested that the story itself carried the impact of the gospel of the day and that the preaching would have been more effective if the preacher had trusted the power of the human narrative, if carefully crafted, to retell the gospel story. Not all the participants in the workshop agreed, particularly because in this case the preacher was not also the presider at the liturgy. The discussion that followed raised issues about the use of story in preaching that continue to be disputed among both homileticians and theologians.

Preaching is frequently described today as "telling the story."[2] Yet the prevalent practice of beginning the homily or sermon with a story drawn from human experience, literature, or the media has met recently with critical resistance from the pew as well as the academy. The complaint lodged in earlier years was that preaching never connected with life experience. While that remains true in far too many pulpits today, a new problem is emerging. Those who come to the Sunday assembly to hear the word of God protest that too often they hear only the life-story of the preacher or images derived from the popular culture that, at best, trivialize the depth and power of the gospel.

Reflecting on this "extensive use of first person narration to which congregations are subjected on a typical Sunday morning," Richard Lischer has charged that "no discipline has invested more heavily (or more uncritically) in story than preaching."[3] Further, he challenges: "How long after theology has tired of story and our culture has grown bored of finding itself, will preaching be burdened by the weight of this cargo that washed aboard one stormy night in the seventies?"[4] In two articles in which he has analyzed the strengths and limitations of narrative preaching,[5] Lischer identifies crucial theological issues at stake in the foundational areas of revelation, anthropology, and christology.

One of Lischer's primary concerns is that narrative or story preaching distorts both human life and divine revelation.[6] Forgetting the reality and power of sin and the ambiguity of human experience, the preacher can underestimate the hermeneutical distance between "my story" and "the story," according to Lischer. While the human story can be used as it was by Martin Luther to express "the story of human misery,...the preface to the story of salvation,"[7] an infinite qualitative gap exists between the word of God, which is "wholly other," and sinful human beings. Luther's own narratives were useful to point out the human dilemma, outline the contours of the problem, or draw out the chaos in human life, but Luther never pretended that the human story could serve as a contemporary manifestation of the gospel. Rather Luther insisted that "we never preach to people who are perfectly whole or hopelessly corrupt, but only to those who are being healed or getting sick." The members of the congregation are "wholly righteous in Christ and at the same time wholly plunged into their own sin and this 'big whorehouse' of a world....[T]he great dragon [is] in each of us."[8]

Viewing the human story as at best "the preface to the story of salvation" suggests further that the story of salvation is told exclusively, or at least uniquely, in the story of Jesus Christ. Hence Lischer writes of the move "from the thousand spurious stories to the *one* true one" and remarks that the *only* clue to Jesus is the sign of Jonah — the Christian story is founded on the "catastrophe" of death and resurrection.[9] This question of the uniqueness of Jesus Christ and the Christian gospel, which is one of the central points debated in the fields of christology and foundational theology today, must be confronted by preachers as well. Is it true that the *only* clue to Jesus is to be found in a sign of utter contradiction? What of the Christian claim that Christ is the mystery hidden in creation from the very beginning (Eph 1:3–10; Col 1:15–16) and the conviction that God's will to salvation is universal (1 Tim 2:4)? If all things were created in Christ and all was created for Christ, is there no touchstone in human experience of that promise? On the other hand, if the mystery of Christ is found implicitly in all religious experience and even in deeply human experience, why preach the Christian gospel at all? What of the Pauline claim that we preach the gospel of Christ crucified, who is both "stumbling block to the Jews" and "folly to the Greeks" (1 Cor 1:23)? Can the story of Jesus be reduced to one of many expressions of religious experience?

Significant homiletic issues emerge precisely at this point. Can the preacher's use of narratives drawn from the world's religions and from profoundly human, but not specifically religious, experience be described adequately as the use of "spurious stories"? Does the human story function only as a preface describing human need for

the salvation found in the gospel of Jesus Christ, or can a concrete
human story function as a contemporary parable, a new hermeneutic, of the gospel? Do we preach as Jesus did, or do we preach Jesus?
When we tell God's story in Jesus, does story operate differently
(more deeply? more powerfully? in a "wholly other" fashion?) than
when we tell a "merely" human story or even stories drawn from
other religious traditions? Is it always necessary to make explicit the
connection between the human story and the gospel, or can that
connection remain implicit? Can the preacher rely on the liturgical
context of a homily to further interpret the human story in light of
the death and resurrection of Jesus Christ?

At the heart of Lischer's plural criticisms is the danger that a contemporary approach to preaching that begins with human experience
or narrative will remain on that level and fail to communicate the
gospel, the presence and power of God-among-us. The purpose of
the homily as described in multiple liturgical documents is precisely
to connect ordinary human experience with the scriptures and liturgy
of the day.[10] Turning to the ways in which the story of Jesus was
proclaimed in the earliest Christian communities as reflected in the
biblical and liturgical narratives, contemporary preachers can discover key elements for our contemporary announcing of the gospel.
Because of its rich liturgical overtones and the possibility of its liturgical origins as well as its carefully crafted structure, the Emmaus
narrative in chapter 24 of Luke's Gospel presents a valuable model
for contemporary narrative preaching.

The Emmaus Narrative

The eucharistic overtones of the Emmaus narrative (Luke 24:13–35)
are noted frequently.as preachers and catechists point to the breaking
of the bread as the crucial moment of recognition for the itinerant,
disappointed disciples of Jesus: "With that their eyes were opened
and they recognized him" (Luke 24:31). Given a renewed appreciation of the interrelationship of word and sacrament, however, the
passage also presents an opportunity to reflect on what might be
called the preaching of Jesus in the passage.

As Luke narrates the story, two friends of Jesus are on a journey
from Jerusalem, where all their hopes have been called into question
by the crucifixion of Jesus. In the midst of their own lively exchange,

a stranger approaches and walks with them, but they do not recognize him as Jesus. As they recount "all that went on here these past days," the story they tell is of "a prophet powerful in word and deed" who was delivered to his enemies, condemned to death, and executed. While they had held a memory of freedom and hope in the Messiah, its fulfillment has been contradicted in the suffering and death of Jesus: "We were hoping that he was the one who would set Israel free" (Luke 24:21). A final surprising twist complicates their experience even further: some women disciples have returned from the tomb they claim is empty telling of visions of angels and proclaiming that Jesus lives.

Having walked with them on their journey and listened to their story, Jesus the stranger becomes the preacher who reinterprets all they have experienced with a metaphor of the impossible: a suffering Messiah. Breaking open their imaginations to the unexpected possibility that the glory of God has been revealed precisely through and beyond the crucifixion, Jesus reinterprets the whole heritage of Moses and the prophets in light of the confusing events of their recent history. The words of Jesus, his way of connecting their tragic human experience with the tradition of hope they thought had been destroyed, move them to invite a stranger to share their table. Even before the deeper recognition of Jesus in the breaking of the bread, the words of the preacher opened their hearts and touched their lives, as they were to recall later: "Were not our hearts burning within us as he talked to us on the road and explained the Scriptures to us?" (Luke 24:32). Upon their return to Jerusalem, the disciples proclaim the story of not only "how they had come to know him in the breaking of the bread" but also "what had happened to them on the road" (Luke 24:35).

The pattern of this narrative illustrates what Paul Ricoeur has identified as the threefold mimetic structure of narrative.[11] Borrowed from Aristotle's *Poetics,* the term "mimesis" refers to an artistic or creative representation or imitation of life. Ricoeur suggests that we are all born storytellers in that we make sense of the events of our lives through some sort of story or pattern of unity whether we do so consciously or not. This preunderstanding of the experience of their lives and culture that hearers bring to any new situation (and thus every preaching event) is what Ricoeur calls prefiguration (mimesis-1). In the Emmaus story the disciples had come to understand and live their lives in light of their hope that Jesus would prove to be the

anointed one of God, the Messiah who would finally liberate Israel.
His execution had destroyed that hope, or so it seemed.

In the passage as narrated, Jesus walks with his friends and listens
to their prefiguration of their lives in terms of confusion and dashed
hopes, before speaking a word of new possibility. Only then does
Jesus as preacher make the key narrative move: he configures experience in a new pattern or plot through the imaginative "grasping
together" of disparate or previously unrelated events (the crucifixion, the women's story, an empty tomb, their previous tradition and
hopes). This new configuration (mimesis-2) transforms the succession of events into one meaningful whole and imposes the "sense of
an ending" on the indefinite succession of incidents. Rereading the
past from the perspective of a new ending produces new possibilities of action and response. Reality is redescribed, thus calling into
question all previous presumptions. The clash of images in the new
metaphor of a "suffering Messiah" opens up the possibility that the
story of the women is true: Jesus lives. Given the resurrection as the
"ending" of the events they described, their expectations of freedom
and a future take on new dimensions. The new pattern configured by
the preacher Jesus is God's plot that encompasses the possibility of
both execution and new life, both cross and resurrection. The whole
story of salvation history can be reread in light of the root metaphor
of a "suffering Messiah" whom God has raised to new life.

That imaginative configuration thus opened up new possibilities
for the refiguration of the lives of the disciples (mimesis-3). In the
Emmaus narrative that refiguration begins with the disciples' invitation to the stranger to share their hospitality and join them at the
table, an openness that leads to the even deeper recognition of Jesus
in the breaking of the bread and the later return to Jerusalem to
share their story.

This initial analysis of the Emmaus story in light of Ricoeur's theory of narrative suggests that effective narrative preaching involves
the threefold pattern of prefiguration of past human experience, configuration of the human story in light of the divine plot of the story
of Jesus, and refiguration of imagination and life through the ongoing process of conversion. Both Ricoeur's theory and the broad
framework of the sacramental imagination suggest that narratives of
human experience can be used to proclaim the word of God and effect conversion if the preacher consciously attends to four homiletic
concerns: (1) the function and value of the human story in the proc-

lamation event, (2) the goal of preaching as call to conversion, (3) the preacher's role as narrator of the story, and (4) the importance of "the sense of the ending" in narrative and liturgical proclamation.

Homiletic Concerns

The Function and Value of the Human Story in Preaching

Ricoeur's description of the narrative process as a threefold mimesis offers a deeper understanding of the appropriateness of proclaiming the gospel in and through human stories. What Ricoeur and others have identified as "the narrative structure of human experience"[12] is reflected in the Emmaus text in the disciples' prefiguration of their experience in retelling their story, the configuration of the narrative Jesus weaves, and the account of the refiguration of the disciples' lives.

The same pattern applies to contemporary disciples and would-be disciples. Christian identity, like human identity, is both formed and revealed by the stories through which we bring meaning to the disparate and chaotic events of our lives and world. Many come to the hearing of the gospel in a moment of confusion similar to that of the disciples on the road; former patterns of meaning have broken down or been called into question in a radical way. While the present, as Augustine remarked, is the only moment that exists,[13] human persons remain profoundly affected by memories and images of the past as well as by hope, or lack of hope, for the future. Those who long to hear a word that is a word of God hope that their past memories and present confusion can be woven into a new pattern, that the configuration of the gospel can open up new possibilities for their future.

As the one who retells the story of salvation in the Emmaus passage, Jesus offers personal witness to the truth of the new version of the disciples' familiar story. Hearing the griefs and joys of their people and nation retold in a configuration that is refocused by the possibility of a suffering Messiah allows the disciples to recognize that story as their own.

Part of the power of narrative preaching derives from the insight that life's most powerful experiences can be shared only in and through personal testimony. Hearing the story of human pain or rejoicing gives access to an experience where abstract description and analysis fail. Precisely because of this ability of stories to communicate experiences that exceed the boundaries of other human language, many would claim today that narrative is the most appropriate, even the necessary, category for the holy within the limits of human experience.[14] Further, the narrative structure of human experience points to the inherently social dimension of being human. Narratives both express and create the experience of human communities. "Stories weave into shared fabric the destinies of many persons."[15] A final aspect of the narrative structure of human experience is revealed in the conclusion to the Emmaus passage, when the disciples, profoundly touched by the story and the experience of Jesus, are moved to return to Jerusalem and tell the story to others — the desired dynamic in all preaching.

The homiletic recommendation that proclamation begins with ordinary human experience not only follows the parable patterns of the preacher Jesus but also provides, at the very least, the element of a common prefiguration of experience among the hearers of the word. When the preaching event is not an explicit dialogue, the prefiguration of the hearers' experience can be clarified or brought to focus in the preacher's use of story drawn from human life or culture and used as "the preface to the story of salvation." Sometimes the preacher goes further, however, and uses human stories not only as preface but precisely to mediate the gospel. In that case the preacher has moved beyond prefiguration and is involved in a conscious configuration, selecting and weaving the elements in the story according to the pattern of the gospel. When a human story is used as a hermeneutic of the biblical story, however, clearly the latter controls the development of the plot. Narrative does not simply repeat history; it shifts its configuration, thus changing it fundamentally.

Story-Preaching and the Call to Conversion

Ricoeur's contention that to retell a story is to reshape reality is critical since many would argue that preaching as "telling the story" underlines the continuity between ordinary human experience and the story of the gospel, but what remains disputed is the power of narrative preaching to bring about radical change or conversion. The dialectical imagination insists that the gospel creates its own context (a world quite unlike this world), the world of the parables where God's extravagance and unpredictability reign and where the paradox of the cross challenges the continuity of all narrative.

If, however, the process of conversion is ultimately "a shift of horizons," a transvaluation of all past values and a radical reorienting of one's life,[16] a shift of narrative is no small exchange: one's human identity at the deepest levels of values, character, and relationships is at stake. To offer others a new vision of reality, a new way of understanding and interpreting life, is in fact to offer them new life. As Stephen Crites explains, conversion occurs through a new awakening of consciousness: "not only [one's] past and future, but the very cosmos in which [one] lives is strung in a new way."[17]

But can the telling of stories effect conversion not only of personal identity but also of social and political commitments and structures? Another of Lischer's concerns about preaching as storytelling is to the point here: too often the poetic fails to become prophetic. He questions whether story can provide the resources necessary for implementing ethical growth or sociopolitical change and concludes that "story is incomplete as a vehicle for change until it is interpreted."[18] In response to the charge that stories belong not to the political sphere but to the "purely private sphere" or the "aesthetic sphere of good taste," J. B. Metz replies: "If they give this impression, our stories will only reveal the extent to which we have forgotten how to tell them."[19] Narrative holds the power to preserve forgotten memories of past history and to anticipate a radically new future. Retelling the story of the past harbors the possibility of retrieving the history of those who have been dismissed as insignificant. As the stories and spirituals of black slaves illustrate so powerfully, retelling the story of a suffering people becomes a "subversive" way of reinterpreting history, criticizing oppressive power, and empowering the impulse toward liberation. Precisely because they foster freedom, anticipate a new social order, and release the imagination, poetic and artistic expressions of the human spirit have always been among the first areas of repression by totalitarian regimes. As they know well, stories can be dangerous. Stories of suffering call forth ethical resistance and protest on the part of those who hear the story.

Among those whose narratives clearly move their hearers and readers to ethical decision and action are Elie Wiesel, the Jewish storyteller who insists that the memory of the Holocaust be kept alive precisely so that it never happen again, and Nadine Gordimer, the South African writer whose carefully crafted and imaginative descriptions of life and relationships within the apartheid structures of South Africa carried a powerful impulse toward outrage and resistance. In their writings it becomes clear that stories have a political and practical interest. They bear the power to change lives and move to action.

The power of narrative preaching, however, goes beyond the power of the human story to convey experience or to move human beings to ethical action. The power of preaching is rooted in the power of the Spirit of God to bring life out of death, to undo the power of sin, to liberate and heal. Thus the stories chosen to retell the gospel must be carefully selected and narrated if they are to function as contemporary parables. The use of the story is always at the service of the proclamation of the gospel. When the hearers of the word enter into the world disclosed by the gospel, a whole new order of reality is disclosed. Ordinary human life is redescribed as an encounter with God. Radical revision of one's life according to the values of the reign of God is the only response that fits the new order of reality. Eschatology does indeed remind us that "faith is a slash across the symmetry or predictability of history," as Lischer insists,[20] but this occurs precisely through the creative configuration of narrative, just as the extraordinary world of God broke into the ordinary world of Jesus' hearers in and through his parables.

Contemporary story-preaching, however, too often lacks this deeper dimension of the parable — the metaphorical twist — the moment of shock that is at once shock of recognition and call to transformation. Ricoeur's description of narrative as extended metaphor is key to an understanding of the power of narrative to call forth conversion or transformation. The strategy of metaphor is to exploit a creative use of language in which two disparate realities are brought together in a "metaphorical twist." As Ricoeur describes it, the power of metaphor is "to break through previous categorization and to establish new logical boundaries on the ruins of the preceding ones."[21] Literal interpretation results in absurdity; hence metaphor demands a process of self-destruction or transformation; new and unexpected meaning emerges from the "semantic impertinence" of metaphor. If, however, all experience is interpreted experience, new experience of reality emerges when new meaning emerges. As Ricoeur remarks, metaphor shatters and increases our sense of reality precisely by shattering and increasing our language. "Reality redescribed is itself novel reality."[22]

In narratives we have not only the clash of images but the "synthesis of the heterogeneous"; a new congruence is claimed in the organization of events through the creativity of plot. To grasp the plot of narrative is to understand quite different circumstances, even "reversals of fortune," from a new perspective of unity that is unavailable until the plot reaches its end.

The process of therapy, or of any form of consciousness-raising, illustrates the conversion that a new version of one's life-story can effect. Reflecting on the dynamic between the patient and the psychoanalyst, Ricoeur describes the client's presentation of bits and pieces of lived stories, of dreams, of primitive scenes, and of conflictual episodes as a "potential story" or an "(as yet) untold story." The goal of the analytic sessions is the emergence of a life-story that "the subject can take up and hold as constitutive of personal identity."[23] However, the therapeutic process always involves an element of surprise, whether that involves the emergence of repressed memories, the embracing of truths formerly hidden, the reversal of initial expectations, or the embracing of deeper questions. Both narrator and hearer are called to the creative perception of a new configuration or meaning in previously unrelated, or even conflicting, events.

The Role of the Preacher as Narrator

Perhaps the problem with much contemporary narrative preaching is not the genre of narrative but the stories chosen or the storyteller's lack of clear homiletic purpose. The conscious weaving of a plot for the purposes of faith has nothing to do with the inappropriate use of a story or joke to "warm up an audience." When the preacher introduces a homily with a story drawn from human experience or even structures an entire homily in the form of a story, she or he is operating as the narrator — consciously choosing the story to be told, the details to be revealed, the direction in which the plot will unfold, the description of the characters, and, most importantly, the ending toward which the story moves.

Here the role of inspiration, as explored in the last chapter, is crucial. The preacher's configuring of the plot of the homily is an act of the creative imagination that tends toward a future beyond human conception. But that plot is determined by the plot of the scripture passage. The connection between the two should be obvious to the hearer. Not every powerful human story can be used to proclaim a specific gospel passage. It is the gospel that norms the use of the human story, not vice versa.

Lischer suggests one form of how the preacher as narrator moves from human experience to the gospel. Some human stories are used, as were Luther's, to bring the hearers to a consciousness of their need and sinfulness. Human existence is filled with tragedy as well as comedy, as Frederick Buechner's contemporary homiletic classic has reminded us,[24] and the gospel speaks to both. If the preacher would tell the whole truth of the human story as addressed by the gospel, then part of the story to be told is of radical failure and even evil — the free choice of human beings to be "people of the lie." Such stories serve, as Lischer notes, as "only the preface to the story of salvation." Then the preacher as narrator designs the homily in such a fashion as to show the contrast between the human situation and the gospel.

The narrator can relate other human stories, however, that actually convey the surprise of the kingdom, the lavish extravagance of God, the reversal of roles and expectations that characterizes the gospel. The human story narrated as a story of grace *is* itself a hermeneutic of the gospel. Told from one perspective, the award-winning film *Babette's Feast,*[25] for example, tells the story of the eucharist — abundant feast, community celebration, table of forgiveness, the host pouring out all for the sake of those invited, even the ability to receive being expanded. There are human stories and life experiences that serve as "fragments of salvation," as Schillebeeckx would say, moments in the here and now when we are given a "taste of future glory," to use more traditional liturgical language. Any human story of genuine forgiveness, for example, is already a story of what God can do and has done among us, a story of redeeming power that is beyond merely human capacities. The art of preaching is knowing how to tell the human story in such a way that it becomes clear that something beyond the human — grace — is at work in human life and thus to connect the human story with the world of the scriptures.

The "Sense of an Ending" in Narrative and Liturgical Proclamation

Whether the human story used in preaching is a portrait of sin or of salvation, any narrative is woven toward its conclusion.[26] Hence

both the eschatological dimension of all preaching and the liturgical context of much of Christian preaching need to be further
highlighted. Neither the stories of human failure and sin nor the narratives of grace discovered within human experience constitute the
final word of the human situation: all human experience occurs in
the "not-yet" stage of anticipation of the final reign of God.

A return to the eucharistic structure of the Emmaus passage offers
the opportunity to reflect specifically on the function of the homily in
the context of liturgy or, in Ricoeur's terms, on the move from configuration to refiguration. In the Emmaus narrative the preaching of
Jesus reaches its culmination in the breaking of the bread, in which
finally "[the disciples'] eyes were opened and they recognized him"
(Luke 24:31). In a similar way, when preaching occurs in the context
of the eucharist, the homily is not the primary narrative but an integral part of the larger narrative of the eucharist itself. The homily
is part of the total movement toward the proclamation of faith in
the death and resurrection of Jesus until he comes in glory. As Mark
Searle has suggested, "each text of the liturgy represents a more or
less fragmentary attempt to relate the story-that-cannot-be-told."[27]
This is perhaps most obvious in the structure of the eucharistic
prayer — the "foundational story" in which the community is summoned to remember and give thanks to God for the entire history
of salvation culminating in the death and resurrection of Christ and
anticipating eschatological completion.

The narrative of the homily and the narrative of the eucharistic
prayer are not simply juxtaposed, however. The movement of the
liturgy suggests that the proclamation of the biblical stories recalling
God's fidelity in the past history of the community of faith calls forth
a homiletic interpretation of contemporary experience as also part
of "the plot of God." The proclamation of the homily is calculated
to move hearers to prayer within the context of the celebration and
ultimately to conversion of life, growth in holiness, and service to
God and neighbor.[28]

The refiguration of life called forth by the configuration of the
human story in light of the story of the gospel involves the necessary move through the liturgy toward a deeper involvement in
life, through doxology to praxis. Appropriation of God's promise
(to which the scriptures give testimony) takes place within the liturgy itself as the community turns to intercession and lamentation,
to praise and thanksgiving. Activity on behalf of the reign of God is

rooted first in this turning from self and toward God in expressions of repentance, praise, and gratitude.

In lamentation the community admits its own sinfulness and thus opens a space for the "dangerous memory" of the gospel to challenge the community to a more faithful following of Jesus. As David Power explains:

> Lamentation expresses the community's perception of its own and of humanity's sin and of the shackles which are placed on human freedom and on God's word and gift. Griefs which have been suppressed and hopes which have been stilled are allowed expression. In this act, the community remembers the questions to which the gospel speaks instead of stilling them.[29]

Since the proclamation of the gospel always is grounded in the power of the resurrection, however, the community is moved beyond lamentation to praise, thanksgiving, and life in the power of the Spirit. In the homily the community hears of God's fidelity and promise in the third person, but in the liturgy of the eucharist the community addresses God in the direct relationship of the second person: "Blessed are you, Lord, God of all creation. . . . You are the one God, living and true. . . . We come to You with praise and thanksgiving. . . . Remember your people. . . . We bring you these gifts. . . . We ask you to make them holy through the power of your Spirit." Remembering God's fidelity in the past and calling on the power of the Spirit for the present and future empower the community to refigure their lives according to the gospel.

Since the liturgical context of the homily and the proclamation of the gospel that precedes the preaching provide the field of reference for interpreting a homily, a powerful human story or a first-person narrative based on the gospel may convey the power of the biblical word without any further interpretation or explicit connections being made. When that kind of creative preaching works effectively, it is obvious that the preacher has carefully thought through the connections and the central message of the homily but has chosen to communicate the message implicitly or imaginatively, rather than in a didactic or proclamatory style.[30] The homilist's hope is that in that way the hearers of the word will experience the gospel as an event and be "caught" with immediacy by the "metaphorical twist" of the gospel's call to conversion and action.

Retelling the human story in light of the story of the death and resurrection of Jesus can be a powerful form of preaching the gospel if the gospel determines the selection of the human story and the preacher functions as narrator with a definite sense of the purpose and ending of the story. The plot unfolding in a homily, however, is necessarily "the plot of God" and as such will always move beyond the human story. This discontinuity may involve a moment of reversal. But it may also occur through the preacher's pointing to the "how much more" of the radical extravagance of God's grace within the apparent continuity between the human situation and the gospel. In the liturgical context it is important to remember that the preaching serves as only one connecting piece in a larger narrative. Nevertheless, the homily is an essential moment connecting the earlier development of salvation history with the present day and moving the community from remembering through proclamation to doxology and action. These homiletic concerns about narrative preaching point to even more fundamental theological questions in the areas of revelation and anthropology as well as christology.

Underlying Theological Issues

A Point of Contact? Revelation and Anthropology

Does this approach to narrative preaching distort human life and divine revelation, as Lischer fears? The question of the relationship between the divine and the human recalls the debate between Brunner and Barth discussed in chapters 1 and 3: Is there a point of contact in human experience such that the proclamation of the gospel can be heard? Those who agree with Barth's early writings insist that if the preacher draws on human experience, the homily will not express the word of God. As Barth proclaimed in his commentary on the Letter to the Romans: "[The truth] is not accessible to our perception.... In Jesus the communication of God begins with a rebuff, with the exposure of a vast chasm, with the clear revelation of a great stumbling-block."[31] Many from the Reformation traditions agree that sin has destroyed the "image of God" in humanity — there is no point of contact for the gospel. Thus Lischer argues that in Luther's highly skilled narrative preaching, the human story could function only as "a story of human misery, ... only the preface to the story of salvation" since "humanity has exchanged the truth of God for a lie."[32]

In a more positive vein, Paul Tillich's method of correlation could be applied to preaching to suggest that the story drawn from human experience focuses the ultimate human questions to which the proclamation of the gospel provides a divine response. However, the perspective of the sacramental imagination connects the two stories even further. The theological anthropology at work here places more emphasis on the goodness of creation that is never totally destroyed by sin, on the human community as imaging God, however ambiguously and proleptically, and on the power of grace as "abounding still more" in the face of the sin of the world.[33] From that perspective, the human story contains not only the most profound human questions but also traces of the divine response. The human story is not only a story of human misery, not only the preface to the story of salvation, but the context where salvation continues to occur — or fails to occur — today. Salvation remains always the work of God's grace, but, understood from an incarnational perspective, that grace is at work in and through human history.[34] Hence grace can be proclaimed when the believer who "has eyes to see" relates the human story from a faith perspective as a "fragment of salvation."

The Uniqueness of Jesus Christ and the Gospel

Even if one grants that the human story in its depths is ultimately religious, however, can the gospel of Christ crucified be reduced to another rendition of universal human religious experience, the experience of reality in its depths as gracious? Behind the debate here are profound differences among the variety of theologians who claim to be doing narrative theology today — differences about the uniqueness of the biblical narrative and, more fundamentally, the exclusive singularity of Jesus and the Christian tradition. Those who have been called "postmodern narrativists" (e.g., Hans Frei and George Lindbeck) insist that the singularity of Jesus can be discovered only in the narratives of the Christian scriptures and that the Bible is the primary way of making human experience intelligible. "Correlationists" (e.g., David Tracy, Edward Schillebeeckx, Karl Rahner, Anne Carr, and Rosemary Ruether),[35] by way of contrast, view religious experience as occurring within human experience. Christian experience is a paradigmatic case of religious experience. Thus correlationists make a critical correlation not only between the unique revelation of Jesus and the manifestation of the divine within other religions but also between the claims of the Christian tradition and the claims of secular disciplines and between the Christian story and the human story.

Postmodern narrativists critique the correlationist position on precisely this point: "[T]he scriptures are not about our experience, but about the experiences of Christ Jesus."[36] "These stories tell us about God,...[not some] idea of a new possibility for ourselves."[37] Reflecting what we have called the "sacramental imagination," the correlationists respond with a characteristic "both/and." The scriptures are about both human experience and the experience of Jesus Christ; they tell us both about God *and* about the new possibility available to us in an anticipatory way in the grace of Christ and in fullness in the reign of God. While the postmodern narrativists emphasize the paradox and particularity of God becoming human in Jesus Christ, the correlationists plumb the implications of the incarnation for all of humanity.

The underlying issue here is one that is central to discussions of christology today: Is salvation from God revealed uniquely and exclusively in Jesus Christ? From the time of early Christianity the church has grappled with this issue of the "scandal of particularity" in the face of Christianity's claim that Jesus is universal savior. Further, in the scriptures themselves traces can be found of two different approaches to preaching based on differing approaches to the uniqueness of Christianity that are still being debated today.

On the one hand, Paul's Letter to the Romans is often quoted by those who hold to Christianity's exclusive claim: "If you confess with your lips that Jesus is Lord, and believe in your heart that God raised him from the dead, you will be saved. Faith in the heart leads to justification, confession on the lips to salvation.... Everyone who calls on the name of the Lord will be saved" (Rom 10:9–10, 13). On the other hand, Paul's homiletic method as imaged by Luke in the Acts of the Apostles recognizes a broader religious experience already available to those who worshiped an "unknown God." Hence Paul speaks to the people of Athens about "the God who made the world and all that is in it." Because the God who raised Jesus from the dead is also the creator of heaven and earth, Paul speaks to the Athenians about all humankind seeking God, groping, and eventually even finding the one in whom "we live and move and have our being." This same God, Paul announces, is the one who has "endorsed" Jesus by raising him from the dead (Acts 17:24, 28, 31). Paul names the one who had been experienced and worshiped as the unknown God as the God of Jesus Christ. Paul is convinced that "reform of life" will necessarily follow that recognition (Acts 17:30), but he preaches by building on the religious experience that is already present; he does not speak as if he is bringing a foreign word to those who have had no experience of the God of whom he speaks. God is revealed uniquely, but not exclusively, in Jesus Christ.

Versions of those two divergent approaches to proclaiming the Christian gospel are to be found in differing approaches to narrative theology and narrative preaching today. Those who would emphasize the singularity of the Christian story argue that the relationship between human experience and the Christian narrative is best described as "collision" since the encounter is jarring and world-transforming.[38] As Stanley Hauerwas claims: "[T]he dominant story of the would-be disciple clashes with that of the master. The costly demands of the gospel clash with our innate tendency to make immediate self-satisfaction the ultimate norm of life."[39] Clearly the emphasis here is on the particularity of the Christian narrative, the self-centered ego of the would-be disciple, and the radical transformation that the gospel requires.

However, identification of the terms "particularity" and "exclusivity" overlooks the possibility that the Christian gospel may be unique and radically transformative, but not exclusive. Hence David Tracy, among others, suggests that the revelation of God in Jesus is universal and decisive, but also "inclusivist." While allowing for other classic experiences and expressions of religious experience, Tracy nonetheless describes God's self-disclosure in Jesus the Christ as "transforming." He maintains that the event of the transformative possibilities for human existence disclosed in Jesus the Christ "has all the force of a decisive revelation of God, one's self and the final meaning of the whole of reality."[40] Just as religious classics take the process of other classic texts and events "a step further" and provide a "more intense disclosure" of the ultimate meaning of human life, so for the Christian the scriptures serve as "the classic judging and transforming all other classics — the *norma normans non normata* of all Christian religious and theological language."[41] While Christians maintain that the *ultimate* meaning of the human story is fully explained only in the story of Jesus, that does not deny that other expressions of the meaning of the human story are also powerful and true.

This chapter suggests that it is possible that the preacher, as a Christian believer, can recognize stories of salvation, events that provide glimpses of the reign of God, in other religious traditions and in ordinary human experience and preach the gospel of the day from those contemporary parables.[42] A sacramental-incarnational perspective grounds this inclusivist approach to the mystery of salvation in the Word/Wisdom of God, the paradigm for all creation, enfleshed in Jesus of Nazareth through whom all human beings have been offered the possibility of transformation. While Christians remain convinced that Jesus most fully embodied and embraced that transformation, the salvation of God is nonetheless present in human experience beyond the framework of the Christian story.

Turning to the parables as paradigmatic Christian preaching underscores the key elements in effective narrative preaching. Through the use of ordinary images such as bread and seeds or business or domestic relationships, Jesus described the reign of God. But within each story was a moment of surprise and reversal of the expectations of the hearers. God's world is disclosed within the workings of this world *if we have but eyes to see and ears to hear*. Yet the "world in front of the text," the reign of God that the parables disclose, is not some "wholly other" world, but this world and very human relationships now experienced anew in light of faith in a God who promises to be the future of humanity and of all of creation.

Chapter 7

Grace at the Edges:
Preaching and Lament

The sacramental imagination proclaims that God's grace is to be found in human experience, that the same Spirit of God who was active in the life of Israel and in the earliest Christian communities is still at work in our lives and world. In the stories of their own lives, the Christian assembly knows the mystery of life/death/life that the preacher names as paschal mystery. The power of the Spirit of God has been at work in moments of communion and celebration, in shared laughter and joy, in companionship and a common table, in breakthroughs to new life beyond depression, grief, and loss. The drama of grace reaches a climax in the restoration of right relations, whether through words of reconciliation in a marriage, family, or friendship, in the breakdown of the Berlin Wall, or in the dismantling of structures of apartheid in South Africa. We have witnessed grace at work in coalitions for justice and peace, in radical human courage, in the wisdom shared between generations, in creative political strategies, in truth-telling, compassion, and solidarity, in human fidelity and forgiveness.

But every assembly also knows its own share of grief and death that has not yet come to new life. Images from the media enflesh the pain: the Bosnian mother embracing her starving child, the eyes of the man dying of AIDS, the smiling picture of the child most recently abducted and murdered in our cities, the frustrated faces of the unemployed, polluted waters standing stagnant. Whether we are reflecting on the experiences of our own life or on the local, national, or global realities that confront us every day in newspapers, over radio, or on television, profound experiences of suffering bring us to the limits of our lives and of the meaning-systems we embrace.

Listening for a word of God from that context of global suffering, believers continue to wrestle with what Karl Barth identified in 1922 as "every hearer's question" about the good news: "Is it true?" Barth remarked on the contrast between what the liturgy proclaims and people's concrete lives:

> The whole liturgy says: God is present. The whole situation witnesses, cries, simply shouts of it, even if in the minister or people there arises questioning, wretchedness, or despair.... But what does "God is present" mean in the face of the great riddle of existence? ... Is it true? — this talk of a loving and good God who is more than one of the friendly idols? ... A passionate longing to have the word spoken that promises grace is the desire of every church-goer no matter how they express their want in so-called real life.[1]

The word of grace that all human beings, not only churchgoers, long to hear cannot be spoken too quickly, however. Announcing the paschal mystery in the midst of a world of suffering is possible only if preachers take seriously contemporary experiences of anguish, impasse, and the absence of God. The ongoing experience of the crucified of this world calls for a rethinking of the mystery of the cross and the retrieval of the tradition of lament in Christian prayer and preaching if communities of faith are to proclaim an authentic word of hope in the power of the resurrection in today's global context.

The Contemporary Experience of Impasse

Martin Luther's search for a gracious God continues in our day, not in terms of religious or moral guilt but rather in psychological and interpersonal struggles as well as in social and political terms. The question of salvation is (as *salus,* the root of the word "salvation," suggests) a question of well-being, of the healing and flourishing of humankind and of all creation. Those members of our assemblies who have known serious illness remind us of the fragility, vulnerability, and limits of all our lives. Those who describe the experience of sickness consistently speak about the profound alienation that serious illness brings — a sense of betrayal by one's own body, separation from everyone we have known and loved, the loss of identity and roles and meaningful work, and, most threatening of all, a profound sense of distance, even alienation, from God.[2]

Even those who are healthy, who live in fairly stable families or relationships, and who have regular employment are not exempt from
the unraveling of the social fabric in the world's wealthiest nation.
The breakdown of family life, the increasing violence in neighborhoods, schools, and cities, the drug culture, the increase in racism
and hate crimes, the spread of AIDS, the abandonment of infants and
the elderly, and the prevailing consumer mentality affect the lives and
futures of all of us.

For some in the community, pain and abuse continue to isolate
precisely because they remain invisible and unspoken. The lament of
Tashi, one of the main characters in Alice Walker's novel *Possessing
the Secret of Joy*, reflects the feelings of many women whose voices
are never heard from pulpits but who have known the violation and
degradation of the cross in their own bodies:

> I am a great lover of Jesus, and always have been. Still, I began
> to see how the constant focus on the suffering of Jesus alone ex-
> cludes the suffering of others from one's view. And in my sixth
> year as a member of Adam's congregation, I knew I wanted
> my own suffering, the suffering of women and little girls, still
> cringing before the overpowering might and weapons of the tor-
> turers, to be the subject of a sermon. Was woman herself not
> the tree of life? And was she not crucified? Not in some age
> no one even remembers, but right now, daily, in many lands
> on earth.
>
> One sermon I begged him.
>
> He said the congregation would be embarrassed to dis-
> cuss something so private, and that, in any case, he would be
> ashamed to do so.[3]

Silence and the suppression of pain are not limited to crimes of
domestic violence, rape, and abuse, nor to our churches. Peter Vaill,
a professor of management science at George Washington University,
noted in his consultations with various companies and corporations
vast amounts of pain, but little public recognition or acceptance of
it, among personnel managers, loan officers, credit union people,
vice presidents, and union stewards. Speaking to his colleagues at
an annual conference he called for "the rediscovery of anguish," ob-
serving that "[w]e just can't share our pain and confusion with each
other.... There is a massive suppression of anguish going on in the
organizations and communities of the developed world — no one's

fault in particular; just a fundamental part of culture."[4] K. C. Ptomey Jr. echoes Vaill's analysis in the personal and domestic spheres: "We live with fractured relationships, troubled marriages, problems with our children, addictions, grief, unreconciled differences with people we deeply care about. But, for whatever reasons, our pain does not find an avenue for public expression."[5]

When we extend our awareness to include the victims of international politics and economics, the rebirth of nationalism, racism, vicious acts of "hatred of the stranger," and the devastation of natural resources, we can understand why Constance FitzGerald, a Carmelite, has extended the term "dark night of the soul" to what she calls a "dark night of the world."

Reflection on the experience of the contemporary world, she suggests, whether the experience of women, of the poor and oppressed, of the aging, or of the woundedness of the earth itself, brings the human imagination to the limits of its resources. FitzGerald describes this experience as one of impasse:

> There is no way out of, no way around, no rational escape from, what imprisons one, no possibilities in the situation. In a true impasse, every normal manner of acting is brought to a standstill, and ironically, impasse is experienced not only in the problem itself but also in any solution rationally attempted.... Any movement out, any next step, is canceled, and the most dangerous temptation is to give up, to quit, to surrender to cynicism and despair, in the face of the disappointment, disenchantment, hopelessness, and loss of meaning that encompass one.[6]

The preacher "names grace," but, especially in the contrast experiences of life, it is equally important that the preacher name the situations of impasse and "dis-grace" or sin that confront creation and call out for redemption. One of the main critiques of the claim that grace can be found throughout creation and human history is that the sacramental imagination does not account adequately for the reality of evil. While Catholic traditions may not agree that every human situation can be described as "hopelessly corrupt" or "in need of being healed," the scope and extent of suffering in the world confirm the dialectical imagination's assertion that grace is interlaced with sin throughout human history. The sacramental imagination celebrates the presence of God, but that presence is available for many only in the mode of absence.

For preachers called to speak the good news, this presents a particular challenge. In situations of radical suffering or impasse, how do Christian communities continue to believe and proclaim that "where sin abounds, grace abounds still more" (Rom 5:20)? How is the preaching of Jesus Christ, and him crucified, good news? The very mystery of the cross needs to be rethought in a context of global and cosmic suffering.

The Folly of the Cross

Proclamation of the cross and resurrection of Jesus is at the very heart of Christian preaching. In contrast to both Greeks and Jews, Paul boldly proclaimed: "We preach Christ and him crucified" (1 Cor 1:23). But Christians do not exalt suffering and death.[7] Neither do they necessarily see suffering as God's will for Jesus or for humankind.

Christians never have had only one understanding of the mystery of the cross; it is far too profound to be explained by any one theological perspective. One of the earliest Christian responses to the death of Jesus was horror at the meaningless execution of an innocent man. The resurrection, rather than the crucifixion itself, was seen as the saving event. Multiple passages in the Acts of the Apostles that may have been drawn from early preaching events emphasize the victory of the resurrection in contrast to the evil of the crucifixion: "You put to death the Author of life, but God raised him from the dead" (Acts 3:15). Two other interpretations of the cross, also rooted in scripture and the liturgical life of the church, took stronger hold in Christian teaching and piety, however — the view of Jesus as suffering servant whose death is somehow in the plan of God and a theology of Jesus' death as expiation offered to atone for our sins.[8]

The Christian scriptures present diverse theologies of salvation, redemption, and human suffering appealing to multiple metaphors: buying back the enslaved, the temple ritual of atonement, legal acquittal, freedom from slavery or imprisonment, and health and well-being, among others.[9] In the early Christian tradition, the East emphasized incarnation itself as redemptive, using the language of recapitulation (Irenaeus) or deification (Athanasius). The Latin tradition focused on the cross as source of redemption. Christ "ransomed" or bought back humankind from the devil, who had "rights" to human souls because of sin. Many Christians, strongly influenced by the medieval theology of Anselm, think of the cross in terms of "vicarious satisfaction" — Jesus died on the cross to restore God's honor and to make restitution for the sins of human beings. Only one who was divine could "restore God's honor" for the infinite offense of sin, but it was also necessary that a human being "make satisfaction" for the sinful offense of human being(s).[10] Luther's theology of "penal satisfaction" has also had a profound hold on the Christian imagination, especially among those in the Lutheran and Reformed traditions. Jesus Christ became the suffering servant, the scapegoat, who took upon himself the punishment for sin that humankind deserved, the wrath of God. He was punished in our place. "He was pierced for our offenses, crushed for our sins. Upon him was the chastisement that makes us whole; by his stripes we were healed; ... the Lord laid upon him the guilt of us all" (Isa 53:5–6). God is revealed not in glory and majesty but where God remains hidden: in the humility and shame of the cross.[11] Other medieval theologians, such as Abelard and Aquinas, underscored that it was the love, rather than the suffering, of Christ that was redemptive.

No one of these theological perspectives on the mystery of the cross and salvation is the "right interpretation." Preachers and theologians would be well advised to remember the words of the physicist Nils Bohr: "The opposite of a profound truth is another profound truth." Nevertheless, contemporary preachers are called to preach on the mystery of the cross in a specific time and culture. What aspects of that mystery are forgotten in our day? How might traditional doctrines be heard in the context of massive global suffering and by the suffering members of Christian churches? What are the images of God and theologies of the cross that are implicit, if not explicit, in the imaginations of the hearers of the word? The question is not whether to preach the cross, but how.

Brazilian liberation theologian Leonardo Boff, for example, has raised the questions: "How ought we to preach the cross in a crucified society today?" and "how ought we to preach the resurrection in a world under threat of collective death?"[12] Jürgen Moltmann, J. B. Metz, and Edward Schillebeeckx raise similar questions from the context of northern European theologians operating in the global context of excessive, senseless, and systematic human oppression and suffering. How can we continue to proclaim Jesus as universal savior in a world where so many human beings are deprived of basic human rights and the ecosystem is rapidly being destroyed? Feminist theologians from a variety of cultures, classes, and races are also grappling with the experience of suffering, the paschal mystery, the compassion of God, and contemporary metaphors for salvation.[13] All of these emphasize that the preaching of the cross in our day requires a critical appropriation of the mystery. The last word about the cross may be that it is indeed a mystery of divine love, fidelity, and solidarity, but the first word that must be spoken is of its scandal, injustice, and absurdity.

Like political and liberation theologians, most theologians reflecting on christology today emphasize that the cross must be put in the context not only of the resurrection but also of the life and ministry of Jesus. As many have noted, it is no coincidence that Jesus did not die in bed. Jesus was executed as a political criminal and a religious blasphemer as the consequence of his "dangerous preaching" of the reign of God. His healing ministry and his inclusive table companionship threatened traditional boundaries that distinguished insiders from outsiders in both religious and political realms. Jesus shocked religious authorities as he announced the forgiveness of sins, a proclamation that was the prerogative of God alone. He touched lepers and spoke with Samaritans. He formed bonds of friendship with women and with tax-collectors who collaborated with the oppressive Roman Empire and invited both into the circle of his disciples. A faithful Jew, he radically reinterpreted Jewish tradition and laws of Sabbath observance and ritual purity. His liberating lifestyle, his shocking parables and beatitudes, and the unconditional compassion of God that he embodied in his person and style of relating were all profound challenges to religious and political structures of the day.[14] Even the joy and freedom he invited others to embrace were unpredictable; as liberation theologians have noted, festivity, too, is subversive.[15] In the end the one whose entire life proclaimed "God's 'no' to human suffering"[16] was betrayed by an intimate disciple, abandoned by many of his closest friends, handed over to the empire by religious leaders, sentenced by a political leader who knew him to be innocent, mocked and tortured by soldiers, and executed as a criminal, dying on a cross between two thieves.

The stress of political and liberation theologians on the human evil and injustice that brought about the cross gives rise to the further question of Jesus' experience of death and suffering. It is not possible to know the inner experience of Jesus with certitude. But those who take seriously the full humanity of Jesus can begin to imagine the stark reality behind the gospel portrait of Jesus' anguish in the garden of Gethsemane or his cry from the cross, "My God, my God, why have you forsaken me?" The one who preached absolute trust in the reign of a compassionate God was left in darkness to face rejection of his mission and the utter silence of God. Jesus knew the experience of impasse. Some theologians even speak of abandonment by God or at least the apparent abandonment that Jesus may have experienced.[17]

The cross of Jesus, like all human suffering, raises profound questions about God and God's fidelity. Preachers turn to the language and symbolism of the cross to name the depth of human pain as religious, to show that the human struggle with suffering is ultimately a spiritual crisis. Jesus' cry continues in our world: "My God, my God, why have you forsaken me?" Some theologians are retrieving the importance of the symbol of Jesus' descent into hell in the face of the tragic suffering of so many who are abandoned, forgotten, and unmourned. Elizabeth Johnson traces the symbol of Jesus' descent into Sheol, the kingdom of shadows:

> What this symbolic way of speaking signifies is that even those who die victimized, those who disappear, those who are no longer part of the living history of the earth, those no longer remembered — all these people are not beyond the reach of the living God. The crucified Jesus has joined them, identifying with them, and bringing the power of the reign of God even there.[18]

Rejecting any religious legitimation of human suffering as God's will in an age of massive and senseless suffering including two world wars and the Holocaust, Edward Schillebeeckx underlines the scandal of the cross. He has even suggested that in one sense we are saved in spite of the cross of Jesus, rather than because of it. Nevertheless, in the end Jesus faced the cross as the final consequence of fidelity to his preaching mission with a radical hope in the compassionate God he knew as Abba. He filled an experience that was in itself meaningless and absurd with meaning, love, and a sense of solidarity with all the innocent who suffer. What Christians celebrate is not the cross, nor the sufferings of Jesus, but the power of a love that is faithful even unto death. The triumph of the cross is the tri-

umph of God's mercy bursting the bonds of sin and death. Preaching
about atonement and redemption — or whatever the metaphor for
salvation — is preaching about that kind of unlimited mercy and forgiveness, not the exacting of a blood ransom as the price to be paid
for human sinfulness.

It is not the cross that Christians preach but the entire paschal
mystery of the death and resurrection of Jesus. What Christians celebrate is that death and evil do not have final victory; the power of
God does. The earliest Christian preaching was the good news that
the death of Jesus was not the end. In and through Jesus' love and
fidelity God has taken on the evil and suffering of this world and
broken their hold once and for all with the stronger power of love.
What is humanly impossible is possible for God. Hence the mocking
tone of Paul: "O death where is your victory?" (1 Cor 15:55). Christians continue to hope that God can and will bring life out of death,
that, like Jesus, those who have lived faithfully will be vindicated
and transformed beyond death, that the power of love is stronger
than the power of evil. But the dynamic of hope, like the power of
resurrection, is beyond human control or possibility. Only God can
restore the dead to life. The temptation for the Christian preacher is
to try to "offer solutions" rather than to attend to the anguish of the
assembly and to entrust the pain to God. The preacher's own faith
that God can and will bring life beyond death is pressed to the limits
in situations of impasse, when lament may be the most honest form
of proclamation and prayer.

Retrieving a Tradition of Lament: God at Risk

In recent years scholars have begun to reflect on the "costly loss
of lament"[19] in Christian prayer and worship. Both the genre of
lament and the tradition of arguing with God were firmly established
in the Jewish tradition of prayer, which reflects a great "boldness
with regard to heaven."[20] Such bold speaking to God derives from
Israel's basic understanding of the covenant as a relationship bind-
ing on both divine and human partners. As Walter Brueggemann has
suggested, prayer in the mode of lament "shifts the calculus and *re-
dresses* the redistribution of power between the two parties, so that
the petitionary party [the psalm speaker] is taken seriously and the
God who is addressed is newly engaged in the crisis in a way that

puts God at risk."[21] The psalms of lament are sometimes juridical appeals to the justice of God when human enemies have violated the rights of the psalmist or the people of Israel. As in Psalm 109, these psalms appeal to the *hesed* (covenant love) of YHWH against the failed *hesed* of the human agent. But even more problematic is the failure of God's justice, as in Psalm 88.[22]

The mode of lament reflects the psalmist's experience of profound disorientation or dislocation in terms of both external enemies and ills (war, disease, false accusation, attacks on every side) and internal loss and confusion ("My spirit is faint;...there is no one who takes notice of me; no refuge remains to me; no one cares for me" [Ps 142:3–4]). Worst of all, however, is the absence or silence of God: "My God, my God, why have you forsaken me?" (Psalm 22). While the majority of psalms of lament end with a confession of trust, some are more stark, never reaching a point of resolution or even explicit hope (Psalms 39 and 88). Yet even here, the psalmist has not yet broken off relationship; anger is a mode of relatedness. Will Soll has suggested that perhaps the language of lament is all the more necessary in this state of profound disorientation, "in not playing hypocrite to one's heart, but in keeping, as it were, a channel open to God."[23]

The tradition of lament stretches throughout the history of Israel but reaches the breaking point in the Holocaust. In the experience of many Jews, the channel to God was definitively closed in the abandonment of six million Jewish men, women, and children. As Elie Wiesel states so starkly in recounting his experience as a fifteen-year-old boy in the Nazi death camps of Auschwitz and Buchenwald:

> Never shall I forget the little faces of the children, whose bodies I saw turned into wreaths of smoke beneath a silent blue sky.
> Never shall I forget those flames which consumed my faith forever.
> Never shall I forget that nocturnal silence which deprived me, for all eternity, of the desire to live. Never shall I forget those moments which murdered my God and my soul and turned my dreams to dust.[24]

The Jewish Holocaust stands as a profound "interruption" not only of Jewish faith but also of that of Christians. As David Power remarks:

These stories are as much for Christians as they are for Jews.
This is not only because such atrocities as those committed by
the Nazis would question belief in God were they committed, as
in part they have been, by any race against another. Not only
it is so because the Holocaust stands as a modern expression
of the myth of *homo homini lupus,* and a reminder of all attempts at genocide. Not only is it so because Christians cannot
dare to forget their corporate complicity, however blatant or
ignorant or unknowing, in this racial hatred.... [The most important reason for remembrance] is that this is the suffering of
the *Jewish* people, the people of Yahweh's Covenant and promise. If God suffered this people to suffer, what is to be made of
God's Covenant with the world and with human history?[25]

The realities of the Jewish Holocaust and the other holocausts of
this century cast new shadows on the Christian symbol of the cross.
There a faithful and innocent Jewish man cried out in a psalm of
lament he would have known since his youth: "My God, my God,
why have you forsaken me?" (Psalm 22). Numerous authors commenting on this passage hasten to remind Christians that Psalm 22
ends on a note of confidence in God:

> You who fear the Lord, praise him!...
> [S]tand in awe of him, all you offspring of Israel!
> For he did not despise or abhor
>   the affliction of the afflicted;
> he did not hide his face from me,
>   but heard when I cried to him....
> [F]uture generations will be told about the Lord,
> and proclaim his deliverance to a people yet unborn.
>   (Ps 22:23–24, 30–31)

The psalm does conclude with a note of hope, as does Christian worship, but preachers fail to do justice to the dynamics of
the paschal mystery when they move too quickly to exhortations to
hope. Where is there room for grief in Christian liturgy, even in the
funeral liturgy? The risen one remains for all time also "the crucified one"; the one who has redeemed all of human history and the
cosmos was also "a man of sorrows, acquainted with grief."

If liturgies and preaching are to draw Christian assemblies more
deeply into the paschal mystery that constitutes their daily lives, the

community needs ways of remembering and ritualizing the scandal of the cross as well as of celebrating the victory and hope of resurrection. Authentic faith in our day requires more dissonance within the almost wholly harmonious relation between the sacramental imagination and celebration. Lament disrupts the mood of praise and thanksgiving, but liturgy is meant to reflect as well as transform human life.

Naming Grief: Preaching as Lament

Naming grief is an integral part of the process of preaching hope in the resurrection because the first step toward overcoming suffering is finding a language that leads one out of the prison of silence.[26] Good news is to be found already in the language of lament and tears. Naming pain and claiming forgotten memories are parts of a larger journey toward healing, wholeness, and joy, although that future hope cannot be seen at every step on the journey.

In situations of radical impasse human beings are moved to deeper levels of hope or to despair, whatever subtle forms each takes. Christians hope in the possibility of being transformed by a grace that moves through darkness, but that transformation occurs through the very human process of taking possession of one's pain and confusion, recognizing and claiming the contrast experiences of our time in the church and world, and courageously embracing the present moment in history. FitzGerald describes this contemplative stance as "[holding] this impasse in [our] bodies and [our] hearts before the inner God [we] reach for in the dark of shattered symbols."[27]

Even when shattered, the symbols and stories of faith can hold clues to hope. Grief over the loss focuses our attention on what we value most deeply. Sometimes grief comes in the form of the pain of relinquishment that is a necessary loss for the dominants in any social system of oppression if the equal dignity of all members of the human family is to be respected. The language and symbols of grief are threatening to "the way things are" because they carry the seeds of hope that the future can be different from the present. The resurrection stories suggest that human hopes are often far too limited. Mary Magdalene had to move through her grief over not being able to find the dead body of her beloved friend before she could be open to hear her name and discover new life, new relationship, and a new mission. As Walter Brueggemann has noted, "[W]ithout [grief] there is no newness."[28]

If preachers are to speak in the name of the community, then preachers are called not only to name grief but also to express the community's "complaints" against God.[29] The anger against God that results when hopes have been disappointed or betrayed, or when sacred symbols have been shattered, can be a step toward a deeper and more authentic faith. Long considered one of the seven capital sins, anger provides a key to what one values and an energy that can be focused toward justice and love. As Beverly Harrison has noted:

> Christians have come very close to killing love precisely because anger has been understood as a deadly sin. Anger is not the opposite of love. It is better understood as a feeling-signal that *all is not well* in our relation to other persons or groups or to the world around us. Anger is a *mode of connectedness* to others and it is always a *vivid form of caring*. . . . [A]nger is a signal that change is called for, that *transformation in relation* is required.[30]

The anger that arises as we witness injustice can give rise to protest and resistance as we embrace more deeply God's passion for life and for all the living. Especially in contexts of persecution and injustice, hope is often expressed by naming the powers of evil that will be defeated: "There shall be no more death or mourning, crying out or pain, for the former world has passed away" (Rev 21:4). Or as the African-American spiritual proclaims: "No more cryin' there; . . . no more dyin' there; we are goin' to see the King."[31] The grace of anger goes beyond words however, to the hard work of transformation, to making right relations. In the shared struggle for a more just world, for more authentic relationships, for a church that images more clearly the body of Christ in the world, contemporary disciples discover the companions for the journey who sustain their hope and with whom they can celebrate. As Jürgen Moltmann observed: "Resistance is the protest of those who hope and hope is the festival of those who resist."[32]

Lament expresses, as well as leads to, grieving, anger, resistance, and protest. However, some situations of suffering are so severe and dehumanizing that there is no redemptive dimension to the suffering and active resistance is simply impossible. As Elizabeth Johnson describes the degradation that Simone Weil has named "affliction": "The effect is to squeeze out life, dry out power, introduce unwarranted guilt and self-hatred, plunge the sufferer into darkness."[33] At this level of human suffering, the sacramental imagination must know its bounds. As Johnson concludes: "There is no solution here.... Only a terrible sense of the mystery of evil and the absence of God, which nevertheless may betray divine presence, desecrated."[34]

Faced with that kind of evil, preachers, like all other Christians, are reduced to silent witness and solidarity with those who suffer. Only from that silence and solidarity can preachers credibly recall Jesus' own struggle and death and begin to point to the presence of God in even the most desperate of moments. Here David Power's suggestion for preaching at the time of a suicide may have broader application for Christian preaching in diverse situations that call for lament over the desecration of all that is sacred:

> Rather than focusing on Christ's resurrection, or on resurrection in Christ, the funeral liturgy on such an occasion serves to recall the death of Jesus Christ and his struggle with the forces of death, throughout his ministry and at the point of his own consummation. The solidarity of Christ with the human race in its struggle is more likely to touch the hearts of the bereaved than words about our solidarity with him in paschal joy. Indeed, it is only out of the memory of Christ's solidarity with human strife that hope can be born whenever the ambiguities and tensions of life's meaning are as prominent as they are in the story of a suicide.[35]

Precisely in the midst of the darkness Christians await the birth of the kind of "hope against hope" that is at the heart of Christian belief in the resurrection.

Hoping against Hope: Proclaiming the Resurrection

Christians do not have an explanation of either suffering or hope, but only the story of Jesus and a cloud of witnesses who throughout history have testified to their experience of resurrection. The gospel narratives provide clues of where the unexpected grace of hope happens: two companions journey on a road telling the story of their dashed hopes and welcome a stranger who listens to their pain and suddenly reshapes their story from the perspective of the promise and fidelity of God. A woman stands at a tomb weeping, mourning the loss of all she held dear. In one she could see initially only as a gardener she encounters her beloved speaking her name and commissioning her to share the good news with others. A man who betrayed his closest friend is forgiven and entrusted with the mission to "feed my sheep." A fearful community hears a word of peace spoken; a doubtful disciple touches human wounds and recognizes the transformation of a friend. All the resurrection experiences testify to hope born amid loss and pain. Hope emerges in the power of God breaking forth in new imaginings and new energy. Beyond grief the disciples discover it is possible to love again, to trust that one is forgiven, to get on with life, to invest new energy in the people and mission that have been entrusted to them. The details of the stories of impasse for the original disciples differ, but in each case the Spirit of God brings about what appears to be impossible.

Christian martyrs, too, from those who died in the persecutions of the early church to those tortured and murdered today for living and preaching the gospel, give radical witness to hope in the face of the powers and structures of sin and injustice. Many have spoken explicitly of the possibility of their own death but at the same time expressed their firm conviction that sin and death hold no final power. As Archbishop Desmond Tutu boldly proclaimed to the Eloff Commission of Inquiry in South Africa:

> God's promises are certain. They may remove a Tutu; they may remove the South African Council of Churches, but God's intention to establish his kingdom of justice, of love and compassion will not be thwarted. We are not scared, certainly not of the government, or any other perpetrators of injustice or oppression, for victory is ours through Him who loved us.[36]

Oscar Romero's very similar words take on even deeper meaning when we realize that two weeks after he spoke them he was assassinated while celebrating eucharist:

> I have frequently been threatened with death. I must say that, as a Christian, I do not believe in death but in the resurrection. If they kill me, I shall rise again in the Salvadoran people.... If they manage to carry out their threats, I shall be offering my blood for the redemption and resurrection of El Salvador. Mar-

tyrdom is a grace from God that I do not believe I have earned. But if God accepts the sacrifice of my life, then may my blood be the seed of liberty, and a sign of hope that will soon become a reality. May my death, if it is accepted by God, be for the liberation of my people, and as a witness of hope in what is to come. You can tell them, if they succeed in killing me, that I pardon them, and I bless those who may carry out the killing. But I wish they could realize that they are wasting their time. A Bishop will die, but the church of God — the people — will never die.[37]

The lives of all those who have gone to death like Jesus, alone and in silence, but nevertheless with a radical trust in God's mercy, give the clearest testimony to the possibility of Christian hope. As the apostle Paul insisted: "Hope is not hope if its object is seen; ... and hoping for what we cannot see means awaiting it with patient endurance" (Rom 8:24–25). While patient endurance,[38] or what Dorothee Sölle calls "revolutionary patience," cannot in itself bring about new life, it is a central aspect of the experience of what it means to "hope against hope." FitzGerald suggests that whether in personal or social experiences of impasse, it is possible to discover an energy to live, even in the midst of dying. From the perspective of the mystical tradition, she proposes that the "dark night" is at the same time a call to "move on in hope to a new vision, a new experience."[39]

What many families, communities, and assemblies may be experiencing as limits and loss can be, from the mystic's perspective, a crisis of growth that offers a possibility of transformation if they are able to weather the storm and entrust the darkness to a God who has promised to be faithful, but who seems absent. The patience, or perhaps better courage, that is demanded here is truly "revolutionary," particularly in a culture that is oriented toward success, control, and "quick fixes." Thus FitzGerald observes:

It is in the throes of this crisis that people abandon God and prayer, a marriage, a friend, a ministry, a community, a church and forfeit forever the new vision, the genuine hope, the maturity of love and loyalty, dedication and mutuality that is on the other side of darkness and hopelessness.... [I]t is the birthplace of a vision and a hope that cannot be imagined this side of darkness.[40]

Throughout history, human beings have been able to endure and transcend situations of incredible oppression and suffering. Viktor Frankl, the Jewish psychiatrist who survived the Nazi concentration camps during World War II, developed a major form of psychotherapy around a conviction that developed from his own experience: the person who has a "why" to live can withstand almost any "how."[41] Hope is born and sustained in the depths of human consciousness and is profoundly connected with the ability to imagine the future, to find meaning in one's relationships and life situation, to desire to live. The relationship between grace and human freedom remains beyond human comprehension. Neither is it possible to understand fully the complex and interrelated dimensions of the mystery of the human person. What is clear, however, is how profoundly human lives are shaped by memories and meaning-systems, by imagination and desires, and by the communities in which we live.

Dangerous Symbols and Stories

That realization provides an insight into the formation of the sacramental imagination — the profound confidence that God will be faithful; the deep trust that where sin abounds, grace abounds still more; the radical hope that in the end "all will be well." The assembly of the baptized can proclaim "Dying you destroyed our death; rising you restored our life; Lord Jesus come in glory" because that "hopeful imagination"[42] has been cultivated by symbols, stories, and lives that subvert a culture of death and despair. In an age of individualism and hatred of the stranger, Christian communities gather at an inclusive table and promise to attend to the needs of the poor and the sick. In an age of apathy and despair, Christians gather to give thanks and praise, to sing songs of joy and resistance. At both the beginning and the end of life, Christians gather around symbols of the tomb and proclaim that the Spirit of God brings new life out of death. When sickness threatens to destroy all that we have known and loved, Christians keep vigil at the bedside of the sick and the dying. In a culture that cannot imagine faithful relationships sustained over time, Christian communities witness covenant promises of fidelity and speak words of forgiveness beyond betrayal. In a culture of power and domination, Christian communities anoint leaders ordained to wash feet and to call forth the gifts in the community. As human celebrations, even the most basic symbolism of the church can of course be manipulated and used to reinforce, rather than subvert, systems of injustice, but the power of the basic Christian symbols escapes final human control.[43] For precisely that reason, the symbols are also dangerous; they hold the power to re-form the human imagination.

So, too, is retelling the Christian story dangerous. Explicitly calling to memory human suffering and the passion and death of Jesus is already part of the process of engendering Christian hope. Those memories are considered "dangerous" precisely because they criticize present systems of power and dominance and move the hearers to action and solidarity with those who suffer. To express anger or lament over the violation of human dignity or the earth is implicitly to express hope that the future can be different from the present. Shared stories fuel hopes, forge solidarity, and empower action. But retelling the story of Jesus is "dangerous" for an even deeper reason. The ultimate claim of Jesus' life, ministry, and death was that the compassion of God is the power at the heart of human history and of the universe — the reign of God is at hand. Christians are convinced that tragedy can be transformed precisely because the death of Jesus was not the end of his story. In the resurrection, the Spirit of God has broken the power of the bonds of sin and death and does indeed "make all things new." That same Spirit has been poured out on all creation, holding open future possibilities in the most desperate of circumstances, sustaining the human capacity to endure and to hope, empowering a core of freedom in the depths of the human spirit. The vision of a "new creation" is not "good news" for those who benefit from present systems of power. The promise of the "dangerous story" of the gospel is that another power, the power of love at the core of all creation, is the grace that "abounds still more" in the face of human suffering and injustice. Christians claim that in the resurrection of Jesus, God's power has been poured forth in the world in a radically new way. The Spirit of God holds the future open and is active in the world, fashioning a new creation, making all things new.[44]

Dangerous Memories Enfleshed

Here the sacramental imagination emphasizes, however, that God's Spirit is active precisely in and through creation and human communities. The symbols and stories of Christian hope "capture the imagination" only when they are enfleshed in living communities of hope and resistance. Jesus did not proclaim the reign of God only in words; he enfleshed the good news he announced. If the Christian hope that death is not the end is to be a source of hope for those whose lives are being cut off by AIDS, the gospel proclamation must be enfleshed. The sacramental embodiment of Christ's compassion is expressed not only by a community gathered for anointing and healing but also in faithful families and friends who "keep vigil," in those who, through fashioning a piece of the AIDS quilt, promise to remember the lives of those who have died, in those who work to change discriminatory legislation and attitudes that isolate the sick and dying, in those who work to find a cure for AIDS, in those who console the grieving and listen to their pain, and in those who speak of love in the face of their own loss.

The stories of resurrection are born in the midst of confusion and pain, but they end in joy and hope — signs of a presence and power that go beyond the human imagination. To celebrate the presence of God in the face of suffering is to say that pain and evil shall not have the final victory. To celebrate that hope authentically is to be drawn into living witness, to do everything possible to counter evil with love. In Amy Tan's novel *The Joy Luck Club,* four Chinese women gather every week for the sharing of stories, feasting, and for remembering "good times in the past and good times yet to come." One of the women recalls,

> People thought we were wrong to serve banquets every week while many people in the city were starving.... Others thought we were possessed by demons — to celebrate when even within our own families we had lost generations, had lost homes and fortunes, and were separated, husband from wife, brother from sister, daughter from mother.... How could we laugh, people asked.

She explains that

> it's not that we had no heart or eyes for pain. We were all afraid. We all had our miseries. But to despair was to wish back for something already lost.... So we decided to hold parties and pretend each week had become the new year. Each week we could forget past wrongs done to us.... We feasted, we laughed,

we played games.... We told the best stories. And each week, we could hope to be lucky. That hope was our only joy.[45]

Christian communities gather each week and celebrate not a new year but the end of time — the feast of the eighth day. It is not that the baptized have no heart or eyes for pain. But in the face of it all, the assembly gathers to celebrate the resurrection, to hear again "God's great joke." Christians come together to feast, to celebrate rituals, and to tell "the best stories." Each week the community remembers what lies ahead and declares as the early Christians did: "We remember your coming in glory." This is indeed to "hope against hope."

Chapter 8

Handing on "the Pledge Entrusted" (1 Tim 6:20; 2 Tim 1:14): Doctrinal Preaching

Because the ability to name human experience in its depth is so central to preaching, many would argue that the role of the preacher is more akin to the poet than the teacher. As Walter Brueggemann has remarked: "The deep places in our lives — places of resistance and embrace — are not ultimately reached by instruction."[1] Nevertheless a growing number of believers are registering dissatisfaction with the "slim fare" they are being fed from the pulpit. In a variety of ways the concern is being expressed that while contemporary homilies and sermons may provide psychological insight and personal inspiration, they lack theological substance and fail to hand on the doctrinal tradition of the church.

According to the Notre Dame study of Catholic parish life, for example, core Catholics find contemporary homilies "inspiring and interesting, but uninformative and not helpful to the growth of their faith."[2] William J. Carl III raises a similar concern from a Presbyterian perspective: "If believers do not know what they believe, how can they live the Christian faith? Inspirational sermons go only so far."[3] Some would blame the move toward more experiential and narrative modes of preaching for the loss of solid doctrine in contemporary preaching. Within the Roman Catholic tradition, others have seen Vatican II's restoration of the biblical and liturgical homily as restrictive of doctrinal and ethical preaching. They fear that "preaching from the Bible only will leave some basic Christian truths untaught, some great ethical questions unexamined"[4] and have welcomed the recent *Catechism of the Catholic Church* as a basic guide for doctrinal preaching.[5]

This concern for more solid "doctrinal," "catechetical," or "topical" preaching, voiced recently from a variety of ecumenical perspectives,[6] has particularly strong roots in the Roman Catholic tradition.[7] From the time of the catechism of the Council of Trent until the twentieth century,[8] preaching in the Catholic tradition was viewed primarily as doctrinal instruction and/or moral exhortation. Bernard Cooke notes that although the Council of Trent's decree on preaching exhorted bishops to preach "the holy gospel of Jesus Christ," the objective of regular parish preaching was "to feed the people with salutary words, teaching them what they must know for salvation, telling them clearly and briefly what vices they should avoid and what virtues they should acquire in order to avoid eternal punishment and gain heavenly glory."[9]

Underlying the Tridentine conviction that preaching should consist of doctrinal and ethical instruction was a propositional model of revelation that identified revelation and church teaching. At its best, this neo-scholastic approach to revelation and preaching preserved the Thomistic insight that "faith ends not in propositions, but in the reality [of union with God]."[10] Ideally, priests were encouraged to explain the church's doctrines to the laity in a pastoral way that called believers more deeply into the whole mystery of faith, but all too often that was not the case. Rather, as noted in chapter 2, preaching had become "the vulgarization of theological tracts."[11] Jungmann and others involved in the kerygmatic renewal movement of the 1950s called for a return to the biblical understanding of preaching as the proclamation of the good news of salvation.[12]

While that summons to renewal in all forms of proclamation affected the broader catechetical movement significantly, the restoration of the ancient liturgical homily within the eucharist was not officially mandated until Vatican II. Catholic authors in the 1960s could still describe preaching as "presenting Christian doctrine in a manner adapted to the needs of the times." Examples drawn from scripture or the lives of the saints were for the purpose of giving the sermon "a lasting effect."[13]

With Vatican II's Constitution on the Sacred Liturgy, however, the liturgical homily was clearly distinguished from pastoral preaching, catechetics, and other forms of Christian doctrine. The constitution stressed that the homily is an act of worship, an integral element of the liturgy itself (nos. 35, 52).[14] Deriving its content from "the sacred text," the homily is to draw the assembly into "full, active,

and conscious participation" in both the liturgy and the daily living of the Christian life. The return to the ancient term "homily"
was intended to highlight that preaching in the context of the sacraments should be biblical, liturgical, kerygmatic, and familiar. Thus
Robert Waznak concludes that "proclamation is not about a teaching, but an event, . . . not about doctrines defended but saving acts
boldly announced."[15]

While in full agreement with Waznak that preaching is not a matter of defending doctrines, Gerard Sloyan has identified the problem
lamented by many:

> People do not seem to know much about grace any more. They
> are fairly unenthusiastic and certainly ill-informed about purga-
> tory and the communion of saints. . . . What Christians do and
> do not believe about the incarnation is important. . . . These are
> important matters to a church which has been committed to
> them in some form of expression since apostolic times. How
> can one honestly say that people live by these traditions if they
> do not have them regularly recalled to their minds in adult
> fashion?[16]

In response to the call for more clear doctrinal instruction, Vatican II's reminder is valuable: the homily is not the only form of
Christian preaching. William Skudlarek and others would argue that
while it may be difficult to reach more than a small minority of
a parish or congregation apart from the Sunday morning service,
"the solution to these problems is not to turn the church into a
classroom."[17] Skudlarek suggests instead that programs of Christian
education should flow out of the liturgical assembly and might focus
on a study of the scriptures that specifically addresses doctrinal and
ethical issues. Recognizing that the lack of ongoing catechesis in the
Christian community is a problem, Sloyan and Skudlarek nonetheless both agree that "the homily is not primarily instructional. . . . [Its]
reason is exhortation and encouragement."[18]

Many in the field of catechetics resist the reduction of catechesis
to "instruction," stressing that catechesis shares in the formational
and transformational role of all forms of proclamation.[19] Whether
focusing on the homily or on the larger question of the nature of
catechesis, however, a central issue is the meaning of doctrine or
teaching when the message being handed on is the very mystery
of Jesus Christ. The specific question confronting preachers is: Is it

appropriate to preach Christian doctrine within the liturgy? One's answer to that question depends on one's understanding of both doctrine and liturgical preaching.

Doctrine and Kerygma: Crucial Distinctions

An adequate understanding of doctrinal preaching in our day requires a grasp of the relationship between kerygma and doctrine. That distinction rests in turn on an understanding of the relationship between revelation, sacred scripture, and doctrine. *Revelation* is God's offer of friendship to humankind, an offer that has been made known through creation and history. This Word of God that is God's own self-communication in word and deed has been announced by the prophets and embodied in Jesus Christ, the Word made flesh. The Jewish and Christian communities of faith who experienced a unique relationship with God in the context of their tradition and the events of their history as a people later gathered stories of their faith experience in the texts that came to constitute *sacred scripture*. Those scriptures constitute a record of what the community had come to identify as the history of their salvation in the formative stages of the living tradition. But scripture is also more than a record of a past history of salvation. Christians believe that in the proclamation (kerygma) or announcement of God's action in their past history, the same power of God that was active in the founding stages of the living tradition becomes living and active again here and now. Thus the scriptures proclaimed in faith serve not only as a memory of salvation in the past but also as a sacrament of that experience of God's saving presence now. The language of proclamation, like biblical and liturgical language, is rich, evocative, and multivalent precisely because of the inexpressible mystery from which it arises and which it evokes.

As diverse communities and individuals began to reflect on their communal experience of the mystery of faith in new situations, new questions arose and new language was needed if the Christian heritage was not to be lost in cultural accommodation. The "pledge entrusted" to the earliest Christians was not only teachings about Jesus or even the teachings of Jesus but the entire mystery of God's self-communication in Jesus the Christ and in their ongoing experience of the Holy Spirit in the community.

The biblical, liturgical, and kerygmatic language with which Christian communities had "handed on what they had received" was poetic, symbolic, and reflective of plural experiences of faith, but it proved ambiguous when confronted with new questions in a Hellenistic context. Was the Logos "of the same substance" with the unoriginate Godhead? If so, how was one to interpret the Johannine passage: "The Father is greater than I" (John 14:28)? If not, how could the community explain the tradition of prayer to Jesus? Did Jesus have a rational and spiritual soul? Was he "fully human"? Or were the gnostics and docetists right in claiming the backing of Paul's Letter to the Philippians: "He emptied himself, taking the form of a slave, being born in human likeness" (Phil 2:7)?

The more precise and limited second-order language of *doctrine,* or official church teaching, evolved precisely to protect and preserve the kerygma from fundamental distortion. Hence the resolution of multiple christological disputes in Chalcedon's declaration: Jesus Christ was one in being with the Father as to divinity and one in being with us as to humanity, truly God and truly human, yet remaining one person. The mystery of Jesus Christ could never be defined, nor explained, but it was beyond the limits of orthodox Christian belief to deny either the full humanity or the full divinity of Christ.[20]

Does Doctrine Belong in the Pulpit?

Even this cursory, and necessarily unnuanced, review of the development of christological doctrine suggests two conclusions regarding the relationship between doctrine and preaching. First, the language of doctrine is not appropriate for the task of preaching (kerygma). The language of proclamation, like biblical and liturgical language, is first-order symbolic and poetic language. It is intended to address the hearers of the word on multiple levels of their being — imagination, emotions, memory, and senses as well as rational intellect. Doctrine, on the other hand, is second-order language designed to clarify the boundaries of belief in polemical contexts. Its purpose is to clarify, distinguish, and provide limits for the imagination, rather than to evoke the community's religious experience.

Nevertheless, solid doctrine is essential for Christian preaching. While we do not preach doctrine directly in the liturgical setting, right doctrine (orthodoxy) keeps us from preaching heresy. The pulpit is not the place for speaking about monophysitism, yet Karl Rahner's insight in 1951 that most Catholics were crypto-monophysites (failing to believe that Jesus is fully human)[21] is still clearly reflected in some preaching. Further, if it is true that today students and younger preachers have been raised on christology "from below," perhaps the issue is shifting in the other direction as Jesus is portrayed by some as a secular humanist or a courageous prophet, with the unfortunate result that the preaching never quite reaches the kerygma — the good news of what God has done in Jesus.

Doctrinal errors are not limited to the field of christology. Many Catholics think human beings work to earn salvation — regardless of the nuances of the Council of Trent's statement on justification. Many Christians are at least semi-Pelagian in thinking that the human person takes the first initiative in turning to God in prayer or in seeking forgiveness and conversion. Maybe that is why twelve-step spirituality, with its clear emphasis on trusting entirely in a higher power, speaks more profoundly to many people's lives and hearts than does the preaching they hear in church.

Contemporary heresies are no less threatening to the full truth of the gospel. Consider, for example, the anti-Semitism inherent in some preachers' presentations of "the Pharisees" in the Gospel of Matthew or "the Jews" in the Gospel of John. A homily preached during a eucharistic celebration in the context of a gathering of a congregation of women religious several years ago illustrates that sexism can be not only subtle but even blatant in the preaching event. The focus of the preaching was the passage from the Gospel of John that has been frequently referred to as "the woman taken in adultery" (John 8:1–10). After an analysis of the Levitical law with which the passage was paired during the Lenten liturgy, the priest concluded his homily with the words: "That woman should never have been stoned. She should have been flogged." The congregation was further educated on a detail of legal interpretation but did not hear the preaching of the Christian gospel from the pulpit that day.

On the other hand, the preacher can also fail to preach the gospel by the use of half-truths that evade difficult gospel mandates. Moral concerns, especially issues of social justice, can seem too controversial or too difficult to connect with the scripture passages of the day. Preachers and congregations alike often are called to conversion

by precisely the passages they would prefer to avoid. Both assembly
and preacher need to be challenged by the "full gospel." Doctrine
functions precisely to protect the fullness of the kerygma (the proclamation). Doctrine exists so that the church does not preach or believe
half-truths (heresy). As Karl Barth once observed, "[O]ne is not required to preach confessions of faith, but to have as the purpose and
limit of one's message the Confession of one's Church, taking one's
stand where the Church stands."[22]

Further, because doctrine develops in diverse cultural and historical situations, a study of doctrine can open up new perspectives
and connections by pointing to the mystery of revelation or expressing a biblical insight in a new cultural context that demands
different expression of the same reality. Study of "what was moving forward" in the history of the doctrine and theology of grace
in multiple historical and cultural contexts, for example, is intended
to expand students' perspectives so that they might recognize and
identify that same mystery of God's presence and power in a contemporary context. Images and examples drawn from literature, film,
and contemporary stories of grace, however, are far more appropriate for use in the pulpit than technical language of prevenient grace,
justification, or merit. Doctrine informs, disciplines, protects, and
enriches the preaching of the kerygma — but it never replaces it.

Biblical, Liturgical, and Doctrinal Preaching: Reestablishing Basic Connections

One sometimes hears discussions of whether preaching should be
biblical, liturgical, or doctrinal, as if the three forms of preaching
were mutually exclusive. In reality, however, while either biblical
or doctrinal preaching may not be liturgical, liturgical preaching is
necessarily both biblical and doctrinal. For those in sacramental traditions who are concerned about the apparent absence of doctrinal
preaching in the contemporary church, further reflection on the essential relationship between scripture, worship, and doctrine in the
early church may suggest a way forward.

First, the relationship between doctrine and scripture is key.
Teaching and preaching were not distinct ministries in the early
church; the focus of both was handing on to others the mystery that
had been entrusted to the church: the mystery of salvation from God

in Jesus Christ. Teaching about Jesus included interpretation of the biblical tradition, witness to the good news of salvation in the contemporary moment, and ethical exhortation. The apostolic tradition was the fundamental doctrine of the church, the "rule of faith" to be preserved and handed on in every generation. The canonical scriptures are the church's normative witness to the apostolic tradition. To preach the biblical heritage is therefore to preach the most basic doctrine, the normative teaching, of the Christian church. As Gerard Sloyan insists, "The best assurance that the ancient faith will be preserved and promoted in the hearing of believers is that the Bible be preached at the Sunday liturgy in and out of season."[23] While some, especially Roman Catholics, would argue that the authentic tradition of the church extends beyond the apostolic tradition, Sloyan again remarks on the normative character of the apostolic tradition: "The Bible is the great corrective to all the false starts and near misses of Christian history. It does nothing to threaten the valid developments of genuine tradition. It does everything to threaten the ephemeral doctrines, ... the human traditions."[24]

Second, the worship of the church served both as a source of doctrinal development in the early church and as the context for the proclamation of the earliest confessions of faith (e.g., the Nicene Creed).[25] The very term "orthodoxy" literally refers to "right praise" rather than "right teaching." To preach on the liturgical text of the creed is to preach the most fundamental doctrine of the church.

Third, the worship of the church provided a fundamental source for the scriptures and at the same time was drawn from the richness of the scriptures. The scriptures focus the liturgical celebration, but liturgical context can also reinterpret biblical images and claims. Calling the Bible the "spine of liturgical preaching," Gerard Sloyan has remarked, "The entire service of churches that use liturgical formularies is biblical. When the church prays publicly it always — repeat always — prays in the spirit of the bible, most often in the adapted words of the bible."[26] True liturgical preaching is always biblical preaching. The liturgical celebration is part of the hermeneutic of the biblical text — an aspect of preaching that cannot be neglected in liturgical preaching.

Further, as Gordon Lathrop has noted, the liturgical reuse of ancient biblical images in new cultural moments fundamentally shifts the images so that a new "revelatory twist" occurs.[27] Readings from the Hebrew scriptures proclaiming messianic hope are radically reinterpreted when liturgically juxtaposed with Christian claims that the crucified one is Messiah or when announced on the Feast of Christ the King or during the season of Advent. The image of priesthood is fundamentally changed when those assembled for liturgy are referred to as "holy priests," when the foot-washing narrative in the Gospel of John is selected for the gospel proclamation on Holy Thursday, or when the presider becomes foot-washer in the assembly. Biblical testimonies to God's fidelity, compassion, and power are heard in new ways when those proclamations occur during a funeral liturgy. Whether through the metaphorical breaking open of an unexpected meaning of a biblical image or through ritual embodiment of the word proclaimed, "the liturgical celebration, based primarily on the Word of God and sustained by it, becomes a new event and enriches the Word itself with new meaning and power."[28]

These basic interconnections between biblical, liturgical, and doctrinal preaching are perhaps best evidenced in the process of liturgical catechesis in the fourth and fifth centuries, a process that has been to some extent restored in the contemporary Rite of Christian Initiation (RCIA). The scriptures and the liturgy clearly formed the context for doctrinal instruction. Not only were the expositions of Christian doctrine often preached "in a powerful cascade of biblical images pounding the imagination,"[29] but also the early bishops were aware that the "rite itself brings insight."[30] The insight the rite brings, however, is not knowledge about liturgy but rather a deepened awareness of what it means to be formed into, and to participate in, the body of Christ. As Catherine Dooley explains: "Mystagogy is not so much about looking at the meaning of the rite as it is about the meaning of relationships.... Mystagogy is a way of interpreting life in the light of the mystery celebrated."[31]

Fundamentally the preacher faces the same issue with regard to the church's worship and scriptures as with its doctrine — all three need to be related to concrete human life. Karl Rahner once observed that all the difficulties that women and men today experience have a common basis: "[T]heological expressions are not formulated in such a way that they can see how what is being said has any connection with their own understanding of themselves which they have derived from their experience."[32]

Doctrine, like liturgy and scripture, is intended ultimately to lead believers into the heart of the mystery of relationship with God. While Catholics especially often think of doctrines as a number of incomprehensible mysteries that are to be believed as a matter of faith, Rahner emphasizes that all doctrines are directed toward aspects of the one mystery of the trinity: God is self-communicating love enfleshed in history in Jesus and made present to us in and through the power of the Spirit. Any other doctrine of the Christian church must be somehow connected with that most fundamental mystery of the love for which all human hearts hunger.[33]

Liturgical Preaching and the One Mystery

Two other aspects of liturgical preaching further establish the connections between doctrine, liturgy, and scripture: the liturgical year and the lectionary. The ordering of time into a pattern of festivals and seasons that once characterized the sacramental traditions of the Roman Catholic, Orthodox, Lutheran, and Anglican churches is now broadly accepted in the majority of Christian churches in North America.[34] The structure of the liturgical year into two basic cycles turns our attention on the two great christological and trinitarian mysteries of death and resurrection (Lent-Easter) and incarnation/manifestation (Advent-Christmas). All liturgy celebrates the one mystery at the center of every dogma: the mystery of God with us in human history through Jesus and in the power of the Spirit. Within the week as the basic unit of liturgical time, the celebration of Sunday as feast of the resurrection and as anticipation of the "eighth day" of eschatological fulfillment focuses all preaching in terms of the paschal mystery. Conscious attention to liturgical season, time, and feast will require reflection on the connection between the most basic Christian doctrines and the scriptures and liturgical celebration.

Doctrinal preaching, however, involves far more than explanation of the history or development of a specific teaching of the church. It is certainly appropriate to preach on the doctrine of the trinity on Trinity Sunday or, in the Roman Catholic tradition, on the doctrines of the immaculate conception or the assumption on those feasts, but always in the mode of biblical and liturgical *preaching*.[35] Just as some notes of biblical exegesis can be used in a homily, so too elements of doctrinal instruction or clarification can be useful. Making some connection with the doctrine is certainly called for by the liturgical feast itself. Nevertheless, the context and goal of liturgical preaching should always determine the mode and extent of that instructional element. In a similar way it is appropriate to highlight the church's teaching on peace, capital punishment, or some other ethical issue especially in relation to a particular occasion (e.g., World Day of Prayer for Peace, a dispute about the execution of a prisoner in a particular state, a specific political issue to be decided by government) or when appropriate in terms of the readings for the day. The goal of the preacher, however, is not primarily to teach moral doctrine, much less to dictate specific ethical or political actions, but rather to echo the gospel's call to radical discipleship.[36] True doctrinal preaching leads the assembly back to the baptismal pool and the eucharistic table, renewing the gathered community's commitment to authentic Christian living.

A lectionary, too, while originally the heritage of the "sacramental churches," now is used widely by other Christian churches and pastors. In the present revised Roman lectionary, adopted (with adaptations) as a common ecumenical lectionary (*Common Lectionary* [1983]; *Revised Common Lectionary* [1992]), the three-year cycle of readings for Sundays is designed so that more of the riches of the scriptures might be heard by the people of God. While there are numerous problems with present lectionaries,[37] including the notable omissions, the "snippet approach" to the texts that are included, and some of the ways in which the Hebrew scriptures are used by Christian churches, most critics of the lectionary argue for its revision rather than the rejection of any sort of lectionary. Paul Marshall suggests that this is because the lectionary broadens, rather than restricts, the scope of preaching:

> A message about the preacher and the church's life is given when the texts studied and proclaimed are threatening, disturbing, or even disinteresting to the preacher. The message says that to encounter, even "routinely," the breadth of the scriptures is an adventure in Christian life, the beginning of a journey whose end is not always fully known.[38]

Like Sloyan, Marshall is convinced that the authentic preaching of the whole biblical heritage is the best guarantee that the fundamental doctrine of the church will be handed on. This can be affirmed, however, only in light of the critical concerns raised in chapter 5 about principles for lectionary selection and the need for a critical biblical hermeneutic. This is particularly true in terms of preaching Christian moral doctrine.

Sloyan, who maintains that all of the inspired writers were moralists in one sense, argues that the scriptures as found in the lectionary provide opportunity for preaching on any possible ethical issue. He is not suggesting that the Bible provides answers to moral dilemmas that did not even exist in earlier times and cultures, but rather more fundamentally that "you cannot think of a human state of heart or mind, a human reaction to any challenge in the following of Christ that is not mirrored deeply in the gospels."[39] Well aware of the misuse of the scriptures, particularly Christian misuse of the Hebrew scriptures in lectionary selection, teaching, and preaching, he nonetheless extends his claim:

> There is nothing human there that is not found in some form. ...One needs to have a jejune imagination indeed not to be able to go from those readings directly — not by some wildly circuitous route — to the greed that inevitably corrupts, to overkill masquerading as the first line of a nation's defense, to the ravishing of women for male pleasure, to the big government lie and the crafty domestic deceit. It is all there crying out to be exposed.[40]

Sloyan's call for exposure of corruption and sin reinforces the claim in chapter 5 that the role of the prophetic imagination is crucial if both preacher and assembly are to distinguish the word of God from the limited and often sinful perspectives and assumptions of the culture in which the text emerged. The prophetic imagination is also necessary if the Christian assembly is to celebrate the Christian liturgy and recognize the true intent of liturgical symbolism in spite of the ways in which the concrete human and ecclesial celebration limits or blocks that meaning. The way liturgical space and ritual are designed, the limitations on who can minister and in what roles, the style of presiding, the language used to name both God and the baptized community, restrictions on who may drink from the cup, the community's failure to welcome the stranger, and the choice and use of biblical texts can all undermine baptismal dignity and equality and the building up of the body of Christ.[41] All of this is to say that the liturgical celebration itself must become a more authentic preaching of the ethics of the gospel.

There is a further connection between the preaching of moral doctrine and liturgical preaching, a connection that is rooted in the very structure of the liturgy. The liturgy of the word always precedes and focuses the ritual action to follow. The liturgical structure of remembering that fosters hope and action provides the key for preaching moral doctrine. Christian ethics is not a list of personal and social duties but an invitation to a covenant relationship that empowers the fidelity it requires. Faith comes from hearing; remembering leads to celebration and action. This structure of liturgy suggests not only the appropriate structure for the liturgical homily but also the basic structure of Christian life. The gathered assembly remembers God's promise, fidelity, and justice so that they might recommit themselves to authentic living of Christian discipleship, both within and outside the Christian community.

The Preacher as Pastoral Theologian

R. E. C. Browne once noted that "doctrine does not tell [the preacher] what to think, but how to think."[42] The call for more doctrinal preaching in the Christian churches is at least partially a call for greater theological depth and skill from preachers. Doctrine, the "theology for which the Church is responsible,"[43] is not the only theology that influences the homily. To make appropriate connections between scripture, liturgy, doctrine, and the life of a concrete Christian assembly, the preacher must in effect be a theologian — not a professional theologian, nor an academic one, but a truly pastoral theologian. M.-D. Chenu, in an article written in the 1950s, talks about every thinking Christian as an "unwitting theologian."[44] Preachers need to become "witting ones." To take on the life of the preacher is to commit oneself to becoming a contemplative and to embrace ongoing study as part of one's vocation. This commitment to study includes not only theological study but also an active interest in other areas of human discovery and knowledge and, most important of all, daily and sustained reflection on human experience. "All of reality" — from daily parish happenings and the life-stories shared by individual members of the congregation to international political events — is the appropriate subject for the preacher's theological reflection.[45]

Precisely because preaching involves the art of mediating between religion and culture or of making connections between the Christian tradition and contemporary human experience, the preacher is involved in a theological act. If one begins with the biblical text or doctrinal feast or liturgical season, preaching necessarily involves "faith seeking understanding" — the hermeneutical effort of translating the kerygma to which all scripture and doctrine point into contemporary images and language. If one begins instead with the experience of the gathered assembly, preaching requires theological reflection on human experience and culture that is able to correlate that experience with the focus of the biblical passages for the day and the larger Christian tradition as well as with a particular feast or liturgical season and the specific liturgical event.[46]

One might be faced, for example, with the situation that occurred at a theological school several years ago. A eucharist was planned for the Feast of Our Lady of Guadalupe during Advent. The readings of the day were from Isaiah 41 (the Holy One of Israel is our redeemer and will not forsake the afflicted and needy) and Matthew 11 (the least born into the kingdom of God is greater than John the Baptist; the violent take the kingdom by force). The congregation was an academic theological community. One of the faculty members who was well known and loved was dying of cancer. Further, this was to be the final liturgy of the semester. To speak even a brief word of faith in that context required serious theological reflection. In addition to exegesis of the biblical passages, a number of theological issues required critical reflection. Among the latter were the following: How does the scripture's claim that God will never abandon the needy relate to the human experience of those who are dying and watching others die? How does that relate to the experience of the poor and oppressed — the Juan Diegos of today's Mexico and Central America and world? How is the community to interpret the symbol of Our Lady of Guadalupe and the legend that is central to the religious experience of many of the people of the Americas?[47] How does the Catholic tradition understand devotion to Mary and the saints? How is the story of a vision of Mary related to the biblical claim about God's compassion? What does it mean to intercede for one another? What is the communion of saints? the mystical body? How does all of this connect with Advent? with eucharist? with students and faculty in a theological school?

Making those connections is a theological act. Using Paul Ricoeur's language, we can name three steps that the preacher must take. Beginning with the symbolic language of the scriptures and the liturgy and the commonsense language in which people name their ordinary human experience (step 1: the "first naïveté"), the preacher engages in a process of critical reflection on both human experience and the symbols of our faith and the multiple "conflicts of interpretation" that arise there (step 2), before finally returning to symbolic, poetic, and evocative language that speaks to all levels of the human person and community (step 3: the "second naïveté").[48] The preacher speaks in the language of story, myth, image, and human experience. A "second naïveté" reflects that he or she has grappled with critical issues, but the preacher does not bring them to the pulpit. One of the fundamental problems with contemporary preaching is that either it remains on the level of the "first naïveté" or preachers try to speak out of the second stage (that of critical reflection — whether doctrinal teaching or exegesis or liturgical instruction) rather than moving through that stage to a level of language that engages both the hearts and the minds of the hearers of the word and challenges the community to deeper conversion. The task of the theologian has been described as "locating the mystery" — not explaining it. The preacher's role goes beyond that of the theologian to that of the prophet: announcing the good news of salvation in such a way that the community is drawn into the experience of grace and moved both to celebrate and to share that good news with others.

However, if preaching is the art of naming the grace discovered in the experience of the community of faith, both past and present, a critical question arises: Whose experience counts?[49] The danger that human traditions might be handed on in the name of the gospel was central to the Reformers' critique of Roman Catholicism. The scriptures remain the critical norm of all later ecclesial developments. Both Anglican and Roman Catholic traditions, while agreeing that later developments in the tradition can never violate or contradict the apostolic tradition within the scriptures, nevertheless grant a significant role to the ongoing experience of the community of faith in the development of the authentic Christian tradition. The Bible is the church's book and must be preserved and interpreted by the church. But if the word of God is entrusted to the entire community of believers,[50] by what criteria and with what leadership does the community distinguish the authentic living tradition from distortion?[51] Detailed discussion of these difficult questions is beyond the scope of this text, but the issues are fundamental to decisions about who proclaims the word of God publicly in the name of the church. The review of the history of women's preaching in the next chapter highlights how issues of authentic tradition, authority, and group bias can become intertwined. What is at issue, finally, is fidelity to the authentic Christian tradition — to both the original apostolic tradition and to the ongoing movement of the Spirit in our time.

Chapter 9

Women Preaching the Gospel

Women called to proclaim the gospel today, whether ordained or not, find striking parallels between their experience and those of the first preachers entrusted with the good news of the resurrection of Jesus. The earliest version of Mark's Gospel concludes with this description of Mary Magdalene, Mary, the mother of James, and Salome, who were sent to tell the disciples the good news that Jesus had been raised: "They made their way out and fled from the tomb bewildered and trembling; and because of their great fear, they said nothing to anyone" (Mark 16:8).[1] The longer ending of Mark reports that Mary Magdalene, the first to whom Jesus appeared, announced the good news to his followers, "who were now grieving and weeping." Yet the passage continues: "When they heard that he was alive and had been seen by her, they refused to believe it" (Mark 16:11).

According to Matthew's Gospel, Mary Magdalene and the other Mary, after experiencing a mighty earthquake, were told by an angel to go quickly and tell the disciples that Jesus had been raised. They "hurried away from the tomb, half-overjoyed, half-fearful, and ran to carry the good news to his disciples" (Matt 28:8). In the midst of their mission, Jesus appeared to them promising them peace and giving his own commission: "Go and carry the news to my brothers" (Matt 28:10).

In Luke's version, the women arrived at the tomb and found the stone rolled back but could not find Jesus. "Still at a loss over what to think of this" (Luke 24:4), they were terrified by the presence of two men in dazzling garments who confronted them with the question: "Why do you search for the Living One among the dead?" (Luke 24:5). Remembering the words of Jesus that the Son of Man would be crucified and rise again, they embraced their mission to tell the disciples. Luke notes, however, that "the story seemed like nonsense, and they refused to believe them" (Luke 24:11).

The Gospel of John provides the most detailed story of the woman who later in the tradition would be called the "apostle to the apostles."[2] Mary Magdalene stood weeping beside the tomb, but "[e]ven as she wept she stooped to peer inside" (John 20:11). The focal question of the passage, asked first by the angels and later repeated by Jesus, is: "Woman, why are you weeping?" (John 20:13). The response of this first preacher: "Because the Lord has been taken away, and I do not know where they have put him" (John 20:13). It is precisely in her loss, confusion, and pain that Mary "[catches] sight of Jesus" (John 20:14). Her greatest hope had been to find the dead body of the one she loved. Instead, that hope was broken open beyond all expectation, and she experienced the mystery and power of the resurrection in the calling of her name. In this version, when Jesus commissioned Mary to go to his brothers, she went immediately and proclaimed boldly from her experience: "I have seen the Lord" (John 20:18).

These biblical accounts suggest ecclesial parallels in the experience of many women called to preach in our day. Some who have been disciples of Jesus are questioning their previous understandings of Jesus and the meaning of their discipleship. They seek new ways of understanding the mystery of Christ, new ways of experiencing God, but find their experience of church to be an "empty tomb."[3] There are women who originally responded to a call to ministry, and who still feel called to "anoint the body of Christ," but who have now fled from any ministry publicly identified with the church. Still others are simply at a loss over what to think of all that is happening to the body of Christ. Fear, failure to trust their own experience, and dismissal of their words and insights continue to be reasons why many women remain silent in Christian churches.

For others, the dangerous memories of the words and deeds of Jesus are often, as Luke's passage suggests, the cause for profound transformation. The gospel of one who was himself despised and rejected takes on new meaning and power as women begin to reflect on the prophetic message and liberating lifestyle of Jesus. In the midst of painful and unjust social and ecclesial situations, many women continue to experience the power of resurrection. Some are discovering and creating new ways to announce the good news to those who are grieving and weeping. Still others speak with joy and conviction of their vocation to preach. Like Mary Magdalene, they have moved beyond grief, loss, and confusion to announce the truth of their experience of the crucified and risen one.

All Christian preaching centers around the proclamation that the one who was crucified has been raised and lives among us now in and through the power of the Spirit. But there is a unique way in which women's preaching of the gospel shares in the very mystery of the resurrection. The resurrection is the ultimate surprise and over-throw of former categories and limitations. The proclamation of the good news is an event in which the mystery of the gospel happens again here and now. For many in the Christian churches today, wit-nessing the word of God enfleshed by women is just such a parabolic experience. Their categories and expectations are shattered as God once again proves to be "doing a new thing" (Isa 43:19).

Behind the Words of Women: A History of Silence and Resistance

The "new thing" the Spirit is doing in the twentieth century among women who are preachers of the gospel is not entirely new how-ever. The Christian tradition, even the specifically Catholic tradition, includes a history of women preaching, but also a history of the pro-hibition of women from the public proclamation of the gospel in the name of the church. According to the most restrictive interpretation of the present Code of Canon Law in the Roman Catholic Church, women and other laypersons are ordinarily prohibited from preach-ing at eucharist since the homily is reserved to the ordained.[4] A number of other Christian traditions also restrict liturgical preaching to the ordained, but they recognize women's call to full participation in the ordained ministry of the church. The history of the Christian tradition, however, reveals that the gift for preaching is a gift given to the baptized, limited neither to males nor to the ordained.

Why rehearse here the history of the gradual prohibition of women from public proclamation in the name of the church? For Roman Catholics, it is important to establish whether present church practice, including lay preaching at eucharist, and potential canoni-cal changes are grounded in the authentic tradition of the church. Beyond the Roman Catholic experience, however, not only the offi-cial silencing of women in the past but also an ongoing resistance to women's ecclesial leadership continue to have an impact on contemporary women and the gathered assemblies in which they preach.[5] From the perspective of the sacramental imagination, the naming and enfleshing of the word by women are essential if the Christian community is to give symbolic witness to the inclusive community of discipleship that Jesus founded and to proclaim the mystery of God that Jesus, the scriptures, and the tradition described in female as well as male language and images.[6]

Naming grace in the Christian tradition can happen only if we are equally committed to naming the "dis-grace" or sin that is also part of our human heritage. The focus of this chapter will be to identify the forgotten history of women and laypersons commissioned to preach the gospel, to analyze the reasons or presumptions surrounding restrictions on women's preaching and/or lay preaching, and to explore briefly questions related to the charism and authority to preach in the liturgical assembly. In the following chapter we will return to the question of the uniqueness of women's experience and suggest that the category of social location broadens the discussion of who is called to preach the gospel in the Christian church.

Christian Scriptures

The Christian scriptures offer clear evidence of women as preachers of the gospel.[7] At the same time, the classic texts used repeatedly to restrict women from preaching are also found there. Distinctions from later periods have to be nuanced, however, since the reality of ministry as described in the New Testament is largely charismatic and diverse. Numerous authors have noted that there is no evidence that women were excluded from any of the Spirit's charisms, nor restricted from any of the ministries in the earliest Christian communities.[8] In terms of preaching, there is, on the contrary, clear evidence that women were so gifted and did exercise ministries of preaching, prophesying, and teaching. Women exercised significant leadership roles in early Christian communities, founding and maintaining house churches.

Women's role as prophet is attested to by the very passage used later in the tradition to argue that women are subordinate to men and that women do not image God as fully as men — 1 Cor 11:3–6:

> I want you to know that the head of every man is Christ; the head of a woman is her husband; and the head of Christ is

the Father. Any man who prays or prophesies with his head uncovered brings shame upon his head. Similarly, any woman who prays or prophesies with her head uncovered brings shame upon her head. It is as if she had had her head shaved. . . . It is clear that she ought to wear a veil. (1 Cor 11:3–6).

It is evident from the text that women did pray and prophesy in the context of public worship. Paul's argument is not that the practice should stop but that when women do exercise this authority in the community, they should have their hair covered or bound up. Detailed exegetical debates concerning this custom and its symbolic value are available elsewhere.[9] The point here is simply to establish that women did preach publicly in worship in the early Christian communities.

Women also are included explicitly in the ministry of teaching, a ministry in the early church intimately connected with, if not inseparable from, preaching. Prisca (or Priscilla) is mentioned specifically, along with her husband Aquila, as having instructed Apollos in the Christian faith (Acts 18:26). She is mentioned again in Paul's Letter to the Romans as one of his co-workers (Rom 16:3). In the same passage Junias[10] is described as an outstanding apostle (Rom 16:7). Another women, Phoebe, is named *diakonos* of the church at Cenchrae (Rom 16:1), a term that is ordinarily translated as "missionary," "minister," "servant," or "deacon" and indicates an itinerant leader of a local congregation involved in preaching and teaching.[11]

These historical traces of women as included in preaching roles in the early church are further supplemented by images of women as preachers and prophets in the Lukan and Johannine narratives. Even a cursory survey reveals Anna and Mary functioning as prophets in the infancy narratives (Luke 2), the four daughters of Philip as prophets (Acts 21:9), Mary of Bethany as the exemplary disciple learning from Jesus, a role ordinarily reserved to men (Luke 10), and the role of witness attributed to women in John's Gospel, notably the Samaritan woman and Mary Magdalene.[12]

Nevertheless, two of the texts used to prohibit women from preaching publicly in the Christian assembly are also found in the canon of the Christian scriptures:

According to the rule observed in all the assemblies of believers, women should keep silent in such gatherings. They may not speak. Rather as the law states, submissiveness is indicated for them. If they want to learn anything, they should ask their husband at home. It is a disgrace when a woman speaks in the assembly. (1 Cor 14:33b–35)

A woman must listen in silence and be completely submissive. I do not permit a woman to act as a teacher or in any way to have authority over a man; she must be quiet. For Adam was created first, Eve afterward; moreover, it was not Adam who was deceived, but the woman. It was she who was led astray and fell into sin. She will be saved through childbearing, provided she continues in faith and love and holiness — her chastity being taken for granted. (1 Tim 2:11–15)

In addition to the fact that the first passage occurs in the same letter in which Paul refers to women praying and prophesying publicly without criticizing that practice, biblical scholars have noted that the verb in 1 Corinthians 14 (to speak = *lalein*) does not refer to the official functions of teaching or preaching.[13] The passage from 1 Timothy, a later Pastoral Epistle, which does admonish women not to teach (*didaskein*), is a later development in conflict with the earlier Pauline evidence that women did pray and prophesy publicly in the assembly at worship. Contemporary critical exegesis reveals that the above texts are pastoral injunctions in light of specific historical-cultural circumstances that included a clear patriarchal bias, rather than texts that were intended to be applied universally or handed down as "the Christian tradition." The patriarchal bias of the texts may seem evident in an age of critical biblical scholarship, but these texts, taken as authoritative and inspired, functioned to prohibit women from preaching in the majority of Christian churches well into the twentieth century.[14]

Early Church

By the end of the second century, the threefold church order of bishop, presbyter, and deacon had developed, the ministries of leadership began to absorb earlier charismatic ministries, and preaching became the prerogative of the bishop who was the recognized guardian of the apostolic tradition.[15] While there is evidence that women preached and presided in the Montanist sect of the second century, the condemnation of Montanism as heretical only reinforced

the suspicion that the practice of women preaching endangered orthodoxy. As the head of the catechetical school in Alexandria in the
third century, Origen was invited by the bishops of Jerusalem and
Caesarea "to preach and expound the scriptures publicly although he
had not been ordained presbyter."[16] By that time, however, women
were explicitly excluded from preaching and teaching, as reflected in
the following text from the *Didascalia Apostolorum:*

> It is neither right nor necessary therefore that women should be
> teachers and especially concerning the name of Christ and the
> redemption of his passion. For you have not been appointed
> to this, O Women.... For He the Lord God, Jesus Christ, our
> teacher, sent us the Twelve, to instruct the people and the gen-
> tiles; and there were with us women disciples, ... but he did not
> send them to instruct the people with us. (3.6)[17]

While the prohibition on women's teaching continued, the *Apostolic Constitutions* of the fourth century confirmed that lay*men* could
be teachers if properly trained: "He who teaches even if he is a layman, let him teach as a skillful person properly equipped in word
and deed, for they shall all be taught of God."[18]

Evidence of officially authorized lay preaching is not available
again until the Middle Ages. While the initial concern was for the
church's authentic tradition, the restriction was stated increasingly in
terms of clerical rank and "good order." In the fifth century, Pope
Leo V censured dissident monks whose preaching was not faithful to
the Council of Chalcedon:

> Apart from those who are priests of the Lord, no one may dare
> to claim for himself the right to teach or to preach, whether
> he be a monk or layman and one who boasts a reputation for
> some learning. For although it is desirable for all the church's
> sons to be learned in what is right and holy, no one outside
> the priestly order is to assume for himself the rank of preacher.
> For it is necessary that all things be ordered in God's church;
> that is in the one body of Christ, the superior members are to
> carry out their office and the inferior members are not to resist
> superior ones.[19]

Deacons were permitted only to read the writings of another —
usually one of the church fathers who were considered recognized

authorities in the community. There was no question of women being authorized to preach publicly in the name of the church in a
system that restricted preaching to the ordained and ordination to
men. Where the practice of lay preaching continued, it was condemned on the grounds that subordinates were usurping the rank
of their superiors.

Middle Ages

By the Middle Ages the hierarchical structure of the church and
the strong distinction between clergy and laity had developed significantly. Yet traces of the earlier approach to preaching based
on charism can be discovered in the lay preaching bands that
were given temporary papal authorization and encouragement. Even
where preaching was based on rank, it was not clearly linked to ordination, nor was it always assumed that women were by nature
subordinate. Consequently, an abbess, because she was the superior
of the community — even of joint monasteries of women and men —
had the right to preach to her "subjects." Hildegard of Bingen, a
twelfth-century Benedictine nun, is said to have preached to clergy,
laity, monks, nuns, and ecclesiastical officials — preaching even to
bishops and clergy during their synods.[20]

Of particular interest is the rise of itinerant preaching bands composed of laywomen and men who, in a period of evangelical renewal
in the church, felt called to live the *vita apostolica:* that is, to im-
itate Jesus and the apostles through lives of voluntary poverty and
the preaching of penance and reform.[21] While the issue of heresy
emerged with regard to several of these groups (Cathari, Humiliati,
Waldensians), it is significant to note that the medieval notion of
heresy comprised not only incorrect doctrine but also departure from
the church's disciplinary norms.[22] At least one group, the Humiliati,
were officially authorized to preach words of exhortation (*verbum
exhortationis*) but not doctrine concerning faith and the sacraments
(*articuli fidei et sacramenta*) since doctrinal preaching required a
solid knowledge of scripture and theology. Members of the Franciscan Order, founded as a lay movement dedicated to the imitation
of Christ and the apostolate of preaching, were given permission to
"preach penance everywhere" if Francis so authorized them.[23] While
lay preaching movements flourished for a time,[24] they were clearly

suppressed by the Fourth Lateran Council (1215) when lay preaching was prohibited as the unauthorized usurpation of the clerical office.

The various medieval disputes about the right to preach — between monks and secular clergy, mendicants and local bishops, lay preachers and local clergy — reveal shifting claims about the source of the authority to preach. Writing on the question of whether women are given the "grace of speech," Thomas Aquinas granted that women were given the charism to preach and therefore had a responsibility to do so. However, given the patriarchal and hierarchical worldview of his time and a literal interpretation of 1 Corinthians 14, he concluded that women should exercise their "charism of speaking" in private, rather than in public.[25] The lay preaching bands claimed a charismatic authority grounded in the living of the gospel life; various religious orders or lay bands traced their authority to preach to the permission of clergy, bishop, or pope; rank or office grounded the authority of the medieval abbess as well as the bishop; and eventually the sacrament of ordination was offered as the basis for the authority to proclaim the gospel in the name of the church.

Although the breadth and vitality of the twelfth-century preaching movements had been repressed, the practice of lay preaching continued to be an issue in the thirteenth and fourteenth centuries (as instanced by John Wycliffe and the Lollards). By the fifteenth century, lay preaching was clearly considered heretical (as in the case of Jan Hus).[26] In the sixteenth century, the Council of Trent confirmed the theology and practice of the time: preaching was clearly connected with office in the official teaching of the Roman Catholic Church.

The Seventeenth to Twentieth Century: Diversity within the Protestant Churches

Following the Reformation the diversity of practice and claims to authority to preach multiplied, but the situation of women did not change significantly. While the view that women should not preach or teach in public remained the stance of the majority of Protestant churches well into the twentieth century, it did not go undisputed. In both practice and theory, women such as Margaret Fell, Anne Hutchinson, Mother Ann Lee, Lucretia Mott, Phoebe Palmer, Sojourner Truth, Salome Lincoln Mowry, Antoinette Brown, Olympia

Brown, Anna Howard Shaw, Frances Willard, Louisa M. Woolsley, Aimee Semple McPherson, and Jarena Lee challenged that claim.[27]

In the context of the United States, women had been preaching since colonial times, but the majority of female preachers in the seventeenth and eighteenth centuries came from free church movements, sects, or various holiness groups that stressed spiritual gifts and direct communion with God rather than ordination, public office, or episcopal authority. In the nineteenth century the number of women preachers increased, but still most were not part of mainline churches, nor ordained. After reviewing the history of women's preaching in the mainline churches in the United States, Barbara Brown Zikmund concludes:

> There is no simple way to document chronologically the struggle for the right to preach, because various Christian groups resolved this issue at different times. In general the Quakers, Universalists, Unitarians, and Congregationalists resolved the question earlier than most Methodists, Presbyterians, Lutherans, and Episcopalians. Part of this discrepancy had to do with church polity and part of it related to the connection between preaching and priestly functions in ordained ministry.[28]

By the early 1800s, there were types of women's ordinations within the Disciples of Christ churches, but the first "full ordination" by a local congregation was that of Antoinette Louise Brown, who was ordained by the First Congregational Church of South Butler, New York, in 1853. The first ordination of a woman to a tradition that required approval beyond the level of the local congregation occurred in June 1863 with the ordination of Olympia Brown. In 1880, Anna Howard Shaw was ordained in the Methodist Protestant Church, but in that same year the Methodist General Conference denied ordination to women and revoked all licenses to preach that had been granted to women. By the late 1880s, women had been ordained in Methodist, Baptist, and Unitarian churches.[29] In the early twentieth century, several additional churches ordained women for the first time.[30] By the end of the century, with the exception of the Orthodox Church, the Roman Catholic Church, and the Lutheran Church—Missouri Synod, women have been ordained in all mainline Christian churches and ordained bishops in the Lutheran, Methodist, and Episcopal churches.[31] Nevertheless, the ordination of women has not meant that women receive regular calls to ministry or are chosen as senior or single pastors, nor that their leadership roles and preaching are accepted by the denomination as a whole or by specific local congregations.[32]

Several focal issues emerged repeatedly in the mainline Protestant churches, where the history of women's preaching was closely intertwined with disputes over women's ordination. Fundamental disputes centered around the authority and authentic interpretation of the Bible, particularly the Pauline texts and Pastoral Epistles. Those who opposed women's preaching argued that the Bible clearly prohibited women's leadership or women's public speaking in the assembly and that women were divinely intended to be subordinate to male leadership. Any claim of divine call by the Holy Spirit, they argued, was ill-founded since the same Spirit was the inspired author of the scripture passages that prohibit women's preaching or teaching. Male and female might be considered equal, but each had a proper sphere. This fundamental biblical prohibition of women's preaching was reinforced by social, historical, and cultural reasons: only a few women had exercised significant leadership in the history of the church; women's primary role as mother and her household duties could not be combined with pastoral duties; women's minds were not suited to ministry; women lacked adequate theological training; and the movement promoting preaching by women was closely tied to a larger secular movement demanding masculine political rights.[33]

Those who supported women's preaching insisted that the biblical texts required critical examination that distinguished cultural and historical conditioning of the first century from God's will for the church in the nineteenth century. Both men and women pointed to biblical texts that gave examples of women active in the ministries of the early church, including preaching. Women consistently spoke of their authority to preach in terms of both a desire and a responsibility that derived from a call from the Holy Spirit. Proponents of women's preaching and ordination highlighted the role of the Spirit's guidance of the church beyond biblical times. Still others pointed to the pastoral experience of the church: women were already preaching effectively in the churches and engaged in full-time ministry, especially in missionary countries. The church, they reasoned, should recognize and celebrate that women's ministries were already enriching the church. Commenting on the African-American experience, Leontyne T. C. Kelly observed that "the unordained black woman has long been preacher-spiritual leader," citing as examples So-

journer Truth, Harriet Tubman, Mary McCleod Bethune, Nannie
Burroughs, Barbara Jordan, and Shirley Chisholm.[34] As one author
noted, pastors who were originally compelled by necessity to allow
women to take on new responsibilities were "amazed at the opening
of the mine of spiritual wealth, unknown and unworked before."[35]

Shifts in Roman Catholic Theology and Canonical Disputes

Within the Roman Catholic Church, ordination remains closed to
women at the present time.[36] Still, a growing number of women are
participating in various forms of the church's preaching ministry as
well as in much of the church's pastoral ministry.[37] Official authority to preach has been extended to women and other laypersons for
pastoral reasons, and the practice is even more widespread on an
unofficial basis. Nevertheless, many canon lawyers hold that even
the revised Code of Canon Law (1983) prohibits lay preaching (and
therefore all women's preaching) at eucharist.[38]

To understand this ambiguous situation, it is important to review
the significant shifts that have taken place in the Roman Catholic
understanding of church and ministry in the twentieth century. In
the Dogmatic Constitution on the Church (*Lumen Gentium*), Vatican II radically revised the Catholic Church's understanding of its
identity and mission. Rather than a juridical or institutional definition of the church, the constitution identified the church as mystery
and communion, sacramental sign of the reign of God that it serves.
Describing the church with the biblical images of "People of God,"
"Body of Christ," "Temple of the Holy Spirit," and "Light of the
Nations," the council made it clear that the church is to be identified with the entire people of God. The constitution also emphasized
that the vocation to holiness and the mission of the church to proclaim the gospel in word and deed are shared by all the baptized
and that the hierarchy's role is one of service that enables the whole
church to fulfill its mission.

A fuller appreciation of the mission and ministry of all the baptized flowed from this renewed ecclesiology.[39] The "mission of the
laity" was no longer viewed as participation in the mission of the
hierarchy, a form of the apostolate of "Catholic Action." Rather,
the council asserted that all baptized persons participate directly in
the common priesthood of Jesus Christ and share Christ's threefold
priestly, prophetic, and ruling office. Through baptism and confir-

mation all members of the church are commissioned "by the Lord himself"[40] to participate in the saving mission of the church. The "universal call to holiness" is a vocation shared by all members of the church since all are called to give witness to the reign of God. The word of God has been entrusted not solely to the magisterium but to the entire church.[41] The whole church is missionary — "the work of evangelization is a basic duty of the People of God."[42] Within the one body of Christ, there are, however, different gifts and functions. The Holy Spirit gives specific gifts to individuals so that they might share in building up the one body of the church (1 Cor 12:4–11, 28–30; Rom 12:4–8). The role of pastoral leadership within this diversity of gifts includes the coordination of the many charisms and ministries within the local church so that "all according to their proper roles may cooperate in this common understanding with one heart."[43] These emphases of the council — that the people are the church, that the word of God has been entrusted to the entire church, that baptism and confirmation are the source of all ministry, that all the baptized share in the priesthood of Christ and are called to participate in the mission of the church, and that the baptized have a responsibility to exercise the charisms they have been given — have all had a pronounced effect on the growth of the desire to preach among those who are fully initiated but not ordained.[44]

Since canonical legislation is to be interpreted in light of the documents of Vatican II rather than vice versa,[45] it is important to note that both the council and the new code embrace this renewed vision of church as the community of the baptized, equal in dignity by virtue of baptism. Ministerial roles are not determined by the status of "superiors" and "inferiors" in the one body of Christ. Rather, baptism gives every member a basic participation in Christ's mission, though members exercise different functions in the community deriving from the different gifts received from the Spirit.

In the new code the baptized are not only encouraged to proclaim the gospel but told that it is their responsibility to do so (ca. 225). "In virtue of their baptism and confirmation lay members of the Christian faithful are witnesses to the gospel message by word and by example of a Christian life" (ca. 759). Most basic to this discussion is that the Christian faithful have "a right to the word of God and the sacraments" (ca. 213). Nonetheless, many would argue that the restriction prohibiting lay preaching at eucharist is clear in canon

767.1: "Among the forms of preaching the homily is preeminent; it is part of the liturgy itself and is reserved to a priest or deacon."

As the German bishops argued in 1973, however, the liturgical nature of the homily need not necessarily restrict preaching to the ordained even in the context of eucharist:

> Because of the close relationship between the liturgy of the word and the liturgy of Eucharist, it is suitable that the preacher and president of the Eucharist be one and the same person, but this is not absolutely necessary. Moreover, since the church teaches that the entire community preaches the gospel and celebrates the liturgy, the responsibility for maintaining the office of preaching should not be given to the priest alone. Finally, lay preaching is a way of making visible the different charisms, services, and offices which exist in the Christian community without detracting from the unity of its mission.[46]

The *Directory of Masses for Children,* published by the Congregation for Divine Worship in 1973 and still in effect, offers another rationale for lay preaching at eucharist when it states that "one of the adults may speak after the gospel, especially if the priest finds it hard to adapt himself to the mentality of children."[47] The central question here is clear: Who can best communicate God's word in this congregation here and now? For pastoral reasons, someone other that the presider may be the more effective preacher at a specific celebration.

Conclusions

Several basic conclusions emerge from this rereading of the history of lay preaching in the Christian (and specifically Roman Catholic) tradition.

1. Regardless of the reasons given for the authorization of preaching, the charism to preach is grounded in baptism and confirmation — the source of all ministry.

2. There is a history of authorized and official preaching by women and other laypersons, even at eucharist.

3. Restrictions on the public preaching of women and laypersons in the name of the church have been intertwined. They stem from (*a*) inadequate interpretations of 1 Corinthians 14 and 1 Timothy 2; (*b*) a hierarchical model of ministry that subordinated laity to

clergy, combined with a patriarchal understanding of the order of creation that subordinated women to men; (c) concern at an earlier point in the church's history that the lack of theological training for lay preachers could result in distortion of the church's authentic doctrine; and (d) the connection of liturgical preaching with ordained ministry so as ensure the unity of word, sacrament, and community leadership. The final point remains the most seriously debated theological and liturgical issue regarding lay preaching at eucharist, but the question of liturgical preaching needs to be situated in the larger context of who is gifted with a charism for preaching and what will best serve the good of building up the body of Christ.

Who Is Called to Preach? Broadening the Context

The question of whether women or other laypersons who are gifted with a charism to preach and adequately trained theologically should preach in the liturgical context cannot be separated from the larger questions of who is called to preach in the broader life of the church and what constitutes the preaching ministry of the church. Without dismissing the fundamental importance of explicit liturgical proclamation by women, the churches need to claim the many ways in which women and men preach the gospel today. The preaching of Jesus is the paradigm for all Christian proclamation, and Jesus announced the reign of God in his person and actions as well as in his words. As a layman in his own religious tradition, Jesus announced the reign of God in ways that were not limited to events of public teaching or preaching, and his preaching rarely took place in a liturgical setting.

So, too, in our day it is important to recognize that all of the activities in which the baptized promote the reign of God are part of "the preaching of the church." Preaching the good news of salvation requires that the Christian community make the experience of salvation more of a concrete reality in our world. Women in prison ministries, women caring for battered women and abused children, women providing shelter for the homeless, women keeping vigil at the bedsides of the sick and the dying, and women involved in legal advocacy or political lobbying on behalf of the poor are all participating in the action on behalf of justice that is a "constitutive part of preaching the gospel."[48]

Equally important, however, is naming the power and source of that experience of salvation — the power of God. Women are also involved in this explicit naming of the power of salvation in our world. In a variety of ministries of the word — spiritual direction, teaching, theologizing, pastoral counseling, the pastoral leadership of parishes — women are involved in discerning and naming the experience of God in the midst of human struggle. Even in the Catholic Church, an increasing number of women from a variety of age groups, backgrounds, and styles of life are now involved in ministries explicitly identified as preaching the gospel: they are full-time missionaries, members of itinerant preaching teams, pastoral associates, leaders of scripture-sharing groups, and so on. Women preach in a number of contexts of prayer and spirituality: directing retreats and days of recollection, presiding at morning and evening prayer and at services of the word, forming the faith of the church as catechists involved with the Rites of Christian Initiation, and proclaiming the word in a variety of forms of worship in both Catholic and ecumenical contexts.

As women have embraced the commission to "spread the good news," sought out opportunities to preach, and engaged in processes of creative imagination, new avenues and modes of preaching the gospel have emerged. There is a real danger in restricting our understanding of preaching to the pulpit or the liturgical context. Most of the people in our world who hunger for the good news of salvation or liberation are not to be found in churches. If preaching is a matter of making connections between concrete human experience and God's word that enables people to hear the gospel as good news *for them,* then the gospel and the preachers have to meet people where they are.

Liturgical Preaching and Sacramental Issues

Within this broader context it is important to reconsider the question of who is called to preach in the eucharistic assembly. The plea for a broader understanding of preaching has been used in the past to relegate women to the broader spheres of evangelization or to a separate sphere of women's "proper realm," while excluding women from public proclamation on behalf of the church, particularly in the sacramental sphere. Properly understood, however, liturgical ministries are profoundly connected with the reality of service in the daily life of the community.[49] Here we find the theological-liturgical explanation for a frequent pastoral experience today: a community or family that has experienced the ministerial gifts, including the ministry of the word, of the nonordained members of a parish team begins to wonder why the "lay minister" cannot preach the homily at a marriage, funeral liturgy, or Sunday eucharist.

Within the Roman Catholic Church, the recovery of the ancient homily at the time of Vatican II has promoted a major renewal within Catholic preaching. However, the emphasis that the homily is "part of the liturgy itself" has reinforced the restriction in canon law that the homily is reserved to the ordained priest or deacon.[50] Some theologians have expressed the concern that lay preaching breaks "the intrinsic bonds between word, sacrament, and community leadership."[51] This does not mean, however, that these theologians necessarily oppose women preaching at eucharist. On the contrary, some argue that to have a layperson exercise this leadership role is in practice to suggest that the discipline of ordination be reconsidered. William Skudlarek, for example, has written: "The link between preaching and the sacraments, especially the Eucharist, is a close one. We need to consider it carefully, not so much to limit who may preach, but to widen our understanding of who may rightfully lead a community in its sacramental response."[52]

The practice of lay preaching at eucharist does raise questions about who in the community may be called to ordained ministry and how the Christian community calls forth those gifted with a charism for leadership, whether for a ministry of word or of word and sacrament. If all ministries of the word are not to be subsumed within the exclusive role of ordained ministers, however, then even if ordination in the Roman Catholic Church were open to women and married men, as it is in the majority of Christian churches, questions about lay liturgical preaching would remain. Is it appropriate that a fully initiated,[53] but not ordained, member of the community gifted with a charism for preaching and suitable theological background preach in the context of eucharist? This in turn raises the question of how we are to understand the role of the presider in the liturgical assembly. Does the unity of word and sacrament necessarily require that a single minister be both preacher and presider? What about the roles of lector and cantor, which are also ministries of the word? Mary Collins suggests that new and more collaborative models of presiding are possible without breaking the unity of word and sacrament. She remarks:

> If Eucharist is the act of the whole church and if the ordained is someone who presides within, not over, the community of believers, then it seems possible and necessary to seek new models for understanding sacramentality in relationship to liturgical presidency. Ecclesial experience confirms that it is possible for one who presides within the liturgical assembly to engage another believer to lead them all together into deeper communion with the mystery of Christ by the power of the Word, and that this collaborative ordering does not fracture the sacrament of unity.[54]

In her proposal Collins does not identify the presider with the preacher. Rather, leadership within the assembly includes calling forth the gifts of other believers within the assembly. Pastoral practice in this area seems clearest in situations where a foreign language is the issue. In numerous Spanish-speaking or Vietnamese parishes, for example, nonordained members of parish teams who speak the language of the people have frequently been formally authorized to preach at eucharist. The pastoral principle applied so easily in the case of children obviously needs to be extended: Who can most effectively proclaim God's word in this situation here and now?

Even from a canonical standpoint, both the practice in West Germany officially approved for eight years by the Vatican and present liturgical law confirm that someone other than the presider may preach the homily. The introduction to the lectionary cites specifically the deacon or one of the concelebrants.[55] Considering the case of permanent deacons who may have considerably less theological training and preparation for preaching than many women in pastoral ministry, the restriction of women from preaching the homily at eucharist becomes even more incomprehensible.

Charism, Office, and Authority

If the gathered assembly is the primary symbol within the liturgy, and if the unity of word, sacrament, and leadership in the community is of central concern, then it would seem fitting for those who gather the community on a regular basis and who exercise leadership and a genuine ministry of the word in the ongoing life of the community to proclaim the good news in the liturgical context as well. While theoretically it is precisely the ordained ministers in the community who combine the three ministries of word, sacrament, and pastoral leadership, in reality many times, particularly in the Roman Catholic context, the primary pastoral ministries in the community, including ministries of the word, are exercised by nonordained pastoral ministers.[56] Given that pastoral reality and the present ban on the ordination of women in the Roman Catholic Church, one can argue that the situation in which an ordained minister is brought into a community for sacramental celebration also breaks the unity of word, sacrament, and community leadership. Given that irregular situation, is it not appropriate for one who knows, leads, and genuinely ministers to the community to exercise the ministry of preaching? This does not mean that there is no role for the itinerant preacher or the sharing of ministries beyond the boundaries of local churches. But it does show the inconsistency of prohibiting liturgical preaching by one of the baptized who is a member of the community on the grounds that it breaks the unity of word, sacrament, and community leadership, when preaching by the ordained often, in reality, does the same.

A further concern is that anyone who preaches the gospel in the liturgical context speaks in the name of the church, at least implicitly. By what authority does one interpret the gospel and attempt to name where God is active here and now in human history and experience? Ultimately, both the ability and the call to preach come from the source of all real power in the Christian community — the Holy Spirit.[57] The sacramental imagination emphasizes that the Spirit's power is mediated through creation, human life, history, and cultural and religious experience. The church confirms and celebrates this in a public, communal way. When women, including those who are ordained in Christian churches, describe the source of their authority to preach, they most frequently identify an inner experience of vocation and the invitation and confirmation of local communities of believers.[58] Recognition and confirmation of the charism to preach by the bishop or other leaders who are responsible for ordering the public exercise of the ministries of the word within the local church are important for the unity and public witness of the church but are not the original source of the ability or authority to preach.[59] From a sacramental perspective, the grounding of all ministries, including ordained ministries, is to be found in baptism and confirmation.[60] Further, the notion of the *vita apostolica,* the apostolic life that flows from fidelity to one's baptism, as source of authority to preach needs to be retrieved in a contemporary context in light of reflection on Jesus' own exercise of authority as well as the commission he left his disciples. Highlighting key aspects of that gospel authority, Elisabeth Schüssler Fiorenza writes:

> Authority within the church as the discipleship community of equals must not be realized as "power over," as domination and submission, but as the enabling, energizing, creative authority of orthopraxis that not only preaches the gospel of salvation but also has the power to liberate the oppressed and to make people whole and happy. Jesus commissioned his disciples not only to preach but also to heal and to set free those dominated and dehumanized by evil powers.[61]

At the same time, a sacramental ecclesiology recognizes that the public recognition and commissioning of preachers by the ecclesial community and its leaders is important. From a sacramental perspective, grace, charism, or inner religious experience cannot be divorced from or set in opposition to its public historical and social manifestation in communities and institutions. Using ordination in an expanded sense to apply to public commissioning, Thomas O'Meara suggests that "ordination is the visible affirmation and invocation of charism, a celebration of the church's diverse life and risky mission, a symbol of the Spirit truly present in the church,...the liturgical and communal bridge between personal charism and a particular ministry."[62] Hence O'Meara argues that ordination should be enhanced, not diminished. Since ordination comes out of the local church, the ordination ritual should involve more communal symbols and more involvement by all the people of God. The process of public liturgical commissioning should be extended to include more ministries; further, different kinds of ordinations are needed. In this context, the role of a ministry of leadership is precisely to stimulate, discern, and order the charisms of the Spirit as they come to a community.[63]

As the history of lay preaching reveals, however, those entrusted with leadership do not always view or exercise their role in that way. Further, within the Roman Catholic Church, the office of leadership is restricted to males. From a sacramental perspective, we might argue that some form of public liturgical commissioning of liturgical preachers is desirable. Nevertheless, that cannot be said without recognizing and criticizing the twofold bias of patriarchy and clericalism that remains deeply ingrained within the leadership structures of the Christian churches.[64] Given that situation the ideal of public liturgical recognition of the ministry of preaching may not always be possible. Nevertheless, the Christian community has a right as well as a hunger to hear the word of God. Further, the primary responsibility of bishops and other pastors of the church is to see that the word of God is proclaimed and heard as fully as possible in their local churches. Here it may be valuable to recall a similar dilemma in the early church alluded to earlier in the chapter. When Demetrius, Origen's local bishop, called him home for what he regarded as a breach of discipline (preaching although he had not been ordained presbyter), the bishops of Jerusalem and Caesarea who had invited Origen to preach took issue with their brother bishop:

> He has stated in his letter that such a thing was never heard of before, neither has hitherto taken place, that laymen should preach in the presence of bishops. I know not how he comes to say what is completely untrue. For whenever persons able to instruct the brethren are found, they are exhorted by the holy bishops to preach to the people.[65]

The operative pastoral principle at work here centers around the question of what will best build up the body of Christ so that the church might be more fully the "sacrament of salvation" for the world. That same concern should be at the center of pastoral decisions in the present context.

The most basic reason for the importance of preaching by women as well as men is that the sacramental imagination recognizes that new imaging of the mystery Christ, new enfleshing of the word, makes available aspects of the mystery of the gospel and the mystery of God that were previously hidden or even repressed. Restriction of the public proclamation of the gospel at the key moment of the community's celebration of its deepest identity — the eucharist — to ordained males suggests implicitly that men have a privileged hearing of the gospel, whether by divine plan or by church discipline. On the other hand, the very reality of women preaching, particularly in the liturgical context, shatters traditional stereotypes and suggests new models of church and ministry, a fuller vision of humanity, both female and male, as created in the image of God, a more fundamental understanding of the image of Christ as located in baptism, and, ultimately, new images of God.[66] This is not simply a question of inclusive language and alternative names and images for the incomprehensible and unnameable God, though that too is fundamental, but is a matter of the community's ongoing discovery of the mystery of God as that has been revealed in the life experience of women as well as men.

Many agree that it is essential to the integrity of the gospel that the word be preached by women as well as men. Nevertheless, some question whether it is yet another form of stereotyping to suggest that women's preaching differs from that of men. In the next chapter we turn to the difficult question of what is meant by "women's experience" and the broader concern of how social location affects an understanding of preaching and of who is called to preach the gospel in our day.

Chapter 10

The Good News in Different Voices

As women participate more fully in the ministry of preaching, the experiences of both preacher and community prompt deeper questions and call for further reflection on the connections between human experience, gender, social location, and preaching. Contemporary literature on women's spirituality, on women's psychology, on feminist, womanist, mujerista, and Asian women's theology, and on feminist theory is so abundant and diverse that it is beyond the scope of one book to sort through the competing claims, let alone to make relevant connections with preaching. A significant recurring thread in much of that literature, however, refers to "women's ways of knowing" or women's "different voice" in ethics.[1] Some have proposed that a similar case can be made for "women's ways of preaching."[2] Just as in disputes about whether women have a distinct learning style or a distinct mode of ethical decision making, however, the question is whether descriptions of what is distinctive about "women's preaching" name a genuine difference based on gender or simply reinforce old stereotypes.

This chapter will survey efforts that have been made to identify what distinguishes the preaching of women from that of men. Because claims for the importance of preaching by women frequently center around the complex term "women's experience," an overview of the diverse use of that term in contemporary feminist theology will follow. Discussions of gender differences and the "politics of the pulpit" are significant in themselves, but also they need to be situated within the broader context of the significance of social location and the multiplicity of human differences and particularities. The implications of these issues for the theology and praxis of preaching are fundamental since the word of God is entrusted to the entire community and is discovered and proclaimed in specific and diverse social locations.

Women's Ways of Preaching?

Assumptions about women's "special nature" or at least unique feminine traits underlay earlier arguments in favor of women's preaching as well as those opposed to it. On the one hand, early in the twentieth century Aimee Semple McPherson maintained that

> [w]oman's personality, her tender sympathies, her simple, direct message — the women, motherheart, working over the world, yearning to help its wayward sons and daughter — these are all qualities in favor of her right to tell the story of God's love.[3]

Mark A. Matthews, a fundamentalist leader in Seattle, on the other hand, insisted that

> [o]nly a man can preach the Gospel.... It takes courage... to preach the infallible Bible and the vicarious atonement.... It takes no courage to go to pink teas and present to the world social service platitudes. There isn't anything effeminate about the Gospel nor... about a real... preacher of the Gospel.... The pulpit offers a greater opportunity for real men, who possess real manhood, than any other position in the world.[4]

While fundamentally opposed in their response to whether women should preach the gospel from the pulpit, both reflect a dual anthropology that stresses the difference of ability, personality traits, and gifts of women and men. This analysis can result in the conclusion either that public preaching is not an appropriate social role for women or that the preaching ministry is sorely in need of "women's special gifts."

The attribution of a "special nature" to the two sexes, which basically can be reduced to the axiom "anatomy is destiny," is widely disputed today. Recognizing the complexity of the "nature versus nurture" discussion, many who would not subscribe to any theory of women's "special nature" nonetheless argue that women and men preach differently due to gender socialization.

A number of authors in the field of homiletics have attempted to describe, if not analyze, the causes of the difference between women's and men's preaching. Carol Norén remarks in her book *The Woman in the Pulpit*: "The Sunday morning service is different when a woman preaches. Church members know this instinctively."[5] In a survey of eight male and two female professors of homiletics,

Christine Smith observed that while all agreed that there is a definite distinctive quality to women's preaching, they had difficulty in naming the specific dimensions of that distinctiveness. Women's preaching was described variously as more imaginative, more creative, more relevant, more relational and contextual, more holistic, more self-revealing, more communal, and less abstract than that of men.[6] When Smith turned to women's psychology to help interpret those impressions, however, she noted that the data were very indecisive regarding inherent differences between men and women or the basic distinctiveness of female and male personality traits. "This is not to say that there are no differences; it is only to say that research still finds these differences difficult to define and their origins almost impossible to chart accurately."[7]

Smith highlighted the need to supplement Gilligan's early claims about a female "ethic of care."[8] She remarked that further attention needed to be given to social analysis of patriarchal parental and family relationships that socialize women toward dependency and connectedness but fail to develop healthy ego boundaries or sense of self. Nevertheless, Smith concluded: "When the preacher is a woman, perhaps there is a radically different relational understanding at work in the art of proclamation. This difference suggests to us that women preachers feel that the relationship established in the moment of preaching is as crucial to life and faith as the truths of the biblical witness."[9]

In another exploration of the uniqueness of women's preaching, Janice Riggle Huie suggests that in their struggle to develop adequate images of a liberating God, many women are exploring their own imaginations and intuition in ways that result in the rediscovery of God in "feminine" terms; the expanded use of metaphor and story; participatory, rather than authoritarian, preaching; and imaginative and passionate preaching.[10] Huie notes explicitly, however, that the use of metaphor, story, and imagination is "clearly not a quality that is confined to women. Rather it is a gift of God growing out of the struggle for an inclusive new creation."[11] Recognition that sex is not the only significant variable in human difference and particularity adds further complexity to the discussion of how women's preaching differs from that of men. The preaching of African-American women is arguably more different from that of white women than from that of African-American men. United Methodist bishop Leontyne T. C. Kelly has remarked:

The black woman preacher draws her strength from the strong sisterhood of the black church, which has historically supported the church and its educational institutions by cooking dinners, sponsoring programs, teaching Sunday school, training sons and daughters in Christian homes, encouraging black males to be the leaders in the church that society denied outside of it.[12]

When Cheryl J. Sanders compared and analyzed sermons by black women and black men, however, she did identify several gender-specific aspects of black women's preaching. She concluded that women tend to emphasize the personal while men stress the prophetic, that storytelling and testifying are generally more important to women preachers than to men, and that women preachers use more inclusive language and images than men.[13] Katie Cannon's critical reflections on African-American preaching by both women and men advocate a womanist hermeneutic and homiletic style in black preaching.[14] In *Weaving the Sermon,* Smith notes that "Black women preach quite differently" but states that the scope of her book applies primarily to the preaching of white Protestant women. She further remarks that the women's psychology sources on which she relied were biased in terms of class, race, ethnicity, physical privilege, and access.[15]

The meaning of the term "women's experience" remains diverse and complex, both in homiletic literature and beyond. Brief analysis of what is meant by that term in various strands of feminist theology[16] can help clarify some of the underlying issues operative in discussions of the importance for the church of preaching by women.

"Women's Experience"

The literature in support of women's role in the preaching ministry reflects three distinct, but related, approaches to women's roles, women's experience, and social change. The liberal approach emphasizes equality and human rights and does not emphasize sexual differences. The cultural approach stresses differences and the uniqueness of women's experience rooted in embodiment and sexuality. The structural-reform or liberationist approach analyzes social structures and the distribution of power and roles in a community and calls for social change on the basis of the professed values of the group.

In terms of preaching, the liberal approach emphasizes women's right to preach and/or to be ordained. Created equally in the image of God, equal in baptismal dignity, and bearing equal responsibility for the spread of the gospel, women have an equal right to preach the word of God publicly in the name of the church and to lead the community in public prayer. This approach emphasizes *human* experience and a multiplicity of diverse personality traits and gifts that vary according to individual differences, not according to gender categories. Often those who contend that women share the vocation, right, and responsibility to preach do not call into question the preaching ministry or traditional understandings or modes of preaching. In a now-familiar image, women have a right to an equal share of the ministerial "pie."[17]

A cultural or romantic defense of women's preaching highlights distinctive female (often identified as "feminine") qualities and gifts. Women preach differently. Women's preaching is more relational, nurturing, collaborative, imaginative, passionate, concrete, personal. The community will discover another aspect of the gospel when they have heard the word proclaimed and seen the word enfleshed by women as well as men. Whether by socialization, by nature, or by a complex combination of the two, women's experience is different from men's. Embodiment and sexuality provide the fundamental differences. Women's experiences of menstruation, pregnancy, birthing, lactation, and menopause and the broader experience of female sexuality constitute a different way of being in the world. Gender, or the socially constructed interpretation of what a particular society or culture considers to be "masculine" or "feminine,"[18] further defines the differences between males and females. Thus the claim is made that "the feminine is a gift"[19] or that "women are more comfortable in settings where community, collaboration, and relationship are emphasized rather than competition."[20] Congregations that do not ordinarily invite women to preach may do so when the readings feature Mary of Nazareth or other female disciples (e.g., Mary Magdalene or Martha and Mary of Bethany) or when the occasion is specifically identified with women or children (e.g., Mother's Day or a Marian feast). To use the baking image, women's preaching adds a unique flavor or "special spices" to the pie. For a better flavor in the pie: "[A]dd woman and stir."[21]

The structural reform or liberationist approach turns instead to social and political analysis of women's historical experience and social location in both church and society. Key to this approach is critical analysis of patriarchal social systems, whether ecclesiastical or secular, because they do not accord equal dignity, power, or responsibility to all human persons and/or to all baptized Christians. Rather, in patriarchal structures, power, authority, and responsibility are in the hands of dominant males. In this complex system of social stratification that includes race, class, and other variables as well as sex, all members of the society are assigned roles, status, benefits, or power in relation to those to whom they are subordinated for the sake of "good order." A liberationist approach emphasizes that just as ecumenical divisions among Christian churches provide stumbling blocks to the church's authentic preaching of the gospel, so too do all forms of social sin. Structures that systematically discriminate against persons or groups on the basis of sex, race, class, ethnic origin, sexual orientation, or other human variables are in fundamental conflict with the gospel. Creation in the image of God and baptism into the body of Christ ground basic human dignity and provide a new basis for radical equality in all human relationships and social arrangements.

While not denying the central importance of embodiment and sexuality, the liberationist approach to women's experience does not claim that women bring unique "feminine" gifts to preaching or to ministry. In fact, the very use of the term "feminine" is rejected as socially constructed and as perpetuating both false stereotypes and patriarchal systems of power.[22] Rather, liberationists emphasize the way that exclusion and marginalization of women from the public proclamation of the word and from full leadership in the Christian community compromise the preaching of the gospel. At the same time, however, that very experience of exclusion or marginalization, when recognized and faced, can give women access to a word not easily heard by those who are in positions of dominance or privilege in social systems.[23] Especially for a woman of a dominant class, race, ethnic group, and/or clerical status, the experience of gender discrimination may be the concrete experience that opens her eyes to the operation of multiple systems of oppression.

A liberationist approach to preaching underscores that the gospel is good news for the poor, those who do not benefit from the domi nant systems of power. Solidarity with the poor and oppressed and a commitment to work for change in oppressive social systems provide a necessary preunderstanding for hearing the "social revolution" inherent in Jesus' preaching of the reign of God as "good news." This is what is often referred to as the "epistemological privilege of the poor."[24] This does not mean that ordained men from a dominant class, race, and/or ethnic group cannot preach the liberating gospel of Jesus Christ. Rather, it highlights that recognition of one's social location, privilege, and positions of power is essential if those factors are not to unconsciously control one's hearing and preaching of the gospel. Further, the conversion that the gospel requires of all members of the Christian community poses different challenges for those who are dominants in the social system than for those who are not. Wrestling with precisely this problem, Jürgen Moltmann and Douglas Meeks describe something of what the "liberation of oppressors" involves:

> [T]here is no solidarity with the victims of racism, sexism and capitalism without the betrayal of their betrayers. Whoever wants genuine communion with the victims must become the enemies of their enemies. Thus if he or she comes from the ranks of the enemy, he or she will become a betrayer. To become free from the oppressive prison of one's society means to become a "stranger among one's own people." Yet it is only through this estrangement that one can show to the oppressors the homeland of humanity.[25]

Similarly, women from dominant races, classes, and cultures, even when officially excluded from preaching and/or ordained ministry, need to recognize the extent to which they also benefit from and participate in multiple structures of domination if they are to preach authentically the death and resurrection of Jesus Christ.[26] The real challenge is not to "arrive" or be accepted within the present systems of power but to work to change those systems in whatever ways they compromise or violate the dignity of every woman, man, and child and the flourishing of the rest of creation. Within the community of the church this means taking seriously the baptismal dignity, equality, and responsibility of all members of the community.

A structural-reform or liberationist approach to women's experience and preaching affirms that instead of merely slicing up the "pie" equally or adding a few special spices, the church needs a whole new recipe for proclaiming and witnessing to the reign of God (and a renovated kitchen as well!). On the one hand, Procter-Smith remarks, "It could be argued that preaching is a patriarchal mode of action that is inevitably authoritarian and alienating and thus has no place in feminist liturgical experience."[27] On the other hand, she concurs with many other feminist theologians and psychologists in alleging that the experience of women finding their voices, breaking the silence, and speaking with authority is part of the liberating good news that the gospel promises.

The underlying question is not whether women can or should preach, or whether women have unique gifts to bring to the pulpit, but whether the church can envision and embody good news in a nonpatriarchal mode that liberates and invites rather than alienates. That challenge involves the formation of inclusive communities that recognize and celebrate diverse gifts and exercise the kind of leadership that Jesus models in the Gospels. This process of conversion will call the community and its leaders to think differently — to imagine new models of preaching that draw on the experience of the assembly gathered to worship, new understandings of authority that are more consonant with the gospel, new images of the human community and the larger beloved community of creation, new images of Christ, and even new images of God.

While the liberal approach argues for equal access to the pulpit and the cultural approach insists that women will speak "in a different voice," the structural-reform or liberationist approach raises more fundamental questions about church, liturgy, and the preaching ministry. However, the three approaches to women's experience are not mutually exclusive. While no one would deny that there are real differences between women and men, the shape those differences might take in nonpatriarchal communities or cultures, where women and men genuinely share equal dignity, voice, power, and responsibility, remains to be seen. Concerted efforts by churches to change sexist rules and practices and to address more subtle forms of sexism within the community will mean that more women will freely exercise their baptismal charisms, including those of preaching and/or leadership. At the same time, as more women who have consciously addressed the effects of patriarchy on their own lives and churches function as preachers, pastors, and leaders within the community, the ministry of preaching and the experience of church and ministry will be profoundly changed.

To emphasize structural change is not to deny that embodiment, sexuality, and socialization make a difference in preaching. Rather, to speak of the gospel proclaimed through the "experience of women" has multiple possible meanings, all of which affect both the preaching and the hearing of the gospel.[28] Women's *bodily experiences,* including pregnancy, birthing, nursing, and nurturing a child, are all used by biblical writers and classic figures in the Christian tradition as well as contemporary theologians and preachers to image the God who created humankind in the divine image, both female and male.[29] Other bodily experiences of women, including menstruation, physical abuse, and rape, are included in biblical texts but rarely alluded to in preaching.[30] Women also include the experience of aging and menopause in their preaching.[31] Other uses of women's experience in preaching focus on women's *socialized experience,* "what a particular culture teaches or has taught about women's roles, character, and virtues, as when a thinker questions cultural expectations or ecclesial rules about the appropriate 'place' of women and their roles in society and church."[32] Preaching that deals with the household codes[33] and the exhortations that wives be submissive to their husbands addresses this "socialized experience" of women. The lectionary selections for Christian marriage also often prompt discussion of women's socialized experience and how the Bible and church teaching have reinforced those roles. Explicitly *feminist experience* includes a liberationist analysis and critique of women's socialized experience in terms of the multiple dimensions of patriarchy. The choice of text, the perspective from which one preaches, the setting and style of preaching, and the use of a feminist critical biblical hermeneutic can all reflect the preacher's attention to "feminist experience." Sometimes the preacher draws on women's *historical experience,* women's lives and activities in the past in a variety of contexts, to preach on the feast of a saint, to recover the memory of women whose stories have been ignored, or to celebrate a specific occasion. In the context of the preaching and hearing of the gospel, women draw on their specifically *Christian religious experience* to speak of the mystery of God, the significance of Jesus, the power of the Spirit, the meaning of Christian discipleship, or the hope the gospel engenders.[34] The use of experience in preaching, by either women or men, can also refer to unique *individual experiences,* but these too are shaped by the social, political, cultural, and ecclesial contexts in which they occur.

Each of those forms of "women's experience" affects the "enflesh-ing of the word" in a specific preaching event. Some or all of those diverse uses of the term "women's experience" may be operative in a specific preaching event. For example, a sermon or homily drawing on "feminist experience" may include feminist critique of women's socialized experience, the use of images drawn from women's bodily experience, stories drawn from women's historical experience as re-constructed through a feminist hermeneutic, as well as the preacher's Christian religious experience and unique individual experience.

Granted the plurality of individual differences among women, sex or gender remains one significant factor that affects the preach-ing of the word. Recent work on gender analysis by sociologists and anthropologists stresses that gender is an integral and consti-tutive aspect of all social organization and interaction.[35] At the same time, there is increasing agreement among sociologists, anthropol-ogists, and theologians that issues of gender, race, ethnicity, and class have to be considered together as part of an interlocking web of significance.[36]

The Importance of Social Location: Lift Every Voice

The voices of women are not the only voices rarely heard from most Christian pulpits.[37] Chapters 9 and 10 have focused on ques-tions of gender and sex as related to the preaching ministry because women have been systematically excluded from preaching and lead-ership in the Christian churches and the matter of women's authority to preach remains an issue within some of the Christian churches today. Nevertheless, as we have noted, womanist, mujerista, and Asian women theologians, among others, consistently critique white feminists for speaking generically of "women's experience" without attending to the interplay of race, class, sexual orientation, age, eth-nic or national origin, and other dimensions of human particularity on the basis of which "the other" is hated, excluded, or marginal-ized. Sexism is a major strand in a whole network of interwoven forms of oppression.[38]

If "women's experience" includes women's historical, cultural, and political experience of marginalization and dismissal, then to preach from that experience includes attention to the experience of other persons and groups who remain invisible, silent, or absent in

our assemblies. But attending to "the other" does not mean bor-
rowing their stories or using examples from their culture or social
location without entering into real relationship with them and join-
ing in the struggle to change unjust social and political systems. To
do so, however, requires that members of dominant groups recognize their own complicity in systems of oppression and the ways in
which they are also oppressed by positions of domination, power,
and privilege.[39] The challenge here is not the mere use of more diverse examples by the dominant group of preachers, but ongoing
conversion of the community and the preacher into a more authentic
enfleshing of the body of Christ.

All of this means that to identify preaching as the naming of grace
operative in human experience requires more careful attention to the
way social location shapes the human experience of both preachers
and hearers of the gospel. Liberation theologians note that "where
you stand and to whom you listen determines what you hear."
Amos's announcement of God's judgment on the Israelite people for
their failure to live justly and to care for the poor is heard quite
differently in a suburban congregation and an inner-city parish. In
early feminist prayer services and rituals, women remembered and
celebrated Sarah's role in salvation history without attending to her
participation in the oppression of Hagar, the slave woman who was
her servant. The claim that the poor shall inherit the earth does not
sound threatening to the prevailing economy until it is announced in
the context of land reform in El Salvador. If the word of God is to be
discovered in the human community in all of its diversity and in the
interdependence of the human community with all of creation, then
limitations of the voices the community hears preaching the gospel
become limits to the hearing of the fullness of God's revelation.

In their text Liberation Preaching,[40] Justo and Catherine González
offer concrete suggestions to help preachers hear and preach a
text in ways that heighten the challenge to conversion in terms
of one's own specific social location. Using political and liberation
hermeneutics to interpret the scriptures, a preacher or faith community will ask specifically political questions: Who holds authority
in the passage? Who are the outsiders and who are the insiders?
Where is God's power active in the story? For those who belong
to dominant cultures and groups, the challenge becomes to hear the
gospel from another perspective. Leonardo Boff, for example, suggests that to stand in solidarity with the poor is to assign priority

to their questions and then honestly face up to the problems that perspective raises.[41]

González and González also recommend creative ways of using one's imagination for a "new hearing" of the gospel beyond the boundaries of one's social location. They urge preachers and congregations to try to hear the story from the perspective of whatever characters seem "foreign" to them — the Pharisees, the woman, the leper. Feminist biblical scholars and preachers often propose a similar method of "creative actualization."[42] New insights into the text and the experience of earlier ancestors in the tradition often emerge when women preach first-person narratives not only in the roles of Sarah, Hagar, Mary Magdalene, Martha or Mary of Bethany, the Samaritan woman, the woman accused of adultery, or the woman who anointed the feet of Jesus, but also in the roles of Abraham, Peter, Andrew, "the beloved disciple," Judas, or even Jesus.

Another way of attending to social location is to imagine the text and its implications in different sociopolitical settings. How is the claim that "all civil authority is from God" (Romans 13) heard in a country living under a repressive totalitarian regime? What are the implications of the Christian mandate to "love one's enemies" for survivors of rape or to forgive "seventy times seven" in a racist society? How does a community in a battered women's shelter hear the text "wives be submissive to your husbands"? How are we called to reinterpret the "divine limit" given to Adam and Eve in the Garden in the context of ecological devastation?

Shifting social locations in one's imagination can be a creative exercise for any preacher or community. But imagining is no replacement for listening to the experience of the other, working to remain in relationship in spite of pain and conflict, and being actively engaged to change systems of injustice. As Shawn Copeland has remarked, these times "demand a critical feminist theological praxis which refuses to rank or order oppression, which takes up the standpoint of the masses, the marginated, and those beyond the margins, and which is committed to justice in the concrete."[43]

To be committed to justice in the concrete requires that preachers not only listen to the experience of the other but also engage in some form of social analysis, however basic.[44] Reading the "text of the community" involves asking the kind of questions that González and González proposed. Who is present? Who is absent? Why? Who are the insiders and the outsiders? What are the questions and struggles of the senior members in this assembly, not only the existential and intellectual questions but the economic, political, and social struggles? What domestic, racial, political, and economic patterns affect the children in this community? What are the secular and ecclesiastical power dynamics operative here? What questions, which groups, are not welcome in this community? That kind of critical analysis of social systems and the assumptions that are operative in any human gathering not only suggest new insights into the scriptures for the established preachers in the community but also highlight which voices are rarely, if ever, heard.

Reclaiming the Power of Naming

If preaching is a matter of "naming grace" in word and deed, a critical question remains: Who does the naming? The question is integral to any theology of preaching precisely because of the claims we make about the power of language. Plumbing the implications of a theology of the word, Michael Scanlon has suggested that naming is "the primordial human *praxis* of 'the image and likeness' of God who created the world through the divine Word.... We are like God because we can speak."[45] The point here is obviously not literally the ability to speak, but the fact that human beings create history and make the kinds of decisions that affect the future not only of humanity but also of the planet.

The other side of this awareness of the power of human beings to name reality, to create history, and to construct social and cultural systems is the realization that the power of the word, including the word of God, has rested for most of history in the words of the men of the dominant culture, class, race, ethnic group, and sexual orientation. Since alternative perspectives can threaten to subvert the system in power, a key dynamic in the politics and psychology of any system of domination/subordination is the control of language.[46] Mary Daly's pioneering work in feminist consciousness-raising identified the problem early on in relation to women: "The power of naming has been stolen from us."[47]

Self-definition and the power to name one's own experience are crucial not only to human identity, moral maturity, and political liberation but also to human experience of God. In their studies of women's intellectual and ethical development, published under the title *Women's Ways of Knowing,* Mary Field Belenky, Blythe McVicker Clinchy, Nancy Rule Goldberger, and Jill Mattuck Tarule discovered that women repeatedly used metaphors of voice and silence to express their sense of self-worth and social connection or isolation.[48] Their interviews showed that women who lived in conditions of violence and enforced silence experienced themselves as "mindless and voiceless and subject to the whims of external authority."[49] Conversely, women frequently described the process of growing in autonomy, self-worth, and responsible moral agency as "gaining a voice." They were no longer defined by "the other" or by the systems in which they had been raised but began to speak from their experience in "a voice of their own."[50]

While characteristic of women in a patriarchal culture and educational system, the experience described by women in the study by Belenky and her associates is typical of all nondominant groups and peoples in hierarchical structures of domination and subordination. The right and power of self-definition lie at the heart of all liberation movements and their correlative processes of consciousness-raising. Thus, for example, Audre Lorde notes that the second day of the African-American festival of Kwanza celebrates Kujichagulia, or self-determination. Central to the celebration is "the decision to define ourselves, name ourselves, and speak for ourselves, instead of being defined and spoken for by others."[51] In situations of multiple forms of oppression, the experience of enforced silence and the struggle to find a voice include multiple layers of complexity, as Chung Hyun Kyung describes in her volume of Asian women's theology, *Struggle to Be the Sun Again.* The very title of the book alludes to the power of naming stolen from Asian women and the process of reclaiming the power to name themselves.[52] Ada María Isasi-Díaz and Yolanda Tarango define one of the main goals of Hispanic women's liberation theology as "self-determination." They emphasize that as Hispanic women share their stories, "they are affirming the ongoing divine revelation that takes place in their lives and within the community."[53]

That insight is key to the importance of hearing the mystery of God named by preachers from diverse social locations as well as of forming communities of diversity that come together to reflect on the meaning of the word of God in their lives. Self-determination in this context is not opposed to, but rather a manifestation of, the action of God's grace. Fundamental to the claim that God's story is at work in the sharing of human stories is the sacramental imagination's conviction that revelation, while not identical with human experience, is nevertheless disclosed in human experience and in creation. It is important for women and preachers from other nondominant groups to claim and exercise their baptismal right and responsibility to proclaim the word of God. But equally important is the need of the community to hear the word of God filtered through the experience and imagination of those in the community who have previously been silenced or relegated to the margins. If we believe that the word of God has been entrusted to the entire Christian community, then wherever voices are silenced or not welcomed, the community has lost some aspect of the good news of the mystery of God in its midst.

Already in the early 1970s Carlo Molari pointed to the "taking over of the word" by the Christian community as a whole as a "sign of the times" to be attributed to the work of the Holy Spirit. Reflecting specifically on the liturgical context, he commented:

> [T]he content [of the announcement of the gospel] emerges only through the experience of the gospel which believers have lived out in their different life situations through the action of the Spirit. For this reason the fact that only the priest comments on the scripture readings and unveils their present-day meaning is not sufficient for the authentic proclamation of the Word of God today.... [I]t is absolutely necessary that all the experiences of the Christian community and not only those of the priest (even if his are authentic and important) come together in the liturgy.[54]

To participate as a community in renaming our social and symbolic worlds is already to participate in their transformation. To speak of humanity as part of the beloved community of creation is to shift our horizons to the reality of our ecological interdependence.[55] Identity, dignity, and responsibility shift when persons are named as "the baptized" rather than as "laity" and when the church is "we" and not "they." New possibilities for experience of the mystery of God are disclosed when the divine mystery is named and symbolized in female as well male metaphors[56] or from the experience of the poor and oppressed.[57] Language functions to shape our identities, hopes, and possibilities, to limit or expand our imaginations. The way we name and imagine ourselves, one another, and God has everything to do with whether and how we can live together.

Nelle Morton suggests that while it is essential that we "tell the truth" in naming sin as well as grace in our experience, there are also "words we cannot yet speak."[58] Calling for women to "hear each other into speech," she suggests that "perhaps there is a word that has not yet come to sound — a word that once we begin to speak will round out and create deeper experiences for us and put us in touch with sources of power, energy of which we are just beginning to be aware."[59] The Holy Spirit who is the origin of all power and energy in the universe is also the Spirit of love who brings the word of God to birth and who remains the breath of life and source of truth in the Christian community. As the Spirit animates an increasingly global and interdependent community, the word of God is being spoken in new voices and enfleshed in diverse communities and cultures. In that context, the task of preachers, especially those from dominant cultures and groups, is not to "give voice to the voiceless"[60] but rather to create new opportunities and processes by which the many diverse members of the Christian community can "hear each other into speech."

Conclusion

The last chapter accented the importance of attending to the unique aspects of the mystery of the gospel that emerge from the context of diverse life experiences as well as to the role of the Christian community in "hearing one another into speech." Given that frame of reference, we might draw together the major themes of this book by exploring the role of the preacher within the Christian community and highlighting how the sacramental imagination, when critically appropriated, contributes to a contemporary theology of preaching as "naming grace."

The Role of the Preacher: New Metaphors

One way of underscoring the connection between the mission of the community and the call of the preacher is by considering new metaphors for the ministry of preaching. South African theologian Larry Kaufmann describes contextual theology with an image that might also be applied to "contextual preaching." He proposes:

> [W]e must change from merchants who sell pearls to hunters who search for treasures....Up to now we have always seen the Gospel as a pearl which we have to market, which we have to sell to others. That was the old idea of theology as something you receive and then give to others....But if we start with the context people are living in, and try to understand that context, then we discover the ways in which God is already at work in that context. In other words, people already have a treasure. Our task as contextual theologians is to discover that treasure and help people interpret it in terms of the wonderful ways God works in the world.[1]

In a similar way, preachers are called to help people discover and identify the "treasure" of God's grace discernible in their lives and world. As those summoned from within the community to speak of "the wonderful ways God works in the world," preachers serve as both archivists and storytellers of the tradition. Attending to the present questions and struggles within the assembly, they call to memory earlier stories and figures in the community's history that hold a word of encouragement, challenge, or hope for the present situation.

In another sense the preacher is one of the "explorers" sent ahead by the itinerant community to look for water, food, or safe shelter. The preacher is commissioned to "scout the territory" and to "propose a way forward," but the mission is for the good of the group, and the preacher can only make recommendations based on what she or he has experienced; the community and its leaders must test that wisdom and decide how to go forward.

The preacher can function also as the crone, the wise elder, or the grandparent too often ignored in the busy daily life of the family, the community, or the marketplace. When others stop to listen to their stories from the past and their insights from the present, those who "hold the memories" of the family or the tradition often call the community to reflect on the treasures that are already in their midst.

Another helpful metaphor suggests that the community is called to give birth to the word of God hidden in their midst while the preacher serves as midwife.[2] As the word of God takes shape in the womb of the Christian community, preachers are called to attend to the pulse of God at the heart of creation, to stand in solidarity with all who labor to give birth to justice and peace in our world, and to stand in awe of, as well as to celebrate, God's new life in our midst.

Developing this image of the preacher as midwife to the community that is entrusted with giving birth to the liberating word of God, Theresa Rickard remarks:

A midwife accompanies a woman as she gives birth. She encourages and reassures the woman of her own strength in moving the child to birth. The midwife has to be comfortable in the labor room; she is skilled and compassionate in the bringing forth of life. The midwife does not create the child; the child has already been formed. The babies she delivers are not her possession, but a gift that she hands over. The midwife listens attentively to the heartbeat of both the mother and child. She is self-possessed; she knows who she is and remains poised to re-

act. The moment the baby is born, the woman is freed from her
pain and the midwife rejoices in her sister's blessing. She sepa-
rates the child from the mother for the first time and re-presents
the newborn into the waiting woman's arms. The new mother
has the opportunity and responsibility to embrace and nurture
her gift.[3]

Rickard observes that in the Hebrew scriptures stories of birth
serve as metaphors of liberation and that the image of midwife is a
familiar one for those called to facilitate liberation or to proclaim
the truth they have witnessed.[4] The portrayal of God as midwife
in the Hebrew scriptures and the derivation of the term for God's
compassion or covenant love (*rahamim*) from the verb "to have compassion" (*rhm*) and the noun "womb" (*rehem,* sing.; *rahamim,* pl.)
suggest further rich connotations to be explored by preachers.[5]

The power of all of these metaphors is that they draw attention
to the world as graced and the community entrusted with the gospel
before turning to the unique role of an individual called to preach.
This shift, like the emphasis in the last chapter on "diverse voices,"
derives not only from contemporary discussions of multiculturalism,
social location, and democratization but also from the experience
of base Christian communities and theological convictions that are
central to the sacramental imagination.

The Sacramental Imagination and the Assembly
of the Baptized: A First Reading

Christians see the world as "charged with the grandeur of God"[6]
because they believe that the divine mystery of self-communicating
love has been disclosed at the heart of creation and human history in
and through Christ and the Holy Spirit. In view of the incarnation,
the word of God is not only promised and announced but also enfleshed. That word has been entrusted not to privileged individuals
but to the Christian community as a whole, the body of Christ. The
Spirit of God is active in creation and human history[7] as the unfail-
ing, but also unpredictable, presence and power of God-among-us.
That same Spirit, the source of all inspiration, insight, power, and
prophecy, anoints both preacher and hearers of the gospel to speak
and live the "word of truth."

The focus in this book on the community's role in preaching is also grounded in a basic liturgical conviction: the primary symbol in the liturgy is the gathered assembly of the baptized. As the body of Christ, the Christian community welcomes new members, proclaims and hands on the faith of the church, and gathers at a table where all are welcome to celebrate the death and resurrection of Jesus. This gathered community of the baptized constitutes a "holy people, a royal priesthood, a nation set apart" (1 Pet 2:9). With incorporation into the Christian community and baptismal identity comes a mission as well. Anointed with the Spirit, the newly baptized are charged with handing on the faith they have received. Both the blessing of the water and the consecration of the chrism in the Easter Vigil liturgy highlight that the baptized are not passive hearers of the word but active ministers called to preach the gospel:

> You call those who have been baptized to announce the Good News of Jesus Christ to the people everywhere.
>
> (Blessing of Water, Form C).

> Through that anointing you transform them into the likeness of Christ your Son and give them a share in his royal, priestly and prophetic work.
>
> (Easter 1, Preface 1; Consecratory Prayer over the Chrism)

Mary Collins underlines the significance of those rituals when she writes: "Rituals are about relationships; religious rituals are about ultimate relationships — about a people's origins and destiny and their true identity and purpose even in ordinary life."[8] The baptized embrace not only a new identity and mission but also a new basis for relationships: "All of you who have been baptized into Christ have clothed yourselves with him. There does not exist among you Jew or Greek, slave or free, male or female. All are one in Christ Jesus" (Gal 3:28).

Different Gifts: The Charism of Preaching

While the theology of baptism grounds radical equality and a fundamentally new basis for relationships as members of one body, friends of God, and disciples sharing a common mission, it nevertheless also recognizes a diversity of gifts given for the common good. "There are different gifts but the same Spirit; there are different ministries but the same Lord; there are different works but the same God who accomplishes all of them in everyone. To each person the manifestation of the Spirit is given for the common good" (1 Cor 12:4–7). The whole community is called to preach in the sense of witnessing to the Spirit's action in their lives and testifying to the word they hear in the scriptures. At the same time some members of the community are given a vocation to preach that arises from, and is intimately related to, the community's mission to preach. Fundamentally the preaching charism is an expression of the charism of prophecy, which is given to the community as a whole as well as to individuals gifted with a special ability for "naming grace." Bernard Cooke notes the two dimensions of the one gift in his discussion of the ministry of the word in the New Testament and early church: "Though more noticeable exercise of this prophetic activity is manifested by certain leaders, preeminently by the apostles but also by others gifted with special charisms, the prophetic function belongs to the entire community; it is a prophetic people (Acts 2:15–33)."[9] Cooke further notes the use of Isaiah 40 at the beginning of each of the Synoptic Gospels and comments that "in the Christian context, 'prophecy' takes on the precise application of the preaching of the gospel (Matt. 4:23). To prophesy is to evangelize, to be a herald of the gospel, to bear witness to the death and resurrection of Jesus."[10]

Within the context of the community, the prophet is called and empowered by the Spirit to speak God's word. Frequently the prophet's role is described as if the word of God comes from outside the community and the prophet speaks a foreign word over against the community. But a sacramental imagination reminds us that all the baptized share in the prophetic mission of the church. Those who are given a specific vocation to be ministers of the word are given that call in relation to, and for the good of, the entire community. Thus the preacher as prophet is called to listen for any traces of the gospel from within the life experience and sharing of faith in the larger community.

When the many voices in the community have been lifted up and we have "heard each other into speech," there is still need for the prophets among us to connect our stories and testify that we are not just isolated individuals but a community longing to hear good news. If the prophet's role is to listen for an "echo of the gospel," it is also to call our attention to that echo, to link our lives and our liturgies, our stories and the story of Jesus, our grief and our God.

Further, as the dialectical imagination reminds us, sin is also operative within the community called to be body of Christ. Both as individuals and as communities we can resist, betray, and even reject the good news of the gospel. Not even Jesus embraced the cross without a struggle. Part of the prophetic vocation, as discussed in chapters 4 and 5, is to announce "hard words." One of Oscar Romero's homilies in 1977 reflects the shift in his own preaching as he began to hear the gospel in light of the "cries of the poor" and the political and economic realities of El Salvador:

> It is very easy to be servants of the word without disturbing the world: a very spiritualistic word, a word without any commitment to history, a word that can sound in any part of the world because it belongs to no part of the world. A word like that creates no problems, starts no conflicts.
>
> What starts conflicts and persecutions, what marks the genuine church, is when the word, burning like the word of the prophets, proclaims to the people and denounces: proclaims God's wonders to be believed and venerated, and denounces the sins of those who oppose God's reign, so that they may tear those sins out of their hearts, out of their societies, out of their laws — out of the structures that oppress, that imprison, that violate the rights of God and of humanity.
>
> This is the hard service of the word.
>
> But God's spirit goes with the prophet, with the preacher, for he is Christ, who keeps on proclaiming his reign to the people of all times.[11]

Discerning where the Spirit of God is at work in the midst of history and what the authentic word of God is in a concrete situation is difficult since the Spirit is both source of unity, peace, and joy and also the one who can be discovered "troubling the water"[12] when all is not well in the church, the human community, or the world. Attending to the life experience of the community includes being rooted in the authentic tradition — the pledge that has been entrusted to the community and its leaders since its foundation (1 Tim 6:20; 2 Tim 1:14). But the prophet is also called to reinterpret that tradition, to speak a new word of where God is leading the community here and now. The prophet calls to mind memories that are often dangerous because they suggest alternate possibilities and ethical challenges for the present and the future. Remembering God's surprising ways and the community's bold decisions in the past, the prophets remind us of the basis for our hope and call for a similar courage in the present.

The Christian prophet reaffirms the Hebrew prophets' call for fidelity to the covenant but also reinterprets that claim in light of the life, ministry, and death of Jesus. At the heart of Christian prophetic preaching is the promise of resurrection, God's final word on the tragedy of the death of Jesus and the basis for hope for all who live faithfully the reign of God he preached. When proclaiming the gospel within the Christian community, the preacher's summons is always a call to the community to reembrace the covenant of baptism — "a birth unto hope" (1 Pet 1:3). In that sense, postbaptismal preaching always remains a form of mystagogical catechesis,[13] an invitation to the community to enter more deeply and consciously into the paschal mystery at the heart of all Christian life. As emphasized in chapter 7, this embrace of the cross is not a passive resignation in the face of human suffering or evil. Rather, it expresses a deep hope in the Spirit of God, who empowers resistance against whatever dehumanizes or oppresses humanity or destroys creation and who enables a radical trust that suffering and death will not have the final word in the human story or the story of creation.

The Sacramental Imagination: A Second Look

If preaching is finally an invitation to enter more deeply into human life as participation in the very life of God,[14] both the preacher and the Christian community are called to cultivate and exercise a sacramental imagination. The word "imagination" has been used throughout this book in the sense of the power to reconfigure reality by seeing it through an alternative lens. Paul Ricoeur refers to the "grace of imagination" as the "surging up of the possible."[15] New interpretations of our lives and our world that suggest that something more or different is possible empower hope, celebration, and action. Because meaning is at the core of human experience, reality redescribed and perceived in a new way is experienced as genuinely new reality. New energy is available to us when we see new possibilities. There is a new impetus for action when symbols and stories awaken our deepest hopes and potential and reveal to us that those most in need are indeed our sisters and brothers.

Formed by the vision of the scriptures and the rituals of Christian liturgy, the sacramental imagination sees the world through the prism of God's promise: the world and its creatures are God's beloved creation; the human is rooted in and open to the divine; evil will not have the final word; there is a future, even for the dead. At the heart of this vision are the central Christian beliefs of incarnation and redemption and resurrection: the mystery of God, who in Jesus has taken on human flesh and human history and defeated the powers of sin, death, and evil, remains with us in and through the power of the Spirit. In the face of all the evidence to the contrary, the prophetic word proclaims: "Grace is everywhere."[16] "All the evidence is not yet in."[17] "This world is not conclusion."[18] Forgiveness is possible, even between enemies. The poor will hear good news. No one will be excluded. The lamb will lie down with the lion. Nations will beat their swords into plowshares. There will be no more mourning or weeping on all God's holy mountain.

But is it true? Karl Barth's phrasing of every believer's question haunts anyone who would preach in the world we call postmodern. Is a sacramental imagination possible any longer? Sallie McFague questions its viability even in modernity.[19] In a post-Holocaust age of radical discontinuity, indeed the very "interruption of history," can we proclaim God's fidelity in human history? In the midst of ecological devastation, can we announce that "vestiges of God are to be found throughout creation"? Can churches that do not effectively recognize the equal dignity and responsibility of all the baptized and that are ecumenically divided be effective symbols of the body of Christ in the world? Do patriarchal and clerical liturgies "effect what they signify"? Can texts experienced as oppressive by some members of the community liberate? Can we speak of "naming grace in human experience" in the face of radical human suffering? Can limited and sinful human beings and human communities preach, even enflesh, the word of God? Can we believe in the presence of God when what we experience is absence? The challenges in our time to the claims of the sacramental imagination confront every aspect of preaching. Preaching a sacramental vision of reality credibly today requires a critical wrestling with the truth of the dialectical imagination's reminders: the divine mystery is hidden and absent; everything human is profoundly affected by sin; the church is always in need of critique and reform; the reign of God is "not yet"; the tragedy of the cross is the key to all reality.

All of this is to say that those who preach from a sacramental imagination need to incorporate the insights of the dialectical imagination if they are to avoid "cheap grace." Preachers cannot speak easily of God's presence or "God acting in human history" without attending to the vast accumulation of evil, violence, and human suffering and the consequent prevalent experience of God's absence. The critique by the dialectical imagination of any overarching theory of God's activity in history or presence to the world is crucial here: the wisdom of God is revealed preeminently in the folly of the cross. Preachers can and must preach that God is active in human history, but not in neat patterns or uninterrupted narratives.[20] The cross is a "human fiasco," the failure of Jesus' ministry, but at the same time it is the definitive overthrow of evil by the power of divine love working through the historical and human Jesus.

What is most amazing about the sacramental imagination also remains most troubling. The promise is given, the power is given, but the enfleshment of the vision in history depends on human beings. If preachers are to point to God's continued action in human history, the incarnational principle remains central: God is active in and through humankind. Without communities of hope who witness to God's vision of what is possible for humanity and the earth, there is no sacramental realization of that promise. In biblical terms, the word returns empty, not achieving that for which it was sent. Hence the emphasis throughout this book on preaching not only in word but also in deed, not only as individual prophetic preachers but as communities who give living testimony to the gospel. Just as Jesus is the primary sacrament of God's presence among us — the making visible of the invisible God — so too the church, living communities of the baptized, are called to continue to bear witness to the mystery that "compassion is at the heart of reality." That also means, however, that to the extent that we fail to make that claim a tangible reality in human life, we compromise and even contradict the promise of the gospel.

Even the concrete liturgical praxis of the community can contradict what the words and symbols promise. Precisely because the sacramental imagination asserts that sacraments "effect what they signify," a fundamental tension remains within the celebration of every Christian assembly, since the gathered community and its institutional structures are marked by sin as well as grace. Collins highlights this reality when she expands her earlier comments on the preconscious formative power of liturgy in reflecting specifically on the role of laypersons and especially women in Roman Catholic liturgical assemblies:

> The Sunday eucharistic assembly has for centuries provided the ritual setting in which all lay Catholics learned that they were not clerics, learned the consequences of their lesser status, and learned about women's special deficiencies based on their sexual identity. Ritual learning is preconscious, not conscious, learning. The overt content the Eucharist celebrates is the mystery of Christ. Yet through the centuries the whole church learned through the restrictions placed on women's liturgical participation that baptized women were still unfit for singing at worship, for reading the scriptures, for preaching the word, for approaching the altar, for leading public prayer.[21]

Collins's analysis underscores that too often concrete liturgical praxis denies the dignity, responsibility, and equality that the sacrament of baptism proclaims. But at the same time the genuine conflicts that arise over the community's liturgical praxis are grounded in the promises of the baptismal liturgy and biblical texts rooted in baptism. It is precisely the baptismal imagination that resists the failures of the church to live up to its charter vision.

Sacramental and liturgical theologians increasingly describe sacraments as "anticipatory signs"[22] to underscore that sacraments conceal as well as reveal the divine mystery, that the symbol is never adequate to express the reality symbolized, and that sacraments express a hope that needs to be concretized in the future praxis of the community. Nevertheless, at the heart of the sacramental imagination is the conviction that in spite of all that is broken or contradictory, the power of God's grace is stronger than the power of human sin. The power of the Spirit will break through human evil or control in the hope and resistance of communities of believers, in courageous actions and prophetic words. Human lives, as well as sacramental celebrations and the preached word, can serve as "humble landmarks" of "God's abiding presence in a wounded world."[23]

Naming Grace: Echoes from the Future

To view preaching as the art of naming grace in human experience through the lens of a critical sacramental imagination, preachers will need to attend to both "God's abiding presence" and the "wounded world." Discerning the presence of God in the world will mean taking seriously the absence of God in a twofold sense.

First, like all sacraments, preached words will fall short of the mystery of God not only because of human sin but also because the God whom they "make visible [or audible]" remains nevertheless ineffable mystery. As Nathan Mitchell reminds us:

> Every sacrament launches a search, a process of discovery through which we reconnect with something absent, something missing, something unknown, something (in short) *transcendent*. That, of course, is the great paradox of symbols — they simultaneously give and take away; they call us to the threshold of *presence* by first leading us through an abyss of *absence*.[24]

That paradox of all symbols is true of words as well as ritual actions. Words bring us to the threshold of presence by "embodying meaning." In word we reveal our deepest selves, and we commit our futures. We open possibilities or cut them off. Depth words — the words of the poet, the preacher, the priest — effect what they signify. They are audible signs of inexpressible realities. In the end we return to Augustine's insight: sacraments are visible words; words are audible sacraments.

This is not to claim that only the words of liturgy or preaching are sacramental, but rather that any word spoken in truth from the depths of human experience is sacramental in the sense of embodying or "making audible" an experience too deep for words. Just as "the 'first' or 'primary' liturgy that a church assembly celebrates is what Rahner called 'the liturgy of the world,' "[25] so too the primary preaching of the Christian community occurs not in pulpits but in the sacred space of the encounters of our ordinary daily lives and relationships. It is there that we lose heart, betray one another, give up our integrity, declare war, or withhold amnesty. But it is also there that we speak words of love, foster hope, make commitments, grant forgiveness, take stands, and give witness. Those "words of truth and life" and the deeds that embody them form the human basis for hearing and speaking words of the God who loves beyond betrayal, who forgives unconditionally, who brings life out of death. There is a fundamental connection between graced human experience and the mystery of God, but also an "infinite qualitative difference." God is present in and through the word when the mystery of preaching happens. But God is also absent, which is precisely why we need the word of faith to remind us of God's "elusive presence" in absence. The art of naming grace, in the first sense, has to do with declaring the presence of the transcendent God within the limits of human experience.

Second, the absence of God is revealed to us when we realize that the world in which we are called to announce "good news" is not only limited but also wounded by sin and evil. In the face of that reality, naming grace becomes even more difficult. Here the preacher has no words of meaning that can make sense of what is senseless or that can defend what is indefensible as somehow part of "God's mysterious plan." The naming of grace can only follow upon silence and solidarity with those who suffer. The words of grace that well up from experiences of radical suffering are words of lament, grief, anger, and protest; they are anguished words of identification with the crucified one. If the voice of God is to be found here, it remains hidden in the human responses of protest and resistance. If the power of the Spirit can be detected, it is in the power of human endurance, compassion, and hope. The incarnation is the key to the sacramental imagination, but the history of the incarnation culminated in the tragedy of the cross. The art of naming grace, in this second sense, has to do with proclaiming the cross in a world of radical suffering and evil.

In the end, however, it is not the cross that the baptized community proclaims but the paschal mystery of life that emerges beyond death. All that Christians have to live on are the stories and witness of those who have gone before them in faith and the power of the Spirit who keeps the story of Jesus alive. Naming grace means "naming the present"[26] — trying to identify where the Spirit of God is active in contemporary human life and in communities of believers who make the gospel a concrete reality in limited and fragmentary, but still tangible, ways. In the end, preachers proclaim a word of promise, a word whose truth remains to be seen, a word of hope. In this sense preaching remains always a profound act of worship. Whether in the mode of thanks and praise or of lament, preaching is a calling on the mystery of the transcendent God who alone can save us. But given the reminder of the sacramental imagination that God works in and through creation and human history, one can begin to see how dangerous this act of worship is, since the "waking god" will indeed "draw us out to where we can never return."

Notes

Introduction

1. Annie Dillard, "Expedition to the Pole," in *Teaching a Stone to Talk* (New York: Harper and Row, 1982) 40–41 (first published in *Yale Literary Magazine* 150, no. 1 [June 1982]).

2. "American Preaching: A Dying Art?" *Time,* December 31, 1979, 64.

3. Paul VI, apostolic exhortation *Evangelii Nuntiandi,* December 8, 1975, no. 4.

4. In a survey of homiletic literature, Ronald Allen noted: "Preaching is pre-eminently a theological act. Yet, there is a near lacuna in our literature: we give little attention to theological analysis of the preaching event" ("New Directions in Homiletics," *Journal for Preachers* [Easter 1993] 21). Similar observations have been made by David Buttrick, *Homiletic: Moves and Structures* (Philadelphia: Fortress, 1987) 486; John A. Melloh, "Publish or Perish: A Review of Preaching Literature 1968–1981," *Worship* 82 (1988) 506–7; and Robert P. Waznak, "A Second Response [to David Buttrick]," *Worship* 62 (1988) 273.

5. Dean R. Hoge, Jackson W. Carroll, and Francis K. Sheets, *Patterns of Parish Leadership: Cost and Effectiveness in Four Denominations* (Kansas City: Sheed and Ward, 1988).

6. For a helpful overview of the distinction between the dialectical imagination and the analogical imagination, see David Tracy, *The Analogical Imagination: Christian Theology and the Culture of Pluralism* (New York: Crossroad, 1981) 405–45. Sallie McFague makes a similar point in terms of Protestant and Catholic "sensibilities." See *Metaphorical Theology: Models of God in Religious Language* (Philadelphia: Fortress, 1982) 13–14.

7. While the description of the "sacramental imagination" is developed in this book primarily from a Roman Catholic perspective, this perspective is shared by the Orthodox and Anglican traditions and to some extent by the Methodist and Lutheran traditions. See, for example, Alexander Schmemann, *Liturgy and Tradition: Theological Reflections of Alexander Schmemann* (Crestwood, N.Y.: St. Vladimir's Seminary Press, 1990); idem, *The Eucharist: Sacrament of the Kingdom* (Crestwood, N.Y.: St. Vladimir's Seminary Press, 1988); idem, *Introduction to Liturgical Theology,* 2d ed. (Crestwood N.Y.: St. Vladimir's Seminary Press, 1986 [1955]); Paul F. Bradshaw, *Two Ways of Praying* (Nashville: Abingdon, 1995); idem, *Liturgy in Dialogue: Essays in Memory of Ronald Jasper* (Collegeville, Minn.: Liturgical Press, 1994); idem, *The Making of Jewish and Christian Worship* (Notre Dame, Ind.: University of Notre Dame Press, 1991); idem, *Daily Prayer in the Early Church: A Study*

of the Origins and Early Development of the Divine Office (London: SPCK, 1981); Leonel L. Mitchell, *Worship: Initiation and the Churches* (Washington, D.C.: Pastoral Press, 1991); Kenneth W. Stevenson, *Eucharist and Offering* (New York: Pueblo, 1986); Marjorie Procter-Smith, *Praying with Our Eyes Open: Engendering Feminist Liturgical Prayer* (Nashville: Abingdon, 1995); idem, *In Her Own Rite: Constructing Feminist Liturgical Tradition* (Nashville: Abingdon, 1990); Don E. Saliers, *Worship as Theology: Foretaste of Glory Divine* (Nashville: Abingdon, 1994); idem, *Worship and Spirituality* (Philadelphia: Westminster, 1984); Laurence H. Stookey, *Eucharist: Christ's Feast with the Church* (Nashville: Abingdon, 1993); idem, *Baptism: Christ's Act in the Church* (Nashville: Abingdon, 1982); Geoffrey Wainwright, *Doxology: The Praise of God in Worship, Doctrine and Life: A Systematic Theology* (New York: Oxford University Press, 1980); Cheslyn Jones, Geoffrey Wainwright, and Edward Yarnold, eds., *The Study of Liturgy* (New York: Oxford University Press, 1978); James F. White, *Introduction to Christian Worship,* rev. ed. (Nashville: Abingdon, 1990); idem, *Protestant Worship: Traditions in Transition* (Louisville: Westminster/John Knox Press, 1989); idem, *Sacraments as God's Self Giving: Sacramental Practice and Faith* (Nashville: Abingdon, 1983); idem, *New Forms of Worship* (Nashville: Abingdon, 1971); Gordon Lathrop, *Holy Things: A Liturgical Theology* (Minneapolis: Fortress, 1993); and Gail Ramshaw, *Worship: Searching for Language* (Washington, D.C.: Pastoral Press, 1988).

8. See Sandra M. Schneiders, "The Pastoral Imagination: Objectivity and Subjectivity in New Testament Interpretation," *Theological Studies* 43 (1982) 52–68; and Walter Brueggemann, *The Prophetic Imagination* (Philadelphia: Fortress, 1978). For further development of this point, see chapter 5.

Chapter 1 / The Dialectical Imagination: The Power of the Word

1. The expression, a reference to Isa 24:18, is borrowed from Paul Tillich's first collection of sermons, *The Shaking of the Foundations* (New York: Charles Scribner's Sons, 1948).

2. David Buttrick, "On Doing Homiletics Today" (paper delivered at a conference of the Societas Homiletica, Deland, Florida, August 21, 1990) 1. Note also Buttrick's comment in *Homiletic* (see intro., n. 4, above) 486: "Both Catholic and Protestant literature on the theology of preaching has dwindled since the sixties. We seem to be waiting for some new beginning in systematic theology."

3. Buttrick, "On Doing Homiletics Today," 5. Buttrick points to American scholars Edward Farley, Francis Schüssler Fiorenza, and David Tracy as representative of this shift. See Tracy's *Blessed Rage for Order* (New York: Seabury, 1975) pt. 1 for the notion of paradigm shift. See also Hans Küng and David Tracy, eds., *Paradigm Change in Theology* (New York: Crossroad, 1989).

4. David Tracy notes that amid all the genuine theological differences among theologians of the word, the one characteristic that unites them all as sharing a "dialectical imagination" is "the necessity of radical theological negations to constitute all theological language,... the negation of all human efforts to save

oneself, the negation of all poisonous dreams of establishing any easy continuities between Christianity and culture, the negation of all claims to a deluded, self-propelling 'progress' within society and culture, the negation of all aesthetic, ethical and 'pagan' religious possibilities" (*The Analogical Imagination* [intro., n. 6, above] 415).

5. Harry Emerson Fosdick, *The Living of These Days* (New York: Harper and Brothers, 1956) vii.

6. While diverse and complex, the liberal theological tradition of the late nineteenth and early twentieth centuries in both European and American contexts was characterized in general by an emphasis on the immanence of God, the location of revelation in human experience and history rather than in inspired scriptures or dogma, recognition of the historical and cultural conditioning of the Bible and all forms of tradition, stress on the human and historical Jesus and an ethical interpretation of his preaching of the kingdom of God, a social and ethical conception of salvation, and an optimistic view of human nature, destiny, and evolutionary progress with a corresponding underemphasis on original sin and its corruption of humanity. For a basic overview of Protestant liberal theology in its European context, see James C. Livingston, *Modern Christian Thought: From the Enlightenment to Vatican II* (New York: Macmillan, 1971) 96–114, 245–70. For the American context, see Kenneth Cauthen, *The Impact of American Religious Liberalism* (New York: Harper and Row, 1962); and Sydney Ahlstrom, *Theology in America: The Major Protestant Voices from Puritanism to Neo-orthodoxy* (Indianapolis: Bobbs-Merrill, 1967).

7. This issue of whether there is a point of contact in human experience for the preaching of the gospel was also a major dispute among dialectical theologians, most notably Karl Barth and Emil Brunner. While Brunner agreed with Barth that human beings were fundamentally sinners, he argued that a formal, rather than a material, point of contact for hearing the gospel was to be found in the human capacity for understanding speech and in human responsibility. Not even sin can destroy the human capacity to be receptive to the word. See Emil Brunner, *Man in Revolt* (Philadelphia: Westminster, 1947) 527–41. For a clear discussion of this dispute and its homiletic consequences, see Thomas G. Long, "And How Shall They Hear? The Listener in Contemporary Preaching," in *Listening to the Word: Studies in Honor of Fred B. Craddock*, ed. Gail R. O'Day and Thomas G. Long (Nashville: Abingdon, 1993) 167–88.

8. David Jenkins, "Karl Barth," in *A Handbook of Christian Theologians*, ed. Martin E. Marty and Dean G. Peerman (Nashville: Abingdon, 1984) 398.

9. Livingston, *Modern Christian Thought*, 325. Livingston provides a helpful overview of Barth's theology, including the christological shift in his later writings (324–44).

10. Karl Barth, *The Word of God and the Word of Man*, trans. Douglas Horton (New York: Harper and Brothers, 1957) 43, 45.

11. Karl Barth, *The Epistle to the Romans*, trans. Edwyn C. Hoskyns (New York: Oxford University Press, 1968) 98.

12. Karl Barth, *Revelation* (London: Faber and Faber, 1937) 51.

13. Karl Barth, *The Preaching of the Gospel*, trans. B. E. Hooke (Philadelphia: Westminster, 1963). For a more complete and revised version of Barth's

lectures on homiletics, see idem, *Homiletics,* trans. Geoffrey W. Bromiley and Donald E. Daniels (Louisville: Westminster/John Knox, 1991). For an early essay on preaching, see idem, "The Need and Promise of Christian Preaching," in *The Word of God and the Word of Man,* 97–135.

14. Barth, *The Preaching of the Gospel,* 22.

15. Ibid., 12.

16. Ibid., 80.

17. Rudolf Bultmann, *Kerygma and Myth,* ed. Hans Werner Bartsch (New York: Harper and Row, 1961) 206–7.

18. The reference is from Fuchs's essay "Translation and Preaching," as cited in James M. Robinson's "Hermeneutic since Barth," in *The New Hermeneutic,* ed. James M. Robinson and John R. Cobb Jr. (New York: Harper and Row, 1964) 63. See also the discussion of the new hermeneutic in Robert W. Funk, *Language, Hermeneutic, and the Word of God* (New York: Harper and Row, 1966) 47–71. For a political, rather than an existential, development of dialectical theology in the service of the preaching of the gospel, see Jürgen Moltmann, "Toward a Political Hermeneutic of the Gospel," in *Religion, Revolution, and the Future,* trans. M. Douglas Meeks (New York: Charles Scribner's Sons, 1969) 83–107.

19. See Avery Dulles, "Hermeneutical Theology," *Communio* 6 (1979) 23.

20. Funk, *Language, Hermeneutic, and the Word of God,* 10–18. Cf. Richard Lischer, *A Theology of Preaching: The Dynamics of the Gospel* (Nashville: Abingdon, 1981) 54–55: "[E]ven in our redeemed state...grace remains an unnatural and often surprising intrusion." See pt. 2 of Funk's book for one approach to the relationship between dialectical theology, the new hermeneutic, and the extensive literature on parable, metaphor, and the "shock of conversion" that is frequently alluded to in homiletic texts. For further development and additional bibliography on parable and metaphor, see Sallie McFague, *Speaking in Parables* (Philadelphia: Fortress, 1975); idem, *Metaphorical Theology* (intro., n. 6, above); John Dominic Crossan, *In Parables: The Challenge of the Historical Jesus* (New York: Harper and Row, 1973); John R. Donahue, *The Gospel in Parable, Metaphor, Narrative, and Theology in the Synoptic Gospels* (Philadelphia: Fortress, 1988).

21. P. J. Burns, "Hermeneutics (Contemporary)," in *New Catholic Encyclopedia,* 16:206.

22. Lischer, *A Theology of Preaching,* 50.

23. Ibid., 65. See also Herman G. Stuempfle Jr., *Preaching Law and Gospel* (Philadelphia: Fortress, 1978).

24. Paul Tillich, *Systematic Theology,* vol. 1 (Chicago: University of Chicago Press, 1951) 5.

25. Ibid., 1:7.

26. Ibid., 1:49.

27. Paul Tillich, "Holy Waste," in *The New Being* (New York: Charles Scribner's Sons, 1955) 48.

28. Paul Tillich, "Is There Any Word from the Lord?" in *The New Being,* 121.

29. Ibid., 124.

30. See Paul Tillich, "Communicating the Christian Message: A Question to Christian Ministers and Teachers," in *Theology of Culture* (New York: Oxford University Press, 1959) 201–13; cf. idem, *Systematic Theology* 1:3–28.

31. See Tillich, *Systematic Theology* 1:159; idem, *The Courage to Be* (New Haven: Yale University Press, 1952); and idem, "The Eternal Now," in *The Eternal Now* (New York: Charles Scribner's Sons, 1956) 122–32.

32. See Paul Tillich, "You Are Accepted," in *The Shaking of the Foundations* (New York: Charles Scribner's Sons, 1948) 153–63.

33. Tillich argued that Christianity requires both "Catholic substance" (the concrete embodiment of Spiritual Presence) and the "Protestant principle" (critique of the demonic and profane within all such embodiments). See Thomas Franklin O'Meara, "Tillich and the Catholic Substance," in *The Thought of Paul Tillich,* ed. James Luther Adams, Wilhelm Pauck, and Roger L. Shinn (New York: Harper and Row, 1985) 290–306.

Chapter 2 / The Sacramental Imagination: Grace Enfleshed in Word and Action

1. "Justification by Faith," *Origins* 13 (October 6, 1983) no. 154.

2. In Ep. 1 ad Thess., c. 2, lect. 2.

3. See Domenico Grasso, *Proclaiming God's Message: A Study in the Theology of Preaching* (Notre Dame, Ind.: University of Notre Dame Press, 1965) xxvi–xxviii.

4. Karl Rahner, "Priest and Poet," in *Theological Investigations,* vol. 3, trans. Karl-H. and Boniface Kruger (Baltimore: Helicon, 1967) 313.

5. Ibid.

6. Rahner, "Nature and Grace," in *Nature and Grace* (New York: Sheed and Ward, 1963) 134.

7. Rahner, "Priest and Poet," 296.

8. Ibid., 317.

9. See Leo O'Donovan, ed., *A World of Grace* (New York: Seabury, 1980), for an excellent one-volume introduction to Rahner's thought that parallels his own *Foundations of Christian Faith* (New York: Seabury, 1978).

10. For Rahner's own treatment of these themes see especially "Priest and Poet," 294–317; "The Theology of Symbol," in *Theological Investigations,* vol. 4, trans. Kevin Smyth (Baltimore: Helicon, 1966) 221–52; "The Word and Eucharist," in *Theological Investigations,* 4:253–85; "Poetry and the Christian," in *Theological Investigations,* 4:357–67; "What Is a Sacrament?" *Theological Investigations,* vol. 14, trans. David Bourke (New York: Seabury, 1976) 135–48; and "Considerations on the Active Role of the Person in the Sacramental Event," *Theological Investigations* 14:161–84.

11. For a development of Rahner's theology as a foundation for a theology of preaching, see Eileen McKeown, "A Theology of Preaching Based on Karl Rahner's Theology of the Word" (Ph.D. diss., Fordham University, 1989). See also Avery Dulles's article "Revelation and Discovery," in *Theology and Discovery,* ed. William J. Kelly (Milwaukee: Marquette University Press, 1980) 1–29, for

clarification of how conversion and real discontinuity and surprise are involved in the explicit discovery of what was already implicitly present.

12. See Edward Schillebeeckx, *Jesus: An Experiment in Christology,* trans. Hubert Hoskins (New York: Seabury, 1979) 669–74. For Schillebeeckx's theology of revelation, see *Christ: The Experience of Jesus as Lord,* trans. John Bowden (New York: Crossroad, 1981) 29–79; and *Church: The Human Story of God,* trans. John Bowden (New York: Crossroad, 1990). For an overview of Schillebeeckx's theology of revelation and its implications for a theology of proclamation, see Mary Catherine Hilkert, "Discovery of the Living God: Revelation and Experience," in *The Praxis of Christian Experience: An Introduction to the Theology of Edward Schillebeeckx,* ed. Robert J. Schreiter and Mary Catherine Hilkert (New York: Harper and Row, 1989) 35–51; and idem, "Towards A Theology of Proclamation: Edward Schillebeeckx's Hermeneutics of Tradition as a Foundation for a Theology of Proclamation" (Ph.D. diss., Catholic University of America, 1984).

13. Schillebeeckx, *Christ,* 78.

14. Note Schillebeeckx's definition of revelation in *Christ:* "God's saving action in history as *experienced* by believers and *interpreted* in religious language and therefore *expressed* in human terms, in the dimension of our utterly human history" (78).

15. Edward Schillebeeckx, "Can Christology Be an Experiment?" *Proceedings of the Catholic Theological Society of America* 35 (1980) 2.

16. Note a similar approach in the U.S. bishops' pastoral *Fulfilled in Your Hearing: The Homily in the Sunday Assembly* (Washington, D.C.: United States Catholic Conference, 1982): "The preacher does not so much attempt to explain the Scriptures as to interpret the human situation through the Scriptures" (20).

17. Edward Schillebeeckx, "God as a Loud Cry," in *God among Us: The Gospel Proclaimed,* trans. John Bowden (New York: Crossroad, 1983) 76–77.

18. The very use of this term is now disputed. See the comments of Ghanaian theologian Mercy Amba Oduyoye: "I was talking with a German woman recently on the use of the term 'Third World,' which she does not like and which some Third World persons too have declared anathema. She told me about a poster used by Bread for the World: it states that we have only 'one world.' We do have one *earth,* granted, but it is also true to say that we live in *different* worlds. The world of the rural woman in Ghana has little in common with that of the rural woman in Germany, nor does the world of the white woman in South Africa bear comparison with that of her black compatriot" ("Reflections from a Third World Woman's Perspective: Women's Experience and Liberation Theologies," in *Feminist Theology from the Third World,* ed. Ursula King [London: SPCK; Maryknoll, N.Y.: Orbis Books, 1994] 24).

19. Gustavo Gutiérrez, *A Theology of Liberation,* trans. and ed. Sister Caridad Inda and John Eagleson (Maryknoll, N.Y.: Orbis Books, 1973) ix. A helpful introduction to liberation theology, especially for preachers, is Mev Puleo's *The Struggle Is One: Voices and Visions of Liberation* (Albany: State University of New York Press, 1994).

20. Synod of Bishops, *Justice in the World* (Washington, D.C.: United States Catholic Conference, 1971) 34.

21. Leonardo Boff describes this stance and its implications: "To adopt the place of the poor is our first deed of solidarity with them. This act is accomplished by making an effort to view reality from their perspective. And when we view reality from their perspective, that reality simply must be transformed. Reality is exceedingly unjust for the majority of men and women in Latin America. It impoverishes them and pushes them out on the margins of society. To adopt the place of the poor means to assign priority to the questions the poor raise, and then honestly to face up to these problems" (*When Theology Listens to the Poor,* trans. Robert R. Barr [New York: Harper and Row, 1988] ix).

22. Oscar Romero, *The Violence of Love: The Pastoral Wisdom of Archbishop Oscar Romero,* trans. and comp. James R. Brockman (New York: Harper and Row) 54.

23. Boff, *When Theology Listens to the Poor,* 32.

24. Carlos Mesters, "Life Is the Word — Brazilian Poor Interpret Life," in *SEDOS Bulletin* (Rome) 13 (September 1985), as quoted in *Ministries and Communities* 47 (1986) 4. See also idem, "The Use of the Bible in Christian Communities of the Common People," in *The Bible and Liberation: Political and Social Hermeneutics,* ed. Norman K. Gottwald and Richard A. Horsley, rev. ed. (Maryknoll, N.Y.: Orbis Books, 1993) 3–16; and Puleo, *The Struggle Is One,* 114–28.

25. Elsa Tamez, "Women's Rereading of the Bible," in *With Passion and Compassion,* ed. Virginia Fabella and Mercy Amba Oduyoye (Maryknoll, N.Y.: Orbis Books, 1988) 174. On the use of the term "Third World women," see n. 18, above.

26. In patriarchal structures, power, authority, and responsibility are in the hands of dominant males in the social system. In this system of social stratification, which includes not only sex but also race, class, and other variables, all members of the society are assigned roles, status, benefits, or power in relation to those to whom they have been subordinated for the sake of "good order." See chapters 9 and 10 for further discussion related to preaching.

27. See chapter 10, esp. nn. 16 and 36; for discussion of feminist biblical hermeneutics in relation to preaching, see chapter 5 and notes.

28. See, for example, Rosemary Radford Ruether, *Gaia and God: An Ecofeminist Theology of Earth Healing* (San Francisco: HarperSanFrancisco, 1992); idem, *New Woman, New Earth* (San Francisco: Harper and Row, 1975); idem, ed., *Women Healing Earth: Third-World Women on Ecology, Feminism, and Religion* (Maryknoll, N.Y.: Orbis Books, 1996); Elizabeth A. Johnson, *Women, Earth, and Creator Spirit* (New York: Paulist, 1993); Anne M. Clifford, "When Being Human Becomes Truly Earthly: An Ecofeminist Proposal for Solidarity," in *In the Embrace of God: Feminist Approaches to Theological Anthropology,* ed. Ann O'Hara Graff (Maryknoll, N.Y.: Orbis Books, 1995) 173–89; Chung Hyun Kyung, "Ecology, Feminism and African and Asian Spirituality: Towards a Spirituality of Eco-Feminism," in *Ecotheology,* ed. D. Hallman (Maryknoll, N.Y.: Orbis Books, 1994) 175–78; Catharina J. M. Halkes, *New Creation: Christian Feminism and the Renewal of the Earth,* trans. Catherine Romanik (Louisville: Westminster/John Knox Press, 1991); Sallie McFague, *Models of God: Theology for an Ecological Nuclear Age* (Philadelphia: Fortress, 1993);

idem, *The Body of God: An Ecological Theology* (Minneapolis: Fortress, 1993);
Carol J. Adams, *Ecofeminism and the Sacred* (New York: Continuum, 1993);
and Catherine Keller, "Women against Wasting the World: Notes on Eschatology and Ecology," in *Reweaving the World: The Emergence of Ecofeminism,* ed.
Irene Diamond and Gloria Feman Orenstein (San Francisco: Sierra Club Books,
1990) 249–63.

29. See Dieter T. Hessel, ed., *For Creation's Sake: Preaching, Ecology, and
Justice* (Philadelphia: Geneva Press, 1985).

30. See Catherine Mowry LaCugna, *God for Us: The Trinity and Christian
Life* (San Francisco: HarperSanFrancisco, 1991); idem, "God in Communion
with Us," in *Freeing Theology: The Essentials of Theology in Feminist Perspective,* ed. Catherine Mowry LaCugna (San Francisco: HarperCollins, 1993)
83–114; Elizabeth A. Johnson, *SHE WHO IS: The Mystery of God in Feminist
Theological Discourse* (New York: Crossroad, 1992); Anne E. Carr, *Transforming Grace: Christian Tradition and Women's Experience* (San Francisco: Harper
and Row, 1988) 134–57; McFague, *Models of God;* idem, *The Body of God.*

31. In her feminist reconstruction of a theology of proclamation, *The Power
to Speak: Feminism, Language, God* (New York: Crossroad, 1989), Rebecca
Chopp claims a Protestant experience of church and Word and roots her call for
"the creation of discourses of emancipatory transformation" in a theology of
the Word as "perfectly open sign." Nevertheless, she is critical of neoorthodox
theologies of proclamation, identifies with an understanding of the church as
"the sacrament of God's grace in the world," and calls for proclamation of
the Word through women's words that "envision new ways of human flourishing." In *Models of God,* McFague develops the metaphorical theology that
she explicitly contrasted with a "sacramental sensibility" in her earlier volume
Metaphorical Theology. However, in *Models of God* she remarks that Rosemary
Radford Ruether identified the tradition of Christian sacramentality that sees the
whole cosmos as sacramental as a view very similar to her own (see *Models of
God,* 200 n. 9).

32. For a critical correlation of feminist thought and Catholic sacramental
theology with implications for a contemporary theology of the body, see Susan A. Ross, " 'Then Honor God in Your Body' (1 Cor 6:20): Feminist and
Sacramental Theology on the Body," *Horizons* 16 (1989) 7–27; idem, "God's
Embodiment and Women," in *Freeing Theology,* 185–209; idem, "Sacraments
and Women's Experience," *Listening* 28 (1993) 52–64. See also Christine M.
Gudorf, "The Power to Create: Sacraments and Men's Need to Birth," *Horizons* 14 (1987) 296–309; Lisa Sowle Cahill, *Women and Sexuality* (New York:
Paulist, 1992); and Margaret A. Farley, "Feminist Theology and Bioethics," in
Women's Consciousness, Women's Conscience: A Reader in Feminist Ethics, ed.
Barbara Hilkert Andolsen, Christine E. Gudorf, and Mary D. Pellauer (San Francisco: Harper and Row, 1987). For feminist perspectives from other traditions,
see June O'Connor, "Sensuality, Spirituality, Sacramentality," *Union Seminary
Quarterly Review* 40 (1985) 59–70; Elisabeth Moltmann-Wendel, *I Am My
Body: A Theology of Embodiment* (New York: Continuum, 1995); Paula M.
Cooey, Sharon A. Farmer, and Mary Ellen Ross, *Embodied Love: Sensuality
and Relationship as Feminist Values* (San Francisco: Harper and Row, 1987);

and McFague, *The Body of God*. See also Grace Jantzen, *God's World, God's Body* (Philadelphia: Westminster, 1984).

33. See, for example, Rosemary Radford Ruether, *Sexism and God-Talk: Toward a Feminist Theology* (Boston: Beacon, 1983) 12–46. For connections between feminist theologies and the Roman Catholic tradition on the question of revelation, see Mary Catherine Hilkert, "Experience and Tradition — Can the Center Hold?" in *Freeing Theology*, 59–82.

34. See Mary Aquin O'Neill, "Imagine Being Human: An Anthropology of Mutuality," in *Miriam's Song II*, ed. Priests for Equality (West Hyattsville, Md.: Priests for Equality, 1988) 11–14; idem, "The Mystery of Being Human Together," in *Freeing Theology*, 139–60; Elizabeth A. Johnson, "The Incomprehensibility of God and the Image of God Male and Female," *Theological Studies* 45 (1984) 441–65; Rosemary Radford Ruether, "Feminist Hermeneutics, Scriptural Authority, and Religious Experience: The Case of the *Imago Dei* and Gender Equality," in *Radical Pluralism and Truth: David Tracy and the Hermeneutics of Religion*, ed. Werner G. Jeanrond and Jennifer L. Rike (New York: Crossroad, 1991) 95–106; Kari Elisabeth Børresen, ed., *The Image of God: Gender Models in Judaeo-Christian Tradition* (Minneapolis: Fortress, 1995); and Mary Catherine Hilkert, "Cry Beloved Image: Rethinking the Image of God," in *In the Embrace of God*, 190–205.

35. For diverse Roman Catholic feminist perspectives on ecclesiology, see Mary E. Hines, "Community for Liberation," in *Freeing Theology*, 161–84; Ada María Isasi-Díaz and Yolanda Tarango, *Hispanic Women: Prophetic Voice in the Church* (San Francisco: Harper and Row, 1988); and Elisabeth Schüssler Fiorenza, *Discipleship of Equals: A Critical Feminist Ekklesia-logy of Liberation* (New York: Crossroad, 1993). For perspectives of feminist theologians from Protestant or neoorthodox traditions, see Letty Russell, *Church in the Round: Feminist Interpretation of the Church* (Louisville: Westminster/John Knox Press, 1993); and Rebecca S. Chopp, *The Power to Speak*, 71–98.

36. See Mary Collins, *Worship: Renewal to Practice* (Washington D.C.: Pastoral Press, 1987); Catherine Bell, "The Dynamics of Ritual Power," *Journal of Ritual Studies* 4, no. 2 (1990) 209–13; Margaret Mary Kelleher, "Liturgy: An Ecclesial Act of Meaning," *Worship* 59 (1985); Marjorie Procter-Smith and Janet R. Walton, eds., *Women at Worship: Interpretations of North American Diversity* (Louisville: Westminster/John Knox Press, 1993), esp. Mary Collins, "Principles of Feminist Liturgy," 9–26; Procter-Smith, *Praying with Our Eyes Open* (intro., n. 7, above) and *In Her Own Rite* (intro., n. 7, above); Rosemary Radford Ruether, *Women-Church: Theology and Practice of Feminist Liturgical Communities* (San Francisco: Harper and Row, 1985); Barbara Walker, *Women's Rituals: A Sourcebook* (San Francisco: Harper and Row, 1990); Teresa Berger, "Women and Worship: A Bibliography," *Studia Liturgica* 19 (1989) 96–110; idem, "Women and Worship: A Bibliography Continued," *Studia Liturgica* 25 (1995) 103–17; Iben Gjerding and Katherine Kinnamon, eds., *Women's Prayer Services* (Mystic, Conn.: Twenty-Third, 1987); Miriam Therese Winter, *Woman Prayer Woman Song: Resources for Ritual* (New York: Crossroad, 1993); resources available through WATER (Women's Alliance for Theology, Ritual, and Ethics [Silver Spring, Md.]; Janet Walton, "Feminism and the Lit-

urgy," in *The New Dictionary of Sacramental Theology,* ed. Peter J. Fink
(Collegeville, Minn.: Liturgical Press, 1990) 468–73; and Diann Neu, "Women
Revisioning Religious Rituals," in *Women and Religious Ritual,* ed. L. Northup
(Washington, D.C.: Pastoral Press, 1993) 155–72.

37. In addition to the ecofeminist resources cited in n. 28, see Denis Ed-
wards, *Jesus the Wisdom of God: An Ecological Theology* (Maryknoll, N.Y.:
Orbis Books, 1995); Leonardo Boff, *Ecology and Liberation: A New Paradigm,*
trans. John Cumming (Maryknoll, N.Y.: Orbis Books, 1995); Jürgen Moltmann,
God in Creation (San Francisco: Harper and Row, 1985); Jay B. McDaniel,
Earth, Sky, Gods and Mortals: A Theology of Ecology for the 21st Century
(Mystic, Conn.: Twenty-Third, 1990); James Nash, *Loving Nature: Ecologi-
cal Integrity and Christian Responsibility* (Nashville: Abingdon, 1991); Thomas
Berry, *The Dream of the Earth* (San Francisco: Harper and Row, 1988); Charles
Birch, William Eakin, and Jay McDaniel, eds., *Liberating Life: Contemporary
Approaches to Ecological Theology* (Maryknoll, N.Y.: Orbis Books, 1990);
John Zizioulas, "Preserving God's Creation: Three Lectures on Theology and
Ecology," *King's Theological Review* 12 (1989) 1–5, 41–45; 13 (1990) 1–5;
J.-B. Metz and E. Schillebeeckx, eds., *No Heaven without Earth,* vol. 1991/4
of *Concilium* (Philadelphia: Trinity Press, 1991); Wesley Granberg-Michaelson,
"Redeeming the Creation: The Rio Earth Summit: Challenges for the Churches,"
Risk 55 (1992) 1–90; and Stephen Bede Scharper, *Redeeming the Time: A
Political Theology of the Environment* (New York: Continuum, 1997).

38. See Ada-María Isasi-Díaz, "*Palabra de Dios en Nosotras* — The Word of
God in Us," in *Searching the Scriptures,* vol. 1: *A Feminist Introduction,* ed.
Elisabeth Schüssler Fiorenza (New York: Crossroad, 1993) 86–97; idem, "The
Bible and Mujerista Theology," in *Lift Every Voice: Constructing Christian Theologies from the Underside,* ed., Susan Brooks Thistlethwaite and Mary Potter
Engel (San Francisco: Harper and Row, 1990) 261–69; idem, *En La Lucha/In
the Struggle: A Hispanic Woman's Liberation Theology* (Minneapolis: Fortress,
1993); Isasi-Díaz and Tarango, *Hispanic Women;* María Pilar Aquino, *Our Cry
for Life: Feminist Theology from Latin America* (Maryknoll, N.Y.: Orbis Books,
1993); Elsa Tamez, *Through Her Eyes: Women's Theology from Latin America*
(Maryknoll, N.Y.: Orbis Books, 1989); Virgil Elizondo, "Toward an American-
Hispanic Theology of Liberation in the U.S.A.," in *Irruption of the Third World:
Challenge to Theology,* ed. Virginia Fabella and Sergio Torres (Maryknoll, N.Y.:
Orbis Books, 1983) 50–55; idem, *Galilean Journey: The Mexican American
Promise* (Maryknoll, N.Y.: Orbis Books, 1983); Jeanette Rodriguez, *Our Lady
of Guadalupe: Faith and Empowerment among Mexican-American Women*
(Austin: University of Texas Press, 1994); idem, "Experience as a Resource for
Feminist Thought," *Journal of Hispanic/Latino Theology* 1, no. 1 (November
1993) 68–76; idem, *Stories We Live/Cuentos Que Vivimos: Hispanic Women's
Spirituality* (New York: Paulist, 1996); Roberto S. Goizueta, *We Are a People:
Initiatives in Hispanic American Theology* (Minneapolis: Fortress, 1992); Allan
Figueroa Deck, ed., *Frontiers of Hispanic Theology in the United States* (Mary-
knoll, N.Y.: Orbis Books, 1992); Fernando F. Segovia, ed., *Hispanic Americans
in Theology and the Church,* vol. 27 of *Listening* (1992); Fernando F. Segovia,
"A New Manifest Destiny: The Emerging Theological Voice of Hispanic Amer-

icans," in *Religious Studies Review* 17 (1991) 102–9; Justo González, *Mañana: Christian Theology from a Hispanic Perspective* (Nashville: Abingdon, 1990); and Carlos Mesters, *Defenseless Flower: A New Reading of the Bible* (Maryknoll, N.Y.: Orbis Books, 1989). For a theology of preaching that emphasizes the sacramental imagination from a Latino perspective, see Jorge L. Presmanes, "Preaching as Inculturation: Towards a Theology of Liturgical Preaching from the Context of the Latino Culture" (M.A. thesis, Graduate Theological Union, Berkeley, California, April 1990).

39. See M. Shawn Copeland, "Black Theology," in *The New Dictionary of Theology,* ed. Joseph A. Komonchak, Mary Collins, and Dermot A. Lane (Wilmington, Del.: Glazier, 1987) 138–41; idem, "African American Catholics and Black Theology: An Interpretation," in *African-American Religious Studies: An Interdisciplinary Anthology,* ed. Gayraud S. Wilmore (Durham, N.C.: Duke University Press, 1989) 228–48; Gayraud S. Wilmore and James H. Cone, *Black Theology: A Documentary History, 1966–1979* (Maryknoll, N.Y.: Orbis Books, 1979); James H. Cone and Gayraud S. Wilmore, eds., *Black Theology: A Documentary History, 1980–1992* (Maryknoll, N.Y.: Orbis Books, 1993); James H. Cone, *For My People: Black Theology and the Black Church* (Maryknoll, N.Y.: Orbis Books, 1984); idem, "Reflections from the Perspective of U.S. Blacks: Black Theology and Third World Theology," in *Irruption of the Third World,* 235–45; idem, *God of the Oppressed* (New York: Seabury, 1975); Diana L. Hayes, "Feminist Theology, Womanist Theology: A Black Catholic Perspective," in *Black Theology: A Documentary History, 1980–1992,* 325–35; idem, *Hagar's Daughters: Womanist Ways of Being in the World* (New York: Paulist, 1995); Jamie T. Phelps, "Joy Came in the Morning: Risking Death for Resurrection," in *A Troubling in My Soul: Womanist Perspectives on Evil and Suffering,* ed. Emilie M. Townes (Maryknoll, N.Y.: Orbis Books, 1993) 48–64; Renita J. Weems, *Just a Sister Away: A Womanist Vision of Women's Relationships in the Bible* (San Diego: LuraMedia, 1988); Delores S. Williams, *Sisters in the Wilderness: The Challenge of Womanist God-Talk* (Maryknoll, N.Y.: Orbis Books, 1993). For emphasis on the connections between African-American spirituality and the sacramental imagination, see *What We Have Seen and Heard: A Pastoral Letter on Evangelization from the Black Bishops of the United States* (Cincinnati: St. Anthony Messenger Press, 1984); and *Lead Me, Guide Me: The African American Catholic Hymnal* (Chicago: GIA, 1987) preface and introductory essays by Thea Bowman and J-Glenn Murray.

40. The title of Leonardo Boff's book, *Liberating Grace* (Maryknoll, N.Y.: Orbis Books, 1979).

Chapter 3 / Preaching as the Art of Naming Grace

1. See, for example, C. H. Dodd, *The Apostolic Preaching and Its Developments* (New York: Harper and Row, 1962) 20–24.

2. Gabriel Marcel's phrase, as cited in Paul Ricoeur, *The Symbolism of Evil,* trans. Emerson Buchanan (Boston: Beacon, 1967) 258.

3. M. Scott Peck's phrase. See Peck's *People of the Lie: The Hope for Healing Human Evil* (New York: Simon and Schuster, 1985).

4. See Gerhard Ebeling, *God and Word* (Philadelphia: Fortress, 1967) 44–45: "However man may interpret his encounter with the mystery of reality, the word of God charges him with the concealment, in one way or another, of his basic situation; it declares that he is not identical with himself, thus not in the truth, and that he is therefore lacking the freedom to be in harmony and peace with the mystery which has power over him.... [A]s one who is god-less, he is man existing in contradiction;... the Word of God alters the situation decisively."

5. Lischer, *A Theology of Preaching* (chap. 1, n. 22, above) 82.

6. See, for example, Ebeling, *God and Word,* 42.

7. See Bernard J. Cooke, "The Experiential 'Word of God,'" in *Consensus in Theology,* ed. Leonard Swidler (Philadelphia: Westminster, 1981) 69–74.

8. See the discussion of "operative belief" in James Tunstead Burtchaell, "A New Pastoral Method in Theology," *Commonweal* 111 (January 27, 1984) 44–49.

9. Karl Barth objected to beginning a sermon with examples drawn from human experience precisely because the preacher can never bridge the infinite gap between the divine and the human. See Barth, *Homiletics* (chap. 1, n. 13, above) 121–25. Others would allow the value of beginning with the human story, but only as the story of human sinfulness and need for the gospel. See chapter 6.

10. See Paul Ricoeur, "Naming God," *Union Seminary Quarterly Review* 34 (1979) 215–27; idem, "Biblical Hermeneutics," *Semeia* 4 (1975) 107–48; Tracy, *Blessed Rage for Order* (chap. 1, n. 3, above) 91–131; Louis Dupre, *The Other Dimension* (New York: Seabury, 1979); Langdon Gilkey, *Naming the Whirlwind: The Renewal of God-Language* (Indianapolis: Bobbs-Merrill, 1969). For Schillebeeckx's approach, which emphasizes a dialectical disclosure of the experience of grace as the basis for naming God at the limits of human experience, see Edward Schillebeeckx, *The Understanding of Faith,* trans. N. D. Smith (London: Sheed and Ward, 1974) 78–101; and idem, *Christ* (chap. 2, n. 12, above) 29–79.

11. Schillebeeckx, *Christ,* 62. Note also Schillebeeckx's further reference to "what proclaims itself *in* experience to be an astonishing and overwhelming event in reality, correcting and crossing all our plans and achievements" (*Christ,* 64). See also Dulles, "Revelation and Discovery" (chap. 2, n. 11, above).

12. Although he is operating out of a different anthropological basis, Ebeling makes the same point in *God and Word.* Ebeling argues that we need the word of God "to save [us] from choking on [our] own self because we no longer [have] any word with which to cry out of the depths of [our] self-contradiction and call upon that mystery that surrounds [us]" (47).

13. Rainer Maria Rilke, *Notebooks of Malte Laurids Brigge,* trans. M. D. Herter Norton (New York: Norton, 1949) 26–27.

14. See Schillebeeckx, *Christ,* 897 n. 158; see also idem, *God the Future of Man,* trans. N. D. Smith (New York: Sheed and Ward, 1968) 136–38, 154–61, 191–99; and idem, *The Understanding of Faith,* 91–101.

15. Note here Leonardo Boff's caution not to glorify or romanticize suffering: "The cross always crucifies.... To preach death and the cross in a genuinely Christian manner is to invite our fellow Christians to embrace this powerful, revolutionary love, which is an identification with sufferers such that we actually join them in their struggle with the mechanisms that produce crosses. What we must *not* do is preach death and the cross for their own sake" (*When Theology Listens to the Poor* [chap. 2, n. 21, above] 120–21).

16. Gustavo Gutiérrez, *The Power of the Poor in History*, trans. Robert R. Barr (Maryknoll, N.Y.: Orbis Books, 1983) 22. See also Boff, *When Theology Listens to the Poor*, and Ernesto Cardenal, *The Gospel in Solentiname*, 4 vols., trans. Donald D. Walsh (Maryknoll, N.Y.: Orbis Books, 1976–1982).

17. Synod of Bishops, *Justice in the World* (chap. 2, n. 20, above) 34.

18. See John Dominic Crossan, "The Life of a Mediterranean Jewish Peasant," *Christian Century* (December 18–25, 1991) 1194–1204.

19. For a discussion of baptism as the foundation for the preaching ministry, whether exercised by ordained or by other baptized members of the community, see Mary Collins, "The Baptismal Roots of the Preaching Ministry," in *Preaching and the Nonordained,* ed. Nadine Foley (Collegeville, Minn.: Liturgical Press, 1983) 111–33 (reprinted in Collins, *Worship: Renewal to Practice* [chap. 2, n. 36, above] 175–95). In the Foley volume, Edward Schillebeeckx argues that the *vita apostolica,* rather than juridical authority, provides the authentic basis for the proclamation of the gospel in the Christian community ("The Right of Every Christian to Speak in the Light of the Evangelical Experience 'in the Midst of Brothers and Sisters,'" 11–39). The disputed question remains that of how this charismatic authority is mediated and confirmed within the church. See further discussion and bibliography on this question in chapter 9.

20. For brief treatments of the relationship between the Spirit and the remembrance of the community (pneuma and anamnesis), see Schillebeeckx, *Christ,* 641–42, and idem, *Jesus* (chap. 2, n. 12, above) 46–48. Note also Robert Schreiter's caution against cultural romanticism since "all cultures are skewed by sin" ("A Framework for a Discussion of Inculturation," in *Mission in Dialogue,* ed. Mary Motte and Joseph Lang [Maryknoll, N.Y.: Orbis Books, 1982] 547).

21. James H. Cone, "The Story Context of Black Theology," *Theology Today* 32 (1975–76) 147.

22. Martin Buber, *Werke,* vol. 3 (Munich, 1963) 71, as quoted by Schillebeeckx in *Jesus,* 674.

Chapter 4 / Words from the Future

1. Yves Congar, "Sacramental Worship and Preaching," *The Renewal of Preaching: Theory and Practice,* vol. 33 of *Concilium* (New York: Paulist, 1968) 62.

2. In Robert Bolt, *A Man for All Seasons* (New York: Random House, 1960) 140.

3. For an in-depth treatment of this approach to a theology of the word from the sacramental imagination, see Rahner's writings listed in chap. 2, n. 10, above; from the dialectical perspective, see Ebeling, *God and Word* (chap. 3, n. 4, above). See also Walter J. Burghardt, "The Word Made Flesh: Does Language Make a Difference?" in *Preaching: The Art and the Craft* (New York: Paulist, 1987) 3–16.

4. For a critical development of a theology of the word that is rooted in creation and incarnation, but also attends to the limits and sinfulness of "flawed human speech," see Mary Catherine Hilkert, "The Word beneath the Words," in *A Promise of Presence: Studies in Honor of David N. Power,* ed. Michael Downey and Richard Fragomeni (Washington, D.C.: Pastoral Press, 1992) 49–70. For a fully developed critical theology of the word, see Chopp, *The Power to Speak* (chap. 2, n. 31, above).

5. See Gerhard von Rad, *The Message of the Prophets* (New York: Harper and Row, 1962); Abraham Heschel, *The Prophets,* vols. 1 and 2 (New York: Harper and Row, 1962); and Brueggemann, *The Prophetic Imagination* (intro., n. 8, above).

6. Marty Haugen, "We Remember," in *Gather* (Chicago: GIA Publications, 1988) no. 249. On this theme, see also Saliers, *Worship and Spirituality* (intro., n. 7, above).

7. Rahner's phrase. See Rahner, "Considerations on the Active Role of the Person in the Sacramental Event" (chap. 2, no. 10, above).

8. Augustine, *Serm.* 227 (*PL* 38, 1099–1100).

9. For an analysis of both the strengths and weaknesses of typological interpretations of the scriptures, see Gerard S. Sloyan, "The Lectionary as a Context for Interpretation," *Interpretation* 31 (1977) 131–38. Note also Gordon W. Lathrop's discussion of the shift of images that occurs in the use of the Bible in the liturgical assembly ("A Rebirth of Images: On the Use of the Bible in Liturgy," *Worship* 58 [1984] 291–304). For further discussion of critical issues related to the selection of lectionary texts, see Peter C. Finn and James M. Schellman, eds., *Shaping English Liturgy* (Washington, D.C.: Pastoral Press, 1990), especially Horace T. Allen, "The Ecumenical Impact of Lectionary Reform," 361–84, and Eileen Schuller, "Some Criteria for Choice of Scripture Texts in the Roman Lectionary," 385–404.

10. U.S. Bishops, *Fulfilled in Your Hearing* (chap. 2, n. 16, above) 20–21. See also Philip H. Pfatteicher and Carlos R. Messerli, *Manual on the Liturgy* (Minneapolis: Augsburg, 1979) 221.

11. William Skudlarek, *The Word in Worship: Preaching in a Liturgical Context* (Nashville: Abingdon, 1961) 98.

12. For critical discussion of a number of these issues and the larger question of the relationship between liturgy and justice, see Collins, *Worship: Renewal to Practice* (chap. 2, n. 36, above) esp. chaps. 9, 10, 11, 12 and 14; idem, "Is the Eucharist Still a Source of Meaning for Women?" *Origins* 21 (1991) 225–29; idem, "Liturgical Spirituality in a Pluralistic Culture," *Doctrine and Life* 41 (1991) 59–67; idem, "Liturgy: Holiness and Justice in Hard Times," *Origins* 25, no. 29 (January 11, 1996) 488–93; David N. Power, *Worship: Culture and Theology* (Washington, D.C.: Pastoral Press, 1990) esp. chaps. 8 and 10; idem, *The*

Eucharistic Mystery: Revitalizing the Tradition (New York: Crossroad, 1992) 3–20, 291–351; idem, "Sacraments: Symbolizing God's Power in the Church," *Proceedings of the Catholic Theological Society of America* 37 (1982) 50–66; Mary Collins and David N. Power, eds., *Can We Always Celebrate the Eucharist?* vol. 152 of *Concilium* (Edinburgh: T. & T. Clark, 1982); Catherine Vincie, "The Cry for Justice and the Eucharist," *Worship* 68 (1994) 194–210; Mark Searle, ed., *Liturgy and Social Justice* (Collegeville, Minn.: Liturgical Press, 1980); James L. Empereur and Christopher G. Kiesling, *The Liturgy That Does Justice* (Collegeville, Minn.: Liturgical Press, 1990); Tissa Balasuriya, *The Eucharist and Human Liberation* (Maryknoll, N.Y.: Orbis Books, 1979); and *Journal of Religious Ethics* 7, no. 2 (1979).

Chapter 5 / Trust the Text or Preach the Gospel?

1. Elie Wiesel, *Legends of Our Time* (New York: Avon, 1968) 31.

2. Barth, *The Preaching of the Gospel* (chap. 1, n. 13, above) 54–55.

3. Reginald H. Fuller, *The Use of the Bible in Preaching* (Philadelphia: Fortress, 1981) 9, 17; Raymond E. Brown, *The Critical Meaning of the Bible* (New York: Paulist, 1981) 18; and Avery Dulles, "Scripture: Recent Protestant and Catholic Views," *Theology Today* 37 (1980) 7–26. See also Sandra M. Schneiders, *Beyond Patching* (New York: Paulist, 1991) 42.

4. Walter Vogels, *Reading and Preaching the Bible: A New Semiotic Approach* (Wilmington, Del.: Glazier, 1986) 18.

5. Walter Brueggemann, *Finally Comes the Poet* (Minneapolis: Fortress, 1989) 8. Brueggemann's project in biblical theology consistently critiques the accommodation of the gospel to social ideology. He insists that the goal of prophetic ministry is the formation of an alternative community. As will be discussed later in the chapter, according to Brueggemann, the *prophetic* construal of the Bible is the primary trust of the church and its preaching (see *Finally Comes the Poet,* 7). For Brueggemann's nuanced approach to the text as "liberating," see especially *Interpretation and Obedience: From Faithful Reading to Faithful Living* (Minneapolis: Fortress, 1991). There Brueggemann calls for "interpretive obedience," which requires "an act of imaginative construal to show how the non-negotiable intentions of Yahweh are to be discerned and practiced in our situation, which is so very different from the situations in which those intentions were initially articulated" (1).

6. Leander E. Keck, *The Bible in the Pulpit* (Nashville: Abingdon, 1978) 99.

7. Elisabeth Schüssler Fiorenza, "The Will to Choose or Reject: Continuing Our Critical Work," in *Feminist Interpretation of the Bible,* ed. Letty M. Russell (Philadelphia: Westminster, 1985) 130. See idem, *Bread Not Stone* (Boston: Beacon, 1984) x–xiv for political analysis of "the power of the word."

8. Phyllis Trible, *Texts of Terror* (Philadelphia: Fortress, 1984) xiii, 1. Cheryl Townsend Gilkes notes that "within the Afro-Christian tradition, these women's stories are familiar and they are preached" (see " 'Some Mother's Son and Some Father's Daughter': Gender and Biblical Language in Afro-Christian Worship Tradition," in *Shaping New Vision: Gender Values in American Culture,* ed.

Clarissa W. Atkinson, Constance H. Buchanan, and Margaret R. Miles [Ann Arbor, Mich.: UMI Research Press, 1987] 82).

9. See Allan A. Boesak, "What Belongs to Caesar? Once Again Romans 13," in *When Prayer Makes Sense,* ed. Allan A. Boesak and Charles Villa-Vincencio (Philadelphia: Westminster, 1986) 138–56. For analysis of the critical use of the Bible in South Africa, see Gerald O. West, *Biblical Hermeneutics of Liberation: Modes of Reading the Bible in the South African Context,* 2d rev. ed. (Maryknoll, N.Y.: Orbis Books, 1995).

10. See Howard Thurman, *Jesus and the Disinherited* (Nashville: Abingdon, 1949) 30–31; Renita J. Weems, "Reading *Her Way* through the Struggle: African American Women and the Bible," in *Stony the Road We Trod: African American Biblical Interpretation,* ed. Cain Hope Felder (Minneapolis: Fortress, 1991) 57–77; and Katie G. Cannon, "Slave Ideology and Biblical Interpretation," *Semeia* 49 (1989) 9–24.

11. See Susan Brooks Thistlethwaite, "Every Two Minutes: Battered Women and Feminist Interpretation," in *Feminist Interpretation of the Bible,* 96–107.

12. Rabbi Marc Tannenbaum, quoting from *Hitler's Table-Talk,* as found in Burghardt, *Preaching* (chap. 4, n. 3, above) 153–54.

13. On the interrelationship and distinction between the terms "revelation" and "inspiration" and related issues, see Thomas A. Hoffman, "Inspiration, Normativeness, Canonicity, and the Unique Sacred Character of the Bible," *Catholic Biblical Quarterly* 44 (1982) 447–69; Sandra M. Schneiders, *The Revelatory Text* (San Francisco: HarperCollins, 1991) 44–59; idem, "The Bible and Feminism," in *Freeing Theology* (chap. 2, n. 30, above) 37–47; and Raymond F. Collins, "Inspiration," *New Jerome Biblical Commentary* (Englewood Cliffs, N.J.: Prentice-Hall, 1990) 1023–33.

The biblical claim that "all scripture is inspired" (2 Tim 3:16) does not mean that all biblical texts can be identified with divine revelation or the divine will, nor that the surface meaning of all biblical texts or injunctions is authoritative and normative for the life of the Christian church. Rather as Vatican II notes, the scriptures teach "firmly, faithfully, and without error that truth which God wanted to put into the sacred writings *for the sake of salvation*" (*Dei Verbum,* no. 11; emphasis added). While the original context for that assertion related to debates about biblical inerrancy in the modern world, the insight has been explored fruitfully in contemporary feminist scholarship with regard to texts that disclose patriarchy or other forms of social or political bias. See Schüssler Fiorenza, *Bread Not Stone,* 23–42; and Johnson, *SHE WHO IS* (chap. 2, n. 30, above) 78–79. Schneiders criticizes any approach that distinguishes certain passages as nonrevelatory as still reflective of a propositional notion of revelation. Instead she speaks of the entire Bible as "revelatory text" but argues for the necessity of a critical hermeneutics that discloses the liberating "word of God" sometimes in direct contrast to the original meaning of a passage.

While both are feminist scholars, Schüssler Fiorenza and Schneiders disagree on the locus of revelation and differ in their approaches to feminist liberation hermeneutics. For Schüssler Fiorenza's approach to feminist hermeneutics and her description of the Bible as historical prototype that is critically open to transformation of its models of Christian faith and community in different social-historical settings, see Elisabeth Schüssler Fiorenza, *In Memory of Her: A Feminist Theological Reconstruction of Christian Origins* (New York: Crossroad, 1983) esp. 26–36; *Bread Not Stone;* and *But She Said: Feminist Practices of Biblical Interpretation* (Boston: Beacon, 1992).

14. See Schneiders, *Beyond Patching;* and idem, *The Revelatory Text,* 27–33.

15. Schneiders, *Revelatory Text,* 38–43. The language of word as sacrament is developed in a systematic way by Karl Rahner (see chap. 2). While the language of sacrament is rarely used, the notion that the scriptures function not as record of revelation but as event of revelation is also central to the dialectical imagination and is developed explicitly by the word-event theologians, as described in chapter 3.

16. Russell, "Introduction: Liberating the Word," in *Feminist Interpretation of the Bible,* 16–17.

17. I am using the term "bias" in this book in the technical sense that Bernard Lonergan identifies as the refusal to admit to consciousness data that might yield unwanted insights, thus blocking the self-correcting process of learning so as to avoid change. See Bernard J. F. Lonergan, *Insight: A Study of Human Understanding* (San Francisco: Harper and Row, 1978) 191–203, 218–42.

18. Sloyan, "The Lectionary as a Context for Interpretation" (chap. 4, n. 9, above) 131. On the development of the canon, see Raymond E. Brown and Raymond F. Collins, "Canonicity," in *New Jerome Biblical Commentary,* 66:48–86; and Bruce M. Metzger, *The Canon of the New Testament: Its Origins, Development, and Significance* (Oxford: Clarendon, 1987). For a critical perspective on the development of the canon as the record of the "historical winners," see Schüssler Fiorenza, *In Memory of Her,* 53–56. Nevertheless, Schüssler Fiorenza argues that as "multiform model," the canon grounds contemporary pluralism in the church and in Christian life (see *Bread Not Stone,* 36–37).

19. In addition to the feminist references in previous notes, see, for example, Felder, *Stony the Road We Trod;* idem, *Troubling Biblical Waters: Race, Class, and Family* (Maryknoll, N.Y.: Orbis Books, 1989); Gottwald and Horsley, *The Bible and Liberation* (chap. 2, n. 24, above); David Jobling, Peggy L. Day, and Gerald T. Sheppard, eds., *The Bible and the Politics of Exegesis: Essays in Honor of Norman K. Gottwald on his Sixty-fifth Birthday* (Cleveland: Pilgrim, 1991); and West, *Biblical Hermeneutics of Liberation.*

20. Schüssler Fiorenza, "The Will to Choose or Reject," 132–33.

21. Proctor-Smith, *In Her Own Rite* (intro, n. 7, above) 116–35. For one selection of suggested supplementary texts, see Barbara Bowe et al., *Silent Voices, Sacred Lives* (New York: Paulist, 1992).

22. Marjorie Procter-Smith, "Feminist Interpretation and Liturgical Proclamation," in *Searching the Scriptures* (chap. 2, n. 38, above) 1:313–25.

23. Raymond E. Brown, "The Passion according to John," *Worship* 49 (1975) 126–34. On this issue, see also Burghardt, "Of Their Race Is the Christ," in *Preaching* (chap. 4, n. 3, above) 139–58; John J. Pawlikowsi and James A. Wilde, *When Catholics Speak about Jews* (Chicago: Liturgy Training Publications, 1987); Darrell J. Fasching, ed., *The Jewish People in Christian Preaching* (Lewiston, N.Y.: Mellen, 1984); Eugene T. Fisher, "The Roman Liturgy and Catholic-Jewish Relations," in *Twenty Years of Jewish-Catholic Relations,* ed.

Eugene T. Fisher, A. James Rudin, and Marc H. Tannenbaum (New York: Paulist, 1986) 135–55; Sloyan, "The Lectionary as a Context for Interpretation"; and Clark M. Williamson and Ronald J. Allen, *Interpreting Difficult Texts: Anti-Judaism and Christian Preaching* (Philadelphia: Trinity, 1989).

24. Schuller, "Some Criteria for the Choice of Scripture Texts in the Roman Lectionary" (chap. 4, n. 9, above) 403–4.

25. In addition to the references in notes 23 and 24, see Allen, "The Ecumenical Impact of Lectionary Reform" (chap. 4, n. 9, above) 361–84.

26. The phrase is taken from Ronald J. Allen, "Preaching against the Text," *Encounter* 48, no. 1 (winter 1987) 105–13.

27. The selection in the Roman lectionary includes a portion of the larger household code, Col 3:18–4:1. For critical analysis of that passage as well as of the household codes located in Eph 5:21–6:9 and 1 Pet 2:11–3:12, see Schüssler Fiorenza, *In Memory of Her,* 251–70, as well as further bibliography, 280–83 nn. 22–74. See also Clarice J. Martin, "The *Haustafeln* (Household Codes) in African American Biblical Interpretation: 'Free Slaves' and 'Subordinate Women,' " in *Stony the Road We Trod,* 206–31.

28. Sandra M. Schneiders, "Feminist Ideology Criticism and Biblical Hermeneutics," *Biblical Theology Bulletin* 19 (January 1989) 4. See also idem, "Living Word or Deadly Letter? The Encounter between the New Testament and Contemporary Experience," *Proceedings of the Catholic Theological Society of America* 47 (1992) 45–60; and Donald P. Senior, "Response to Sandra Schneiders," *Proceedings of the Catholic Theological Society of America* 47 (1992) 61–68.

29. Sandra M. Schneiders, "The Bible and Feminism," in *Freeing Theology,* 51. In addition to the theological importance of the Bible for Christians, Schneiders also argues for its ecumenical and spiritual significance (51). For alternate feminist and womanist perspectives on the authority of the Bible, see Letty M. Russell, "Authority and the Challenge of Feminist Interpretation," in *Feminist Interpretation of the Bible,* 137–46; and Weems, "Reading *Her Way* through the Struggle."

30. Schneiders, "Feminist Ideology Criticism and Biblical Hermeneutics," 7. In *Beyond Patching* (62–71), Schneiders grants that "[a]t times we must judge the witness of the scriptures as inadequate, biased, or even counter-evangelical," but further argues that "some texts in scripture might function today not as prescriptions for Christian attitudes or behaviors but as witness to the understanding of the gospel by earlier (or later) Christians" (70). See also Renita Weems's reminder that African-American women "have to be prepared to resist those elements of the tradition that have sought, even in the name of revelation, to diminish their humanity" ("Reading *Her Way* through the Struggle," 77). See also her treatment of the story of the Egyptian woman Hagar and her slaveholding mistress, the Hebrew Sarah (Gen 16:1–16; 21:1–21), in "A Mistress, a Maid, and No Mercy," in *Just a Sister Away: A Womanist Vision of Women's Relationships in the Bible* (San Diego: LuraMedia, 1988), and "Reading *Her Way* through the Struggle," 75–76.

31. Schneiders, "Feminist Ideology Criticism and Biblical Hermeneutics," 724–25. See *The Revelatory Text* (161–64), for Schneiders's proposal that we

substitute "textual meaning" for "literal meaning." See also her "Faith, Hermeneutics, and the Literal Sense of Scripture," *Theological Studies* 39 (1978) 719–36; and "From Exegesis to Hermeneutics: The Problem of the Contemporary Meaning of Scripture," *Horizons* 8 (1981): 23–39. For another approach to a "feminist hermeneutics of marginality" grounded in an understanding of the word as "perfectly open sign," see Chopp, *The Power to Speak* (chap. 2, n. 31, above) esp. 40–70.

32. Schneiders, "Paschal Imagination" (intro., n. 8, above) 59.

33. Ibid., 63

34. This image is frequently used by feminist scholars, among others. See, for example, Trible, *Texts of Terror,* 4–5.

35. This projected world or possible reality, which Ricoeur calls "the world before the text," is not limited by the actual reality of the writer's historical world even though it is in some sense derived from that world. The text projects reality, not under the modality of what is, but what can be. What the reader does by interpreting the text is to discern that projected world and to respond to the invitation to live according to its structures and dynamics.

36. Schneiders, "Feminist Ideology Criticism and Biblical Hermeneutics," 8.

37. For similar claims by Raymond Brown and Walter Burghardt regarding the preaching of the anti-Semitic passages in John's Gospel and by Allan Boesak regarding the South African context, see notes 9 and 23, above.

38. For Ricoeur's recent writing on narrative as a kind of extended metaphor, see *Time and Narrative,* vol. 1, trans. Kathleen McLaughlin and David Pellauer (Chicago: University of Chicago Press, 1984). On the notion of genre as revelatory, see Ricoeur's "Toward a Hermeneutic of the Idea of Revelation," in *Essays on Biblical Interpretation,* ed. Lewis S. Mudge (Philadelphia: Fortress, 1980) 73–118, and idem, "Naming God" (chap. 3, n. 10, above). See also Paul Ricoeur, *Figuring the Sacred: Religion, Narrative, and Imagination,* trans. David Pellauer, ed. Mark I. Wallace (Minneapolis: Fortress, 1995).

39. David N. Power, "The Holy Spirit: Scripture, Tradition, and Interpretation," in *Keeping the Faith: Essays to Mark the Centenary of Lux Mundi,* ed. Geoffrey Wainwright (Philadelphia: Fortress, 1988) 169.

40. Ibid., 168–70. See also Ricoeur's "Toward a Hermeneutic of the Idea of Revelation." For a fuller development of the implications of Power's writings on critical liturgical praxis for preaching, see Hilkert, "The Word beneath the Words" (chap. 4, n. 4, above).

41. See Brueggemann, *The Prophetic Imagination* (intro., n. 8, above); and idem, *Finally Comes the Poet.*

42. Brueggemann, *The Prophetic Imagination,* 13.

43. Walter Brueggemann, *The Message of the Psalms* (Minneapolis: Augsburg, 1984) 20.

44. Ibid., 20–21.

45. See Brueggemann, *The Prophetic Imagination,* 44–61; Dorothee Sölle, *Suffering* (Philadelphia: Fortress, 1975) 61–86; David N. Power, "When to Worship Is to Lament," in *Worship: Culture and Theology* (chap. 4, n. 12, above) 155–73; Beverly Wildung Harrison, "The Power of Anger in the Work of Love," *Union Theological Seminary Quarterly Review* 36, supplement (January 1981)

41–57 (reprinted in Judith Plaskow and Carol P. Christ, eds., *Weaving the Visions* [San Francisco: Harper and Row, 1989] 214–25); and Mary Field Belenky et al., *Women's Ways of Knowing* (New York: Basic Books, 1986).

46. Power, "The Holy Spirit," 167–68.

47. Weems, "Reading *Her Way* through the Struggle," 77.

48. Power, "The Holy Spirit," 167.

49. Paul Achtemeier, *The Inspiration of Scripture: Problems and Proposals* (Philadelphia: Westminster, 1980).

50. See Rainer Maria Rilke, *Letters to a Young Poet,* trans. M. D. Herter Norton (New York: Norton, 1934) 35.

51. Schneiders, "The Bible and Feminism," 50.

52. In South Africa, Albert Nolan remarked on the "mushrooming in almost every part of the country" of Bible study groups. He wagered that in the context of the major reconstruction needed in postapartheid South Africa, those groups might provide "the way back to church, the way back to spiritual reconstruction, and the way back to the integration of spiritual and material needs" ("Material and Spiritual Needs," *Challenge: Church and People* 24 [1994] 1).

53. Kenneth Untener, "What a Prophet Does and Does Not Do," *Origins* 21 (May 23, 1991) 37.

Chapter 6 / The Human Story and the Story of Jesus

1. The preacher was Andre Kravec, O.P. I am grateful to her for this story.

2. See, for example, Frederick Buechner, *Telling the Truth: The Gospel as Tragedy, Comedy, and Fairy Tale* (San Francisco: Harper and Row, 1977); Richard L. Eslinger, *A New Hearing* (Nashville: Abingdon, 1987); Richard A. Jensen, *Telling the Story* (Minneapolis: Augsburg, 1980); idem, *Thinking in Story: Preaching in a Post-literate Age* (Lima, Ohio: C.S.S., 1993); Eugene L. Lowry, *Doing Time in the Pulpit: The Relationship between Narrative and Preaching* (Nashville: Abingdon, 1985); idem, *The Homiletic Plot: Sermon as Narrative Art Form* (Atlanta: John Knox, 1981); Edmund Steimle, Morris Niedenthal, and Charles Rice, eds., *Preaching the Story* (Philadelphia: Fortress, 1980); Robert Waznak, *Sunday after Sunday: Preaching the Homily as Story* (New York: Paulist, 1983); and John McClure, "The Narrative Function of Preaching," *Liturgy* 8, no. 2 (fall 1989) 47–51.

3. Richard Lischer, "The Limits of Story," *Interpretation* 38 (1984) 35.

4. Ibid., 36. For similar reservations about narrative preaching, see Buttrick (see intro., n. 4, above) 141–43; and Melloh, "Publish or Perish: A Review of Preaching Literature, 1981–1986" (intro., n. 4, above) 513. See also William H. Willimon, "Preaching: Entertainment or Exposition?" *Christian Century* 107 (February 28, 1990) 204, 206; and Carl E. Braaten, "Whatever Happened to Law and Gospel?" *Currents in Theology and Mission* 14 (1987) 111–18.

5. Lischer, "The Limits of Story," 26–38; and idem, "Luther and Contemporary Preaching: Narrative and Anthropology," *Scottish Journal of Theology* 36 (1983) 487–504.

6. Narrative as literary form is distinguished by "the presence of a story and a storyteller" (see Robert Scholes and Robert Kellogg, *The Nature of Narrative* [London: Oxford University Press, 1966] 4). I am using the terms "narrative" and "story" interchangeably in this chapter in the sense described by Gabriel Fackre: "an account of events and participants moving over time and space, a recital with a beginning and ending patterned by the narrator's principle of selection." As he further explains, this general description is roomy enough to include "history" (Gabriel Fackre, "Narrative Theology: An Overview," *Interpretation* 37 [1983] 341). While some authors (Terrence W. Tilley, *Story Theology* [Wilmington, Del.: Glazier, 1985], and George Stroup, *The Promise of Narrative Theology: Recovering the Gospel in the Church* [Atlanta: John Knox Press, 1981]) would argue that this use of the term "narrative" is too broad and further distinctions of genre are necessary, what is primarily at issue in this chapter is the use of human experience drawn from the world's religions or from "secular" stories to communicate the message of the gospel.

For overviews of developments in the field of narrative theology and helpful bibliographies, see Fackre, "Narrative Theology"; Stroup, *The Promise of Narrative Theology;* Tilley, *Story Theology;* Stanley Hauerwas and L. Gregory Jones, eds., *Why Narrative? Readings in Narrative Theology* (Grand Rapids, Mich.: Eerdmans, 1989); Gary L. Comstock, "Two Types of Narrative Theology," *Journal of the American Academy of Religion* 55, no. 4 (1988) 688–717; John Navone, "Narrative Theology and Its Uses: A Survey," *Irish Theological Quarterly* 52 (1986) 212–30; and Michael Goldberg, *Theology and Narrative: A Critical Introduction* (Nashville: Abingdon, 1982).

7. Lischer, "Luther and Contemporary Preaching," 494.

8. Ibid., 500, 492–93. Lischer's claim that Luther did not use the human story to illustrate the gospel, but only to establish the need for the gospel, can be disputed. Note, for example, Luther's use of Moses in the volume on word and sacrament (*Luther's Works,* vol. 35, ed. E. Theodore Bachmann [Philadelphia: Fortress, 1960] 172–73). The Augsburg Confession also clearly states that "saints should be kept in remembrance so that our faith may be strengthened when we see what grace they received and how they were sustained by faith" (The Augsburg Confession, in *The Book of Concord,* trans. and ed. Theodore G. Tappert [Philadelphia: Fortress, 1959] 46–47). I am grateful to Clifford Frederick for these references.

9. Lischer, "The Limits of Story," 33.

10. Constitution on the Sacred Liturgy, no. 52, and Decree on the Ministry and Life of Priests, no. 4, in Walter M. Abbott, ed., *The Documents of Vatican II* (New York: America Press, 1966); General Instruction of Roman Missal, 4th ed. (March 27, 1975) no. 41, and Lectionary for Mass: Introduction, in *The Liturgy Documents: A Parish Resource,* rev. ed., ed. Mary Ann Simcoe (Chicago: Liturgy Training Publications, 1985) no. 24. See also Philip H. Pfatteicher and Carlos R. Messerli, *Manual on the Liturgy: Lutheran Book of Worship* (Minneapolis: Augsburg, 1979) 221.

11. Paul Ricoeur, *Time and Narrative,* 3 volumes, trans. Kathleen McLaughlin and David Pellauer (Chicago: University of Chicago Press, 1984).

12. See Stephen Crites, "The Narrative Quality of Experience," *Journal of the American Academy of Religion* 39 (1971) 291–311. Despite his reservations about the limits of story in preaching, Lischer states clearly that "the essential relationship between story and experience cannot be doubted" ("The Limits of Story," 30). See also H. Richard Niebuhr, *The Meaning of Revelation* (New York: Macmillan, 1941); James W. McClendon Jr., *Biography as Theology* (Nashville: Abingdon, 1974); John S. Dunne, *A Search for God in Time and Memory* (London: Macmillan, 1967); and Tilley, *Story Theology*, 23–26.

13. Augustine, *Confessions* X. See also Ricoeur, *Time and Narrative*, 1:5–30.

14. Stroup, *The Promise of Narrative Theology*, 75. See also McFague, *Models of God* (chap. 2, n. 28, above).

15. Ted L. Estess, "The Inerrable Contraption: Reflections on the Metaphor of Story," *Journal of the American Academy of Religion* 42 (1974) 427.

16. See the discussion of conversion in Bernard Lonergan, *Method in Theology* (New York: Herder and Herder, 1972) esp. 104–7.

17. Crites, "The Narrative Quality of Experience," 307.

18. Lischer, "The Limits of Story," 35. Lischer cites the preaching of Martin Luther King Jr. as a specific example: "The effectiveness of Martin Luther King as a preacher and agent of social change lay not in his ability to tell a story but in his incisive analysis of the situation in America and his prophetic call to justice.... The content and structure of his sermons are not organized around Gospel narratives but gospel principles" (35). For further development in Lischer's approach to King's preaching, see "The Word That Moves: The Preaching of Martin Luther King, Jr.," *Theology Today* 46 (1989) 169–82. James Cone, however, claims that "the theme of liberation expressed in story-form is the essence of black religion" (see "The Story Context of Black Theology" [chap. 3, n. 21, above] 144–50). Cone asserts that African-American spirituals and stories carry a transforming power that white, first world cultures fail to grasp. See also Pius Dlungwane, "African Story-telling and Evangelization," *LUMKO Conference Report on "Inculturation"* (February 21–22, 1995) 46–52.

19. J. B. Metz, *Faith in History and Society* (New York: Seabury, 1980) 209. Both Metz and Schillebeeckx are explicitly indebted to critical theorists from the Frankfurt school for many of their insights on the power of narrative.

20. Lischer, "The Limits of Story," 38.

21. Paul Ricoeur, "Creativity in Language," in *The Philosophy of Paul Ricoeur*, ed. Charles E. Reagan and David Stewart (Boston: Beacon, 1978) 131. See also Ricoeur's "Metaphor and the Main Problem of Hermeneutics," *New Literary History* 6 (1974/75) 95–110; and idem, *The Rule of Metaphor* (Toronto: University of Toronto Press, 1977). For further discussion and bibliography related to metaphor as well as creative theological use of metaphor, see McFague, *Speaking in Parables* (chap. 1, n. 20, above); idem, *Metaphorical Theology* (chap. 1, n. 20, above); and idem, *Models of God* (chap. 2, n. 28, above).

22. Ricoeur, "Creativity in Language," 132.

23. Ricoeur, *Time and Narrative*, 1:74.

24. Buechner, *Telling the Truth*.

25. The original text of Isak Dinesen's story, on which the movie was based, is available in Isak Dinesen, *Babette's Feast and Other Anecdotes of Destiny* (New York: Random House/Vintage Books, 1988).

26. The phrase "sense of an ending" is taken from the title of the book by Frank Kermode, *The Sense of an Ending: Studies in the Theory of Fiction* (New York: Oxford University Press, 1967).

27. Mark Searle, "The Narrative Quality of Christian Liturgy," *Chicago Studies* 21 (1982) 81.

28. Gerard S. Sloyan, *Worshipful Preaching* (Philadelphia: Fortress, 1984) 56.

29. David Power, *Unsearchable Riches: The Symbolic Nature of Liturgy* (New York: Pueblo, 1984) 165.

30. See Jensen, *Telling the Story*, 114–68.

31. Barth, *The Epistle to the Romans* (chap. 1, n. 11, above) 98.

32. Lischer, "Luther and Contemporary Preaching," 494, 493.

33. The power of grace may not be evident, however, from the evidence immediately available in a given cultural or personal situation. Here Schillebeeckx's notion of "contrast experience" as mediation of grace is important. See also Boff, *Liberating Grace* (chap. 2, n. 40, above); and Carr, *Transforming Grace* (chap. 2, n. 30, above) 211–14.

34. See, for example, Edward Schillebeeckx, *God the Future of Man* (New York: Sheed and Ward, 1968) esp. 185–87.

35. See Comstock's "Two Types of Narrative Theology." Comstock uses Tracy as his primary example of a correlationist and refers to the correlationists as "impure narrativists."

36. Ibid., 698.

37. William Platcher, "Paul Ricoeur and Postliberal Theology: A Conflict of Interpretations" (paper quoted in ibid., 699 n. 10).

38. Stroup, *The Promise of Narrative Theology,* 235.

39. Hauerwas's position, as described by Navone in "Narrative Theology and Its Uses," 215.

40. David Tracy, "The Particularity and Universality of Christian Revelation," in *Revelation and Experience,* vol. 113 of *Concilium,* ed. Edward Schillebeeckx and Bas van Iersal (New York: Seabury, 1979) 115.

41. Ibid., 113.

42. The same basic principle applies to preaching on feasts of Mary or another of the saints or when we keep memorial of other leaders in faith such as Dorothy Day, Oscar Romero, or Martin Luther King Jr. We remember these women and men precisely because their lives were unique expressions of the gospel. Preaching on these feasts remains biblical and liturgical preaching, but the concrete life-story of the person(s) remembered offers a way of interpreting and illustrating the gospel. See James A. Wallace, *Preaching through the Saints* (Collegeville, Minn.: Liturgical Press, 1982).

Chapter 7 / Grace at the Edges: Preaching and Lament

1. Barth, "The Need and Promise of Christian Preaching" (chap. 1, n. 13, above) 107–9. Note also Nathan Scott: "Of all the myriad issues of life which the Christian pulpit is required to handle there is none so pressing, so inescapable, and so burdensome for the preacher as the problem of suffering, the mystery of iniquity, the strange and brutal haphazardness with which as it seems at times, acute misfortune is distributed amongst persons" ("The Burdens and Temptations of the Pulpit," in *Preaching on Suffering and a God of Love*, ed. Henry J. Young [Philadelphia: Fortress, 1978] 7).

2. See Jennifer Glen, "Sickness and Symbol: The Promise of the Future," *Worship* 54 (1980) 397–411; David Power, "Let the Sick Man Call," *Heythrop Journal* 19 (1978) 256–70; and Eric J. Cassel, "The Nature of Suffering and the Goals of Medicine" *New England Journal of Medicine* (March 18, 1982) 639–45.

3. Alice Walker, *Possessing the Secret of Joy* (New York: Harcourt Brace Jovanovich, 1992) 273–74.

4. Peter B. Vaill, "The Rediscovery of Anguish," *Creative Change* 10, no. 3 (1990) 18–24, as quoted by K. C. Ptomey Jr., "A Cry in the Night," *Weavings* 8 (1993) 31. On the denial of grief and lack of recognition of how those who are dominant are also oppressed by the very structures by which they oppress others, see Brueggemann, *The Prophetic Imagination* (intro., n. 8, above); Dorothee Sölle, *Suffering*, trans. Everett R. Kalin (Philadelphia: Fortress, 1975); and Jürgen Moltmann and Douglas Meeks, "The Liberation of Oppressors," *Christianity and Crisis* 38 (December 25, 1978) 310–17.

5. Ptomey, "A Cry in the Night," 33.

6. Constance FitzGerald, O.C.D., "Impasse and Dark Night," in *Living with Apocalypse: Spiritual Resources for Social Compassion,* ed. Tilden Edwards (New York: Harper and Row, 1984) 94 (reprinted in JoAnn Wolski Conn, ed., *Women's Spirituality: Resources for Christian Development* [New York: Paulist Press, 1986] 287–311). For a discussion of the notion of impasse in the context of political commitment, see also Belden C. Lane, "Spirituality and Political Commitment," *America* (March 14, 1981) 197–202.

7. See Dorothee Sölle's critique of Christian masochism in *Suffering,* 9–32.

8. While expiation in the Jewish tradition has roots in God's mercy (God wiping away human sinfulness out of love), the term "expiation" began to be understood interchangeably with "propitiation," as if Jesus, in the place of humankind, was "making satisfaction" through paying the price for sin to an angry God. Even worse was the extension into Christian piety that viewed human suffering as a share in this propitiating "work" of Christ.

9. See Joseph A. Fitzmyer, "Reconciliation in Pauline Theology," in *No Famine in the Land: Studies in Honor of John L. McKenzie,* ed. James W. Flanagan and Anita Weisbrod Robinson (Missoula, Mont.: Scholars Press for the Institute for Antiquity and Christianity — Claremont, 1975) 155–71; Schillebeeckx, *Christ* (chap. 2, n. 12, above) 477–514.

10. For contemporary issues in soteriology and a critical perspective on the later appropriation of Anselm's theory in the tradition, see Elizabeth A. John-

son, "Jesus and Salvation," *Proceedings of the Catholic Theological Society of America* 49 (1994) 1–18.

11. "Christ, the Son of God, stands in our place and has taken all our sins upon his shoulders;...he is the eternal satisfaction for our sin and reconciles us with God, the Father" (*Luther's Works,* vol. 51, ed. and trans. John W. Doberstein [Philadelphia: Fortress, 1959] 92). Paul Althaus observes: "Theology of glory leads man to stand before God and strike a bargain on the basis of his ethical achievement in fulfilling the law, whereas the theology of the cross views man as one who has been called to suffer....Luther's statement 'God is known only in suffering' is an ambiguous statement or — more correctly — it points to the deep correlation between the suffering Christ, in whom God makes himself known, and the suffering man, who is the only man able to enter into community with God" (*The Theology of Martin Luther,* trans. Robert C. Schultz [Philadelphia: Fortress, 1966] 27–28). Gerhard O. Forde points out that God cannot simply forget about his wrath and show his mercy to sinners if his righteousness is not satisfied. Arguing against juridical ideas about appeasing God or propitiation, however, Forde interprets the doctrine of atonement in terms of God's radical mercy that has been rejected by sin: "God in mercy and love sends Jesus to die for us so as actually and concretely to have mercy" (*Theology Is for Proclamation* [Minneapolis: Augsburg Fortress, 1990] 130). For one approach to preaching salvation in social terms, see David Buttrick, *Preaching Jesus Christ* (Philadelphia: Fortress, 1988).

12. Boff, *When Theology Listens to the Poor* (chap. 2, n. 21, above) 104–47.

13. See Johnson, *SHE WHO IS* (chap. 2, n. 30, above) 246–72; and Elizabeth A. Johnson, *Consider Jesus* (New York: Crossroad, 1990) 97–128; Jacquelyn Grant, *White Women's Christ and Black Women's Jesus* (Atlanta: Scholars Press, 1989) 195–230; idem, "Subjectification as a Requirement for Christological Construction," in *Lift Every Voice* (chap. 2, n. 38, above) 201–14; Mary John Mananzan, "Paschal Mystery from a Philippine Perspective," in *Any Room for Christ in Asia?* vol. 1993/2 of *Concilium,* ed. Leonardo Boff and Virgil Elizondo (Maryknoll, N.Y.: Orbis Books, 1993) 86–94; Wendy Farley, *Tragic Vision and Divine Compassion: A Contemporary Theodicy* (Louisville: Westminster/John Knox Press, 1990); Sölle, *Suffering;* Emilie Townes, *Womanist Justice, Womanist Hope* (Atlanta: Scholars Press, 1993); idem, ed., *A Troubling in My Soul* (Maryknoll, N.Y.: Orbis Books, 1993); Patricia Wismer, "For Women in Pain," in *In the Embrace of God* (chap. 2, n. 28, above) 138–58; Williams, *Sisters in the Wilderness* (chap. 2, n. 39, above) 161–70.

14. See Crossan, "The Life of a Mediterranean Jewish Peasant" (chap. 3, n. 18), regarding the profound social and political challenge of Jesus' patterns of table companionship and healing. For a synthesis of critical scholarship from a historical-critical perspective, see John P. Meier, "Jesus," in *New Jerome Biblical Commentary* (chap. 5, n. 18, above) 1316–28. See also Albert Nolan, *Jesus before Christianity,* rev. ed. (Maryknoll, N.Y.: Orbis Books, 1992); Schillebeeckx, *Jesus* (chap. 2, n. 12, above); Jon Sobrino, *Christology at the Crossroads,* trans. John Drury (Maryknoll, N.Y.: Orbis Books, 1978).

15. See, for example, Boff, *Liberating Grace* (chap. 2, no. 40).

16. Schillebeeckx's phrase, in *Jesus* (chap. 2, n. 12, above) 178.

17. See Jürgen Moltmann, *The Crucified God* (New York: Harper and Row, 1974); idem, "The Crucified God: God and the Trinity Today," in *New Questions about God*, vol. 76 of *Concilium*, ed. J. B. Metz (New York: Herder and Herder, 1972) 26–37; Edward Schillebeeckx, "The 'God of Jesus' and the 'Jesus of God,'" in *Jesus Christ and Human Freedom*, vol. 93 of *Concilium*, ed. E. Schillebeeckx and B. van Iersal (New York: Herder, 1974) 110–26; Robert J. Schreiter, "The Crucified God," *The Bible Today* 28 (May 1990) 159–64.

18. Johnson, *Consider Jesus*, 59.

19. The phrase is taken from Walter Brueggemann, "The Costly Loss of Lament," *Journal for the Study of the Old Testament* 36 (1986) 57–71. See also Claus Westermann, *Praise and Lament in the Psalms*, trans. Keith R. Crim and Richard N. Soulen (Atlanta: John Knox Press, 1981); William Michael Soll, "The Israelite Lament: Faith Seeking Understanding," *Quarterly Review* 8 (1988) 77–88; Belden C. Lane, "*HUTZPA K'LAPEI SHAMAYA:* A Christian Response to the Jewish Tradition of Arguing with God," *Journal of Ecumenical Studies* 23, no. 4 (1986) 567–86; David N. Power, "When to Worship Is to Lament," in *Worship: Culture, and Theology* (chap. 4, n. 11, above) 155–73.

20. See Lane, "*HUTZPA K'LAPEI SHAMAYA*," 567. See also Sheila Carney, "God Damn God: A Reflection on Expressing Anger in Prayer," *Biblical Theology Bulletin* 13, no. 4 (1983) 116–20.

21. Brueggemann, "The Costly Loss of Lament, 59.

22. Ibid., 62–63.

23. Soll, "The Israelite Lament," 86.

24. Elie Wiesel, *Night*, trans. Stella Rodway (New York: Bantam Books, 1982) 32.

25. Power, "When to Worship Is to Lament," 167. Note the claim of J.-B. Metz that only Jews can speak of the mystery of God when reflecting on the "catastrophe of Auschwitz" and that Christian theology needs to be thoroughly revised with a view toward Auschwitz ("Facing the Jews: Christian Theology after Auschwitz," in Johann-Baptist Metz and Jürgen Moltmann, *Faith and the Future: Essays on Theology, Solidarity, and Modernity* [Maryknoll, N.Y.: Orbis Books, 1995] 38–48, esp. 43–45).

26. See Sölle, *Suffering*, 61–86.

27. FitzGerald, "Impasse and Dark Night," 112.

28. Brueggemann, *Prophetic Imagination*, 60.

29. David Power proposes a serious challenge for Christian liturgists and preachers when he remarks: "In the present time of cultural disorientation and reorientation, there seems to be place for a fuller use of lament in Christian assemblies, but this requires the courage to let beliefs about God and about Providence be questioned. We may indeed grieve over suffering and oppression, bewail the calamities of the Jewish people, weep over the raped earth, look with sorrow on the church's treatment of women, but do we ever allow this to be a complaint against God?" ("When to Worship Is to Lament," 165).

30. Harrison, "The Power of Anger in the Work of Love" (chap. 5, n. 45, above) 49.

31. Andrae Crouch, "Soon and Very Soon," in *Lead Me, Guide Me* (chap. 2, n. 39, above) no. 4.

32. Moltmann, *Experiences of God,* 33. From a homiletic perspective, see Christine M. Smith, *Preaching as Weeping, Confession, and Resistance* (Louisville: Westminster/John Knox Press, 1992).

33. Johnson, *SHE WHO IS,* 261. See the original essay by Simone Weil, "The Love of God and Affliction," in *Waiting for God,* trans. Emma Crauford (New York: Harper and Row, 1973) 117–36.

34. Johnson, *SHE WHO IS,* 264. Johnson joins a growing number of theologians who speak of the grief or suffering of God. Reflecting on the crucifixion of Jesus in light of the ongoing crucifixion of a growing number of innocent persons, especially women and children, today, she states: "Here if anywhere it can be glimpsed that Wisdom participates in the suffering of the world and overcomes, inconceivably, from within through the power of love" (263).

35. David N. Power, "The Funeral Rites for a Suicide and Liturgical Developments," in *Worship: Culture, and Theology,* 261–69. See also Kent D. Richmond, *Preaching to Sufferers: God and the Problem of Pain* (Nashville: Abingdon, 1988). Recognizing that the homily is an integral part of a larger structure of Christian worship, one might debate further whether it is ever appropriate that liturgical preaching be in the mode of lament without explicit naming of the Christian hope of resurrection. Must every homily or sermon speak of the entire paschal mystery even when preaching is in the context of eucharist or a sacramental celebration? Can the preacher ever "name the grief" in retelling the story of Jesus and allow the liturgical symbols and eucharistic narrative to proclaim the Christian hope?

36. Desmond Tutu, *Hope and Suffering* (Grand Rapids, Mich.: Eerdmans, 1984) 188–89.

37. Cited in Jon Sobrino, *Archbishop Romero: Memories and Reflections,* trans. Robert R. Barr (Maryknoll, N.Y.: Orbis Books, 1990) 99–100.

38. Note that the biblical words *hypomené* and *makrothymía* refer not to passive waiting but to an expectation that bears fruit, a courageous persistence. See A. D. Verhey, "Patience," *The International Standard Bible Encyclopedia,* vol. 3, gen. ed. Geoffrey W. Bromiley (Grand Rapids, Mich.: Eerdmans, 1986) 688–90.

39. FitzGerald, "Impasse and Dark Night," 97.

40. Ibid., 102. Note Clarissa Pinkola Estes's counsel of a similar wisdom drawn from alternative mythic traditions, especially the story of "skeleton woman" (*Women Who Run with the Wolves* [New York: Ballantine Books, 1992] 130–65). Thomas Berry observes something similar on a global scale when he claims: "In each state of its development when it seems that an impasse has been reached, most improbable solutions have emerged that enabled the Earth to continue its development" (*The Dream of the Earth* [chap. 2, n. 37] 223).

41. Viktor E. Frankl, *Man's Search for Meaning: An Introduction to Logotherapy,* 3d ed. (New York: Simon and Schuster, 1984) 88.

42. The phrase is taken from the title of Walter Brueggemann's *Hopeful Imagination: Prophetic Voices in Exile* (Philadelphia: Fortress, 1986).

43. See chapter 4, n. 12, especially the work of Mary Collins and David N. Power. See also Power's "The Holy Spirit: Scripture, Tradition, and Interpretation" (chap. 5, n. 39, above) 152–78.

44. For different theological expressions of how the Spirit of God holds open future possibilities and engenders human freedom, see Karl Rahner, "Theology of Freedom," in *Theological Investigations,* vol. 6 (New York: Seabury, 1974) 178–96; Edward Schillebeeckx, "I Believe in God, Creator of Heaven and Earth," in *God among Us* (chap. 2, n. 17, above) 91–102; Jürgen Moltmann, "Creation as an Open System," in *The Future of Creation* (Philadelphia: Fortress, 1979) 115–30; idem, *God in Creation* (chap. 2, n. 37, above).

45. Amy Tan, *The Joy Luck Club* (New York: Putnam's, 1989) 11–12.

Chapter 8 / Handing on "the Pledge Entrusted" (1 Tim 6:20; 2 Tim 1:14): Doctrinal Preaching

1. Brueggemann, *Finally Comes the Poet* (chap. 5, n. 5, above) 109. See also Karl Rahner, "Priest and Poet" (chap. 2, n. 4, above) 294–317.

2. Joseph Gremillion and Jim Castelli, *The Emerging Parish: The Notre Dame Study of Catholic Life since Vatican II* (San Francisco: Harper and Row, 1987) 134–35, as quoted by Robert P. Waznak, "The Homily Fulfilled in Our Hearing," *Worship* 65 (1991) 27.

3. William J. Carl III, *Preaching Christian Doctrine* (Philadelphia: Fortress, 1984) 60.

4. As reported in Gerard Sloyan's "Is Church Teaching Neglected When the Lectionary is Preached?" *Worship* 61 (1987) 126.

5. See the *Catechism of the Catholic Church* (Washington, D.C.: United States Catholic Conference, 1994). For critical analysis of the use of the catechism in relation to preaching, catechesis, and the Bible, see Robert Waznak, "The Catechism and the Sunday Homily," *America* (October 22, 1994) 18–21; Gerard S. Sloyan, "The Vatican's Catechism in Review: The Use of the Bible in a New Resource Book," *Biblical Theology Bulletin* 25 (1995) 3–13; idem, "A Theological and Pastoral Critique of the *Catechism of the Catholic Church,*" *Horizons* 21 (Spring 1994) 159–78; B. L. Marthaler, ed., *Introducing the Catechism of the Catholic Church: Traditional Themes and Contemporary Issues* (New York: Paulist, 1994), especially the chapters by G. Sloyan and P. Phan; and the April 1994 issue of *Chicago Studies.*

6. In addition to Carl's book, see Wayne Brouwer, "Preaching the Heidelberg: A New Look at the Tradition of Catechetical Preaching," *Reformed Worship* 26 (1992) 38–39; and James Arne Nestigen, "Preaching the Catechism," *Word and World* 10 (1990) 33–42.

7. Carl, a Presbyterian, notes, however, that "Protestants may have traditionally started with a text and Roman Catholics with a doctrine, but the tables have turned in this century — especially with the renewed interest in the Bible among Catholics since Vatican II and the continued interest in topical preaching among Protestants since Fosdick" (*Preaching Christian Doctrine,* 59).

8. See John A. McHugh and Charles J. Callan, *Catechism of the Council of Trent for Parish Priests* (New York: Joseph F. Wagner, 1934). In the introduction to the volume, McHugh and Callan describe their earlier work *A Parochial Course of Doctrinal Instructions for All Sundays and Holydays of the Year Based on the Teachings of the Catechism of the Council of Trent and Harmonized with the Gospels and Epistles of the Sundays and Feasts* (New York: Joseph F. Wagner, 1920–21). That four-volume work follows the order suggested in the preface of the catechism: "A dogmatic or moral subject, drawn from the Gospel or Epistle of the day, is accompanied by the appropriate passage of the Roman Catechism in which the subject is explained and developed" (*The Catechism of the Council of Trent for Parish Priests,* xxxi). For an overview of doctrinal preaching in the medieval period, see D. L. D'Avray, *The Preaching of the Friars: Sermons Diffused from Paris before 1300* (Oxford: Clarendon, 1985).

9. Bernard Cooke, *Ministry to Word and Sacraments* (Philadelphia: Fortress, 1980) 288.

10. Thomas Aquinas, *Summa Theologiae* II–II, q. 1, a. 2, ad 2. See Avery Dulles, *Models of Revelation* (Garden City, N.Y.: Doubleday, 1983) 36–52.

11. Josef Jungmann's phrase. See Grasso, *Proclaiming God's Message* (chap. 2, n. 3, above) xxvi–xxviii.

12. See the discussion of the kerygmatic movement's contribution toward a Catholic theology of preaching in ibid., xxvi–xxvii.

13. E. Haensli, "Doctrinal Preaching," *Sacramentum Mundi,* 5:82–83. See also Hugo Rahner's effort to show how the "new" aspect of kerygmatic preaching was related to "the divine truths of revelation" that priests had learned in dogmatic theology (*A Theology of Proclamation* [New York: Herder, 1968] 11–22).

14. This view is shared by the Anglican and Lutheran traditions. See the Lutheran Book of Worship, Ministers' Edition, 25, 27. Paul V. Marshall remarks, in fact, that this is the "emerging ecumenical conception of the sermon" ("The Liturgy of Preaching," *Liturgy* 1 [1980] 47).

15. Robert P. Waznak, "Homily," in *New Dictionary of Sacramental Worship,* ed. Peter Fink (Collegeville, Minn.: Liturgical Press, 1990) 554.

16. Sloyan, "Is Church Teaching Neglected" 130–31.

17. Skudlarek, *The Word in Worship* (chap. 4, n. 11, above) 17.

18. Sloyan, "Is Church Teaching Neglected?" 131–32.

19. See Catherine Dooley, "Liturgical Catechesis: Mystagogy, Marriage, or Misnomer?" *Worship* 66 (1992) 386–97; and idem, "Catechesis, Catechetics," in *New Dictionary of Theology* (chap. 2, n. 39, above) 161–666. See also Adrien Nocent, "Liturgical Catechesis of the Christian Year," *Worship* 51, no. 6 (1977) 497.

20. Note Rahner's description of a dogmatic statement as "a communal linguistic ruling on terminology" ("What Is a Dogmatic Statement?" *Theological Investigations,* vol. 5, trans. Karl-H. Kruger [Baltimore: Helicon, 1966] 54). See also George Lindbeck, *The Nature of Doctrine: Religion and Theology in a Postliberal Age* (Philadelphia: Westminster, 1984).

21. Karl Rahner, "Current Problems in Christology," in *Theological Investigations,* vol. 1, trans. Cornelius Ernst (New York: Seabury, 1974) esp. 157–61, 173–74, and 200.

22. Barth, *The Preaching of the Gospel* (chap. 1, n. 13, above) 31. See also Sloyan's review of major challenges to the gospel throughout Christian history and his conclusion regarding doctrines: "[T]hey do not enable us to comprehend the divine-human relation, they provide us with a language to keep from saying false and foolish things about it as we expound the Scriptures" ("Is Church Teaching Neglected?" 134).

Determining what is the authentic doctrine of the church requires a critical reading of the tradition and of dogmatic and magisterial statements. This topic goes beyond the scope of the present chapter, but for an overview of issues involved, see Avery Dulles, *The Survival of Dogma* (Garden City, N.Y.: Doubleday, 1971) esp. chap. 11; Walter Principe, "When Authentic Teachings Change," *The Ecumenist* (July–August 1987) 7–73; Yves Congar, "Reception as an Ecclesiological Reality," in *Election and Consensus in the Church,* ed. G. Alberigo and A. Weiler (New York: Herder, 1972) 43–68; Rahner, "What Is a Dogmatic Statement?" 42–66; idem, "Considerations on the Development of Dogma," in *Theological Investigations* 4:3–35; idem, "Basic Observations on the Subject of the Changeable and Unchangeable Factors in the Church," in *Theological Investigations* 14:3–23; Piet Schoonenberg, "Historicity and the Interpretation of Dogma," *Theology Digest* 18 (1970) 132–43; and International Theological Commission, "On the Interpretation of Dogmas," *Origins* 20 (1990) 1, 3–12.

23. Sloyan, "Is Church Teaching Neglected?" 126.

24. Ibid., 135.

25. For a helpful overview of this development, see Geoffrey Wainwright, "Doctrine, Liturgy and," in *New Dictionary of Sacramental Worship,* 349–58.

26. Gerard Sloyan, "What Is Liturgical Preaching?" *Liturgy* 8 (1989) 10. Biblical preaching, however, is not necessarily liturgical. See Sloyan's examples of the diverse forms of biblical preaching in the Armenian church, North American black churches, and evangelical white churches (9–10).

27. Lathrop, "A Rebirth of Images" (chap. 4, n. 8, above). See also David N. Power, "Liturgical Praxis: A New Consciousness at the Eye of Worship," in *Worship* (chap. 4, n. 12, above) 127–42; and Mary Collins, "Critical Questions for Liturgical Theology," in *Worship: Renewal to Practice* (chap. 2, n. 36, above) 115–32; and idem, "Liturgical Spirituality in a Pluralistic Culture" (chap. 4, n. 12, above).

28. Constitution on Sacred Liturgy, no. 52.

29. Catherine Dooley's description of Cyril of Jerusalem's catechetical homilies ("Liturgical Catechesis," 392).

30. Burghardt, "Catechetics in the Early Church: Program and Psychology," *The Living Light* 1, no. 3 (1964) 107. While the contemporary liturgical homily is not ordinarily in the mode of extended mystagogical preaching, nonetheless, as John Paul II has pointed out, all authentic liturgy "is bound to have a catechetical aspect" (*Catechesi Tradendae* [October 16, 1979] 23 [DOL 76]).

31. Dooley, "Liturgical Catechesis," 395. On preaching and mystagogy, see Geoffrey Wainwright, "Preaching as Worship," *Greek Orthodox Theological*

Review 28 (1983) 325–36; idem, "The Sermon and the Liturgy," *Greek Orthodox Theological Review* 28 (1983) 337–49; Walter Burghardt, "Do This in Memory of Me: The Homily as Liturgy," in *Preaching: The Art and the Craft* (chap. 4, n. 3, above) 108–18; Gerard Sloyan, *Worshipful Preaching* (Philadelphia: Fortress, 1984); Samuel E. Torvend, "Preaching the Liturgy: A Social Mystagogy," in *In the Company of Preachers,* ed. Regina Siegfried and Edward Ruane (Collegeville, Minn.: Liturgical Press, 1993) 48–65; John Allyn Melloh, "Preaching, Liturgical Ministry of," *The New Dictionary of Sacramental Worship,* 991–93; idem, "Preaching and Liturgy," *Worship* 65 (1991) 414–15; idem, "The Liturgical Homily," *Assembly* 7, no. 2 (1980) 106–7; John Baldovin, "Biblical Preaching in the Liturgy," *Studia Liturgica* 22 (1992) 112–13. For connections between mystagogy and lament, see Lathrop's "Rebirth of Images." Lathrop contends that "mystagogy into the book and the assembly must be mystagogy into the disappointment and pain and prayer which is in the book" (299).

32. Karl Rahner, "Theology and Anthropology," in *The Word in History,* ed. T. Patrick Burke (New York: Sheed and Ward, 1966) 18. Note also David Buttrick's observation that the homiletician is a "reverse theologian" seeking to discover new images to point to the experience that the doctrine is intended to preserve ("Homiletics and Rhetoric" [lecture delivered at Pittsburgh Theological Seminary, April 16, 1979], as cited in Carl, *Preaching Christian Doctrine,* 29).

33. See Karl Rahner, "The Concept of Mystery in Catholic Theology," in *Theological Investigations* 4:36–76. For further discussion of the mystagogical dimension of doctrines, see Rahner, "What Is a Dogmatic Statement?" 58–60; James J. Bacik, *Apologetics and the Eclipse of Mystery: Mystagogy according to Karl Rahner* (Notre Dame, Ind.: University of Notre Dame Press, 1980); Mary E. Hines, *The Transformation of Dogma: An Introduction to Karl Rahner on Doctrine* (New York: Paulist, 1989); and Peter Chirico, "Religious Experience and Development of Dogma," *American Benedictine Review* 23 (1972) 363–78.

34. See Thomas J. Talley, "The Liturgical Year: Pattern of Proclamation," in *Reforming Tradition* (Washington, D.C.: Pastoral Press, 1990) 125. On the relationship between preaching and the liturgical year, see Frank C. Quinn, "Liturgy: Foundation and Context for Preaching," in *In the Company of Preachers,* 7–25; Robert Taft, "The Liturgical Year: Studies, Prospects, Reflections," *Worship* 55 (1981) 2–22; and Skudlarek, *The Word in Worship* (chap. 4, n. 10, above) 11–30.

35. See Catherine M. LaCugna, "Making the Most of Trinity Sunday," *Worship* 60 (1986) 210–24.

36. See Charles E. Bouchard, "Authentic Preaching on Moral Issues," in *In the Company of Preachers,* 191–209; and Edward J. van Merrienboer, "Preaching the Social Gospel," in *In the Company of Preachers,* 176–90. Note Bouchard's emphasis on the close relationship between morality and spirituality and van Merrienboer's stress on clarifying the gospel value involved in a specific social or political issue. See also Walter J. Burghardt, "Let Justice Roll Down Like Waters: Preaching the Just Word," in *Preaching,* 119–38; and Empereur and Kiesling, "Preaching and the Transformation of the World," in *The*

Liturgy That Does Justice (chap. 4, n. 12, above) 82–108. On the relationship between liturgy and moral theology, see Enda McDonagh, *The Making of Disciples* (Wilmington, Del.: Glazier, 1982); and Don E. Saliers, "Liturgy and Ethics: Some New Beginnings," *Journal of Religious Ethics* 7, no. 2 (1979) 173–89. See further references in chap. 4, n. 12, above.

37. See chapter 5, esp. notes 21–27. See also Marjorie Procter-Smith, "Images of Women in the Lectionary," in *Women — Invisible in Theology and Church,* ed. Elisabeth Schüssler Fiorenza and Mary Collins (Edinburgh: T. & T. Clark, 1985) 51–62.

38. Marshall, "The Liturgy of Preaching," 49.

39. Sloyan, "Is Church Teaching Being Neglected," 137.

40. Ibid. For the comment that all were moralists, see ibid., 129. In an earlier article, Sloyan's critiques of the lectionary are far more pointed. See "The Lectionary as a Context for Interpretation," *Interpretation* 31 (1977) 131–38.

41. For bibliography on critical discussion of the relationship between liturgy and justice, see chap. 4, note 12.

42. R. E. C. Browne, *The Ministry of the Word* (Philadelphia: Fortress, 1958) 47.

43. Rahner, "What Is a Dogmatic Statement?" 53.

44. The article is in M.-D. Chenu, *Is Theology a Science?* (New York: Hawthorn, 1959) 14–18.

45. Note Aquinas's description of the theological task as reflection on all of reality in relation to God (*Summa Theologiae* 1a, q. 1, a. 7). See also Simone Weil's essay "Reflections on the Right Use of School Studies with a View to the Love of God," in *Waiting for God* (chap. 7, n. 33, above) 105–16. At the same time, note John Baldovin's plea for "modesty" within the liturgical homily: "It is simply a response in faith by a limited human being in a specific situation. I am convinced that the best a preacher can do week-in and week-out with sensitivity to the liturgical assembly, to the assembly's act of thanksgiving, and to the scriptures that are determined for the day, is to discern one thing that needs to be said in this situation and say it imaginatively enough to have an impact. In my experience many a promising homily flounders on the shoals of overambition." ("Biblical Preaching in the Liturgy," 113–14).

46. See Carla Mae Streeter, "The Role of Theological Communication in the Act of Preaching," in *In the Company of Preachers,* 102–12; and William J. Hill, "Preaching as a 'Moment' in Theology," *Homiletic and Pastoral Review* 77 (1976) 10–19 (reprinted in *Search for the Absent God,* ed. M. C. Hilkert [New York: Crossroad, 1992] 177–86).

47. See Rodriguez, *Our Lady of Guadalupe* (chap. 2, n. 38); and Virgilio P. Elizondo, "Our Lady of Guadalupe as a Cultural Symbol: The Power of the Powerless," in *Liturgy and Cultural Religious Traditions,* vol. 102 of *Concilium,* ed. Herman Schmidt and David Power (New York: Seabury, 1977) 25–33. On popular religion as a source of theological reflection, see Roberto S. Goizueta, "Rediscovering Praxis: The Significance of U.S. Hispanic Experience for Theological Method," in *We Are a People!* (chap. 2, n. 38, above) 51–77; Orlando O. Espin, "Tradition and Popular Religion: An Understanding of the *Sensus Fidelium,*" in *Frontiers of Hispanic Theology in the United States* (chap. 2, n. 38,

above) 62–87; Sixto J. Garcia, "Sources and Loci of Hispanic Theology," *Journal of Hispanic/Latino Theology* 1, no. 1 (November 1993) 22–43; Juan José Huitrado-Rizo, "Hispanic Popular Religiosity: The Expression of a People Coming to Life," *New Theology Review* 3, no. 4 (November 1990) 43–55; and bibliography in chap. 2, n. 38.

48. See Ricoeur, *The Symbolism of Evil* (chap. 3, n. 2, above) 347–53.

49. See Monika Hellwig, *Whose Experience Counts in Theological Reflection?* (Milwaukee: Marquette University Press, 1982). For the critical questions this raises in any dialogue between feminism and Roman Catholicism, see M. C. Hilkert, "Experience and Tradition," in *Freeing Theology* (chap. 2, n. 30, above) 59–82.

50. In one of the most important shifts in Vatican II's Constitution on Divine Revelation, that document says "the Word of God has been entrusted to the entire church" (rather than, as previously, "solely to the magisterium") (*Dei Verbum,* no. 10). For the importance of this article, see Joseph Ratzinger, "The Transmission of Divine Revelation," *Commentary on the Documents of Vatican II,* ed. Herbert Vorgrimler (New York: Herder and Herder, 1969) 111:181–98.

51. In the Roman Catholic tradition, *Dei Verbum* clearly states that the ultimate judgment of the authenticity of an interpretation of the word of God "has been entrusted to the living teaching office of the Church alone." However, that authority is itself subject to a higher authority: "Yet this Magisterium is not superior to the Word of God, but its servant" (no. 10).

Chapter 9 / Women Preaching the Gospel

1. The biblical translations in this chapter are taken from the New American Bible, the translation used most frequently in the Roman Catholic liturgical context.

2. Bernard of Clairvaux, *Sermones in Cantica,* Serm. 75, 8 (PL 183, 1148).

3. For one helpful discussion of the dilemma, see Schneiders, *Beyond Patching* (chap. 5, n. 3, above). The literature on women's spirituality and ministry is too vast to survey here, but several volumes that provide helpful overviews of Christian feminist spirituality, include Conn, *Women's Spirituality* (chap. 7, n. 6, above); Fabella and Oduyoye, *With Passion and Compassion* (chap. 2, n. 25, above); Mary Jo Weaver, *Springs of Water in a Dry Land* (Boston: Beacon, 1992); Miriam Therese Winter, Adair Lummis, and Allison Stokes, eds., *Defecting in Place: Women Claiming Responsibility for Their Own Spiritual Lives* (New York: Crossroad, 1994); and Rodriguez, *Stories We Live/Cuentos Que Vivimos* (chap. 2, n. 38, above). For some women the crisis of confronting patriarchy within Christianity and the Christian churches has led to an "exodus from Christianity" and a post-Christian identity. For an early survey of feminist theology that includes a review of the move toward post-Christian feminism, see Carol P. Christ, "The New Feminist Theology: A Review of the Literature," *Religious Studies Review* 3 (1977) 203–12. See also Mary Daly, *Beyond God the Father: Toward a Philosophy of Women's Liberation* (Boston: Beacon, 1973);

Carol P. Christ, *Laughter of Aphrodite: Reflections on a Journey to the Goddess* (San Francisco: Harper and Row, 1987); and Daphne Hampson, *Theology and Feminism* (Oxford: Blackwell, 1990). For a collection that includes a breadth of contemporary approaches to feminist spirituality, see Judith Plaskow and Carol P. Christ, *Weaving the Visions: New Patterns in Feminist Spirituality* (San Francisco: Harper and Row, 1989).

4. Canon 767.1. See John Burke and Thomas P. Doyle, *The Homilist's Guide to Scripture, Theology, and Canon Law* (New York: Pueblo, 1986); and Joseph Fox, "The Homily and the Authentic Interpretation of Canon 767.1," *Apollinaris* 62 (1989) 123–69. For an alternative interpretation of canon law on this question, see James H. Provost, "Canon Law in a Time of Transition," in *Preaching and the Non-ordained* (chap. 3, n. 19, above) 134–58; idem, "Canon 766," in *Roman Replies and CLSA Advisory Opinions 1986*, ed. William A. Schumacher and J. James Cuneo (Washington, D.C.: Canon Law Society of America, 1986) 71–73; idem, "Brought Together by the Word of the Living God (Canons 762–772)," *Studia Canonica* 23 (1989) 345–71; J. A. Coriden, "The Preaching of the Word of God (cc. 762–772)," in *The Code of Canon Law: A Text and Commentary,* ed. J. A. Coriden, T. J. Green, and D. E. Heintschel, commissioned by the Canon Law Society of America (New York: Paulist, 1985) 551–55; John M. Huels, "The Law on Lay Preaching: Interpretation and Implementation," *Proceedings of the Canon Law Society of America* 52 (1990) 61–79; idem, "The Ministry of the Divine Word (Canons 756–61)," *Studia Canonica* 23 (1989) 325–44; idem, *Disputed Questions in the Liturgy Today* (Chicago: Liturgy Training Publications, 1988) 17–25. See also James A. Wallace, "Guidelines for Preaching by the Laity: Another Step Backward?" *America* (September 16, 1989) 139–41; J. Frank Henderson, "The Minister of Liturgical Preaching," *Worship* 56 (1982) 214–30; and William Skudlarek, "Lay Preaching and the Liturgy," *Worship* 58 (1984) 501–6.

5. Note the stories of contemporary women preachers as chronicled in David Albert Farmer and Edwina Hunter, eds., *And Blessed Is She* (New York: Harper and Row, 1990). Farmer observes that "women who preach still are not widely recognized in mainstream Protestantism — and certainly not in Catholicism — as the equals of male preachers, and the greatest evidence of the fact is the limited opportunity for women to preach" (3). See also "New Voices in the Pulpit," *Emory Magazine* 67, no. 1 (1991) 17–25.

6. See Johnson, *SHE WHO IS* (chap. 2, n. 30, above), and the bibliography included there. For a concise overview, consult Johnson's earlier article, "The Incomprehensibility of God and the Image of God Male and Female" (chap. 2, n. 34, above).

7. Even the Vatican declaration *Inter Insigniores* recognizes that women were the first witnesses to the resurrection and the first charged by Jesus to announce the paschal message. Note, however, that the document distinguishes between women and "the apostles themselves" and states that only the latter are the "official witnesses to the resurrection" (Congregation for the Doctrine of the Faith, "Declaration on the Question of Admission of Women to the Ministerial Priesthood" [October 15, 1976] *Origins* 6 [February 3, 1977] 520).

8. Task Force on the Role of 'Women in Early Christianity, "Women and Priestly Ministry: The New Testament Evidence," *Catholic Biblical Quarterly* 41 (October 1979) 610. See also Schüssler Fiorenza, *In Memory of Her* (chap. 5, n. 13, above). Regarding the specific ministry of preaching, see Sandra Schneiders, "New Testament Foundations for Preaching by the Non-ordained," in *Preaching and the Non-ordained*, 60–90.

9. See, for example, Schüssler Fiorenza, *In Memory of Her*, 226–30; and Jerome Murphy-O'Connor, *1 Corinthians* (Wilmington, Del.: Glazier, 1979) 104–9. Murphy-O'Connor observes that this form of praying and prophesying is "a ministry of the word deriving from a profound knowledge of the mysteries of God based on the scriptures. It would be very difficult to justify a distinction between prophecy in this sense and our contemporary liturgical homily" (105).

10. While the name is a well known one for women at that time, exegetes, before recent challenges from feminist scholars, had commonly interpreted it as the shortened form of the male name Junianus. The operative patriarchal assumption was that a woman could not have been an apostle; hence the name must have been either incorrect or abbreviated.

11. Again, however, because the *diakonos* in this case is female, exegetes and translators traditionally translated the term as "deaconess" and argued that her role was not parallel to that of male deacons.

12. See Sandra Schneiders, "Women in the Fourth Gospel and the Role of Women in the Contemporary Church," *Biblical Theology Bulletin* 12 (1982) 35–45; and Raymond E. Brown, "Roles of Women in the Fourth Gospel," *Theological Studies* 36 (1975) 688–99.

13. Robert J. Karris, "Women in the Pauline Assembly: To Prophesy but Not to Speak?" in *Women Priests: A Catholic Commentary on the Vatican Declaration,* ed. Arlene and Leonard Swidler (New York: Paulist, 1977) 205–8. For an overview of the debate about the Pauline authenticity of this passage and related feminist scholarship, see Caroline Vander Stichele, "Is Silence Golden? Paul and Women's Speech in Corinth," in *The Ministry of the Word: Essays in Honor of Prof. D. Raymond F. Collins,* ed. Joseph A. Selling, *Louvain Studies* 20 (1995) 241–53.

14. See Barbara Brown Zikmund, "The Struggle for the Right to Preach," in *Women and Religion in America,* vol. 1, ed. Rosemary Radford Ruether and Rosemary Skinner Keller (New York: Harper and Row, 1981) 193–205. Note that the texts are still used as the basis for the prohibition of women to "the divinely instituted ministry of Word and sacraments" in some traditions such as the Lutheran Church—Missouri Synod. See "Women in the Church: Scriptural Principles and Ecclesial Practice, a Report of the Commission on Theology and Church Relations of the Lutheran Church—Missouri Synod" (September 1985). While the biblical texts were not the basis for women's restriction from preaching in the Roman Catholic Church, that restriction was taken for granted by most Catholics until the 1970s.

15. See especially the following studies: Yves Congar, *Lay People in the Church* (Westminster, Md.: Christian Classics, 1985); idem, "My Path-findings in the Theology of Laity and Ministries," *The Jurist* 32 (1972) 169–88; Edward Schillebeeckx, *Ministry: Leadership in the Community of Jesus Christ*

(New York: Crossroad, 1981); idem, *The Church with a Human Face* (New York: Crossroad, 1985); David Power, *Gifts That Differ: Lay Ministries Established and Unestablished* (New York: Pueblo, 1980) 59–87; Mary Collins, "The Public Language of Ministry," in *Worship: Renewal to Practice* (chap. 2, n. 36, above) 137–73; Cooke, *Ministry to Word and Sacrament* (chap. 8, n. 9, above); Thomas F. O'Meara, *Theology of Ministry* (New York: Paulist, 1983) 95–133; and Joseph Komonchak, "Church and Ministry," *The Jurist* 43 (1983) 273–88.

For specific discussion of the shift of the preaching ministry from various charismatic ministries to the official ministry of *episkopos* and later of *presbyter,* see Thomas K. Carroll, *Preaching the Word* (Wilmington, Del.: Glazier, 1984); Edward P. Echlin, *The Priest as Preacher Past and Future* (Notre Dame, Ind.: Fides, 1973); Collins, "The Baptismal Roots of the Preaching Ministry" (chap. 3, n. 19, above).

16. *The Church History of Eusebius* 6.19.16, trans. Arthur Cushman McGiffert, in *The Nicene and Post-Nicene Fathers,* ed. Philip Schaff and Henry Wace (Grand Rapids, Mich.: Eerdmans, 1952) 267.

17. *Didascalia Apostolorum* 3.6, trans. R. Hugh Connolly (Oxford: Clarendon, 1929) 133. For a well-documented study of the historical development of lay preaching and its prohibitions with particular attention to canonical issues and developments, see Elissa Rinere, "Authorization for Lay Preaching in the Church" (J.C.L. diss., Catholic University of America, 1981). For critical theological analysis of the question, see Schillebeeckx, "The Right of Every Christian to Speak in Light of Evangelical Experience 'in the Midst of Brothers and Sisters' " (chap. 3, n. 19, above); idem, *The Church with a Human Face,* 174–89; and Congar, *Lay People in the Church,* 271–323.

18. Translation by Rinere, p. 21. Cf. F. X. Funk, *Didascalia et Constitutiones Apostolorum* (Paderborn: Ferdinandi Schoeningh, 1905) 539.

19. *St. Leo the Great: Letters,* no. 119, trans. Edmund Hunt (New York: Fathers of the Church, 1957) 207–8. Cf. the Council of Trullo, quoting Gregory the Theologian: "Why dost thou make thyself a shepherd when thou art a sheep? Why become a head when thou art the foot? Why dost thou try to become a commander when thou art enrolled in the number of soldiers?" (Council of Trullo, canon 64, in *The Seven Ecumenical Councils,* trans. Henry Percival [New York: Charles Scribner's Sons, 1905] 394).

20. Peter Dronke, *Women Writers of the Middle Ages* (New York: Cambridge University Press, 1984) 149. Note G. R. Owst's comment that "it was not without a considerable struggle that this right of preaching in formal fashion in church was completely wrested from [abbesses]" (*Preaching in Medieval England* [New York: Russell and Russell, 1965] 5).

21. See Congar, *Lay People in the Church,* 300–302; and Herbert Grundmann, *Religious Movements in the Middle Ages,* trans. Steven Rowan (Notre Dame, Ind.: University of Notre Dame Press, 1995) 219–26. On the controversy surrounding lay preaching in the Middle Ages, see William Skudlarek, "Assertion without Knowledge? The Lay Preaching Controversy of the High Middle Ages" (Ph.D. diss., Princeton University, 1979), and Rolf Zerfass, *Der Streit um die Laienpredigt* (Freiburg: Herder, 1974).

22. Janet Nelson, "Society, Theodicy, and the Origins of Medieval Heresy," in *Studies in Church History*, ed. Derek Baker, vol. 9: *Schism, Heresy, and Religious Protest* (Cambridge: Cambridge University Press, 1972) 74.

23. Historians who have studied the Franciscan Order note that "any of the brethren, layman or cleric, that had the spirit of God, he gave the permission to preach" (*Legenda trium sociorum* [*Acta Sanctorum*, October 11, 737–38], as quoted by M.-D. Chenu in *Nature, Man, and Society in the Twelfth Century* [Chicago: University of Chicago Press, 1968] 261). Anscar Zawart notes that this permission included both liturgical preaching and the exhortative sermon (Anscar Zawart, *The History of Franciscan Preaching and Franciscan Preachers, 1209–1927*, Franciscan Studies 7 [New York: J. Wagner, 1928] 262). Early on, however, the Franciscan Order became clericalized, though not without "qualms of conscience for Brother Francis" (Chenu, *Nature, Man, and Society in the Twelfth Century*, 260).

24. See Grundmann, *Religious Movements in the Middle Ages*.

25. See *Summa Theologiae*, II–II, q. 177, a. 1, reply, for Aquinas's description of the "charism of speaking" as a grace given for the profit of others to instruct them and to move their affections so that both speaker and hearer may love what is signified by the word and desire to fulfill it. For his argument that women clearly are given this charism, see *Summa Theologiae* II–II, q. 177, a. 2, 1 and ad 1. For the reasons why women should not preach publicly (female sex is divinely intended to be subordinate to the male; men's minds may be enticed to lust; and, generally speaking, women are not perfected in wisdom so as to be fit public teachers), see *Summa Theologiae* II–II, q. 177, a. 2, reply.

26. Note one of the questions used to determine heresy in the interrogations of suspected followers of Wycliffe and Hus at the Council of Constance: "Does the person believe it is permissible for people of either sex, men as well as women, to preach freely the word of God?" (Denzinger-Schönmetzer, *Enchiridion symbolorum*, 1277; translated and quoted by Rinere, 101).

27. See Margaret Askew Fell, *Women's Speaking Justified* (1667) (Los Angeles: William Andrews Clark Memorial Library, University of California, 1979); Phoebe Palmer, *The Promise of the Father* (New York: W. C. Palmer, 1872); Almond H. Davis, *The Female Preacher or Memoir of Salome Lincoln* (New York: Arno, 1972); Frances Willard, *Woman in the Pulpit* (Boston: Lothrop, ca. 1888); Louisa M. Woolsley, *Shall Women Preach? or The Question Answered* (1891) (quoted in Hunter and Farmer, *And Blessed Is She*, 11).

On the history of women's preaching in the U.S. context, see Zikmund, "The Struggle for the Right to Preach," and the original source documents included in *Women and Religion in America* (1:206–41). See also Martha Tomhave Blauvelt and Rosemary Skinner Keller, "Women and Revivalism: The Puritan and Wesleyan Traditions," in *Women and Religion in America*, vol. 2 (San Francisco: Harper and Row, 1983) 316–67; Dorothy Sterling, ed., *We Are Your Sisters: Black Women in the Nineteenth Century* (New York: Norton, 1984); Bert Lowenberg and Ruth Bogin, eds., *Black Women in Nineteenth-century American Life* (University Park: Penn State University Press, 1976); Jualynne Dodson, "Nineteenth-century A.M.E. Preaching Women," in *Woman in New Worlds*, ed Hilah F. Thomas and Rosemary S. Keller (Nashville: Abingdon, 1981) 276–89;

E. Glenn Hinson, "The Church: Liberator or Oppressor of Women?" *Review and Expositor* 72 (1975) 25–26; Georgia Harkness, *Women in Church and Society* (Nashville: Abingdon, 1972) 95–98. For a brief overview and samples of women's sermons, see Farmer and Hunter, eds., *And Blessed Is She.*

28. Zikmund, "The Struggle for the Right to Preach," 193–94.

29. Toward the end of the century, new groups that did allow the ordination of women formed, including the Brethren Church as a split-off of the German Baptist Brethren in the early 1880s and the Church of the Nazarene in 1894.

30. Women were ordained for the first time by the Northern Baptists in 1901; the Nazarenes, in 1908; and the Mennonites, in 1911. The northern branch of the United Presbyterian Church (United Presbyterian Church, U.S.A.) first ordained a woman in 1956; the southern branch (Presbyterian, U.S.), in 1964. The Methodist Episcopal Church decided to open ordination to women in 1956. See Farmer and Hunter, *And Blessed Is She,* 13.

31. For the major official pronouncements of North American religious bodies and ecumenical organizations on women's ordination through 1991, see J. Gordon Melton, *The Churches Speak on Women's Ordination* (New York: Gale Research, 1991). While the first woman minister was ordained within the Southern Baptist Church in 1964, and some women continue to be ordained and receive calls as pastors by individual churches, the majority of delegates at the Southern Baptist Convention in June 1984 voted for a resolution against the ordination of women. The Lutheran Church—Missouri Synod remains firmly opposed to women's ordination on biblical grounds. See Commission on Theology and Church Relations of the Lutheran Church—Missouri Synod, *Women in the Church: Scriptural Principles and Ecclesial Practice* (September 1985). In the Roman Catholic tradition, Pope John Paul II reiterated the view that "the Church has no authority whatsoever to confer priestly ordination on women" in his apostolic letter *Ordinatio Sacerdotalis* (May 22, 1994). On October 28, 1995, Joseph Ratzinger issued a statement as prefect of the Congregation for the Doctrine of the Faith claiming that that teaching is to be understood "as belonging to the deposit of faith" and "has been set forth infallibly by the ordinary and universal Magisterium," although that assertion remains a source of conflict among Roman Catholics. See Ladislas Orsy, "The Congregation's 'Response': Its Authority and Meaning," *America* 173 (December 9, 1995) 4–5; Francis A. Sullivan, "Guideposts from Catholic Tradition," *America* 173 (December 9, 1995) 5–6. For recent discussion of the Orthodox position, see Elisabeth Behr-Sigel, *The Ministry of Women in the Church* (Redondo Beach, Calif.: Oakwood Publications, 1991); Thomas Hopko, ed., *Women and the Priesthood* (Crestwood, N.Y.: St. Vladimir's Seminary Press, 1983); and Kenneth Paul Wesche, "Man and Woman in Orthodox Tradition: The Mystery of Gender," *Saint Vladimir's Theological Quarterly* 37 (1993) 213–51.

32. In 1990 Edwina Hunter noted that "percentages from a number of mainline denominations indicate that ordained women fill 10 to 40 percent of denominational posts and less than 10 percent of parish pastor positions" (*And Blessed Is She,* 89; see also 14).

33. See Zikmund, "The Struggle for the Right to Preach," 200–204, 223–41.

34. Leontyne T. C. Kelly, "Preaching in the Black Tradition," in *Women Ministers: How Women Are Redefining Traditional Roles,* rev. ed., ed. Judith L. Weidman (San Francisco: Harper and Row, 1985) 73-74. See also Gilkes, " 'Some Mother's Son and Some Father's Daughter' " (chap. 5, n. 8, above) 82-87; Cheryl J. Sanders, "The Woman as Preacher," in *African-American Religious Studies* (chap. 2, n. 39, above); Katie G. Cannon, "Womanist Interpretation and Preaching in the Black Church," *Searching the Scriptures* (chap. 2, n. 38, above) 1:326-37; and Ella Pearson Mitchell, ed., *Those Preaching Women: Sermons by Black Women Preachers,* 2 vols. (Valley Forge, Pa.: Judson, 1988).

35. Charles W. Torrey, "Women's Sphere in the Church," *Congregational Quarterly* 9 (April 1867) 170, as quoted by Zikmund, 196. See also Zikmund, "The Struggle for the Right to Preach," 194-200, 208-23.

36. Although "unbroken tradition" rather than specific authoritative biblical texts is at the heart of the dispute among Catholics, the debate continues in the Roman Catholic community as to whether this restriction is by divine will or human law. (See n. 31 for the position of John Paul II, which the Vatican Congregation for the Doctrine of the Faith has declared to be "infallible" and for responses by Catholic theologians.) Note also that some Roman Catholic feminists oppose the movement toward women's ordination in the present church structures as misguided efforts for women to be included in "the clerical hierarchy in its Constantinian form." See Elisabeth Schüssler Fiorenza, "Should Women Aim for Ordination to the Lowest Rung of the Hierarchical Ladder?" in *Discipleship of Equals* (chap. 2, n. 35, above) 23-38.

37. Thomas O'Meara suggests that "Church ministry expanding throughout the world suggests that the Holy Spirit is intent upon a wider service, a more diverse ministry for a church life that will be broader in quantity and richer in quality" (*Theology of Ministry,* 5; see also Power, *Gifts That Differ;* and Kenan B. Osborne, *Ministry: Lay Ministry in the Roman Catholic Church* [New York: Paulist, 1993]).

38. See n. 4.

39. In addition to the Dogmatic Constitution on the Church, see the Pastoral Constitution on the Church in the Modern World (*Gaudium et Spes*); the Decree on the Apostolate of the Laity (*Apostolicam Actuositatem*); and the Decree on the Church's Missionary Activity (*Ad Gentes Divinitus*). For helpful overviews of these major shifts, see Avery Dulles, *Models of the Church,* rev. ed. (New York: Doubleday, 1987); Richard P. McBrien, "Catholic Church" and "Vatican Council II," in *Encyclopedia of Catholicism,* 242-53, 1299-1306; Herman J. Pottmeyer, "Dogmatic Constitution on the Church," in *Encyclopedia of Catholicism,* ed. Richard P. McBrien (San Francisco: HarperCollins, 1995) 425-27; Joseph A. Komonchak, "Vatican Council II," in *The New Dictionary of Theology* (chap. 2, n. 39, above) 1072-77. For further discussion of theology of ministry and specifically "lay ministries," see references in notes 15 and 37.

40. Decree on the Apostolate of the Laity, 3.

41. Dogmatic Constitution on Divine Revelation (*Dei Verbum*) 10.

42. Decree on the Church's Missionary Activity, 35.

43. Dogmatic Constitution on the Church, 30.

44. Although it is not the focus of this chapter, it is significant to note that Vatican II also stressed that preaching is central to the identity and mission of both bishop and priest. See Decree on the Bishops' Pastoral Office in the Church (*Christus Dominus*) 12, and Decree on the Ministry and Life of Priests (*Presbyterorum Ordinis*) 4.

45. Roman Catholic Church law includes not only the Code of Canon Law but also the documents of Vatican II, postconciliar decrees implementing the council renewal, liturgical law, special indults and permissions, and customs of church people. See James H. Provost, "Lay Preaching and Canon Law in a Time of Transition," in *Preaching and the Non-ordained,* 134–58.

46. "Die Beteiligung der Laien an der Verkundigung," 2, 33, trans. William Skudlarek, appendix 3 in "Assertion without Knowledge?" This was part of the reasoning of the West German bishops in their 1973 request to the Congregation for the Clergy for authorized lay preaching at eucharist. In their request, which was granted for eight years, the bishops allude to the shortage of clergy, the number of theologically literate laypersons in Germany, and, finally, their most basic concern: more effective preaching. For the authorization, see the letter of Cardinal J. Wright, prefect of the Congregation for the Clergy, to Cardinal J. Döpfner, president of the German Bishops' Conference, November 20, 1973, in *Archiv für katholisches Kirchenrecht* 142 (1973) 480–82 and in DOL, doc. 344, nos. 2953–63, 914–16. Similar permissions were granted by the Swiss, Austrian, and East German bishops. See H. Mussinghoff, "Predigt des Wortes Gottes," in *Münsterischer Kommentar zum Codex iuris canonici,* ed. K. Lüdicke (Essen: Ludgerus, 1987) at can. 766, pp. 1–2, as cited by Provost, "Brought together by the Word of the Living God," 358, n. 42.

47. Directory of Masses for Children, 24, ICEL translation in *Documents on the Liturgy 1963–1979* (Collegeville, Minn.: Liturgical Press, 1982) 682.

48. Synod of Bishops, *Justice in the World* (chap. 2, n. 20, above) 34.

49. On this point, see David Power, *Gifts That Differ,* 13–15; and Joseph A. Komonchak, " 'Non-ordained' and 'Ordained' Ministers in the Local Church," in *The Right of the Community to a Priest,* vol. 133 of *Concilium,* ed. J. B. Metz and E. Schillebeeckx (New York: Seabury, 1980) 44–49.

50. See n. 4.

51. See Komonchak, " 'Non-Ordained and 'Ordained' Ministries in the Local Church," 47.

52. William Skudlarek, "A Response [to Edward Schillebeeckx]," in *Preaching and the Non-ordained,* 59. Cf. Power, *Gifts That Differ,* 155; and Komonchak, " 'Non-ordained' and 'Ordained' Ministers in the Local Church," 48.

53. Throughout this book I have been using the term "baptized" to connote the full process of Christian initiation. In the Roman Catholic tradition that process includes the three sacraments of initiation — baptism, confirmation, and eucharist. See the general introduction to the Rite of Christian Initiation, *The Rites of the Catholic Church,* study edition (New York: Pueblo, 1976) 3–4.

54. Mary Collins, "Baptismal Roots of the Preaching Ministry," 130. David Power proposes instead: "Rather than argue for the laity's right to give the homily, and thus disrupt the presidency of the assembly, it is much better to

explore the many different ways in which all the members of the assembly can share in breaking the bread of God's word for one another." At the same time, Power notes that the practice of lay preaching of the liturgical homily "can be a practical gesture on the part of an entire congregation, or on the part of its priests or bishops, that by calling on some member or members of the laity to give the homily they influence the situation with regard to the process of choosing candidates for ordination" (*Gifts That Differ*, 154–55).

55. The introduction to the lectionary, 24, 50 (Washington: D.C.: United States Catholic Conference, 1982).

56. Joseph Komonchak registers three concerns regarding the ecclesially approved assumption by lay ministers of roles that were traditionally restricted to the ordained (including liturgical preaching): (1) effective sundering of pastoral ministries from the ordained pastorate; (2) disruption of relationship between church and eucharist; and (3) endangering a proper appreciation of the need for the sacrament of ordination (see "Church and Ministry," *The Jurist* 43 [1983] 286–87). I agree with Komonchak, particularly with regard to his third point, and I would note as he does that it is the restriction of women from all ordained ministry and married men from the presbyterate that is at the root of this situation (p. 286). The refusal to ordain gifted and effective pastoral ministers and the growth of alternative liturgical communities among many who are alienated from the institutional church have begun to seriously undermine the credibility of the need for ordained ministers.

57. See 1 John 2:27 and John 14:26. Note Raymond Brown's discussion of Johannine pneumatology, the gift of every baptized Christian to teach in and through the power of the Paraclete, and the related disputes that arose in the Johannine community (*The Community of the Beloved Disciple* [New York: Paulist, 1979] 138–44).

58. Exploring the essential qualification for authentic preaching, namely, the authority of apostolicity, Sandra Schneiders remarks that "[a]lthough institutional criteria can be useful, they must not supplant the theological criteria of vocation, personal assimilation of the mystery of Christ that one preaches, and the gift of the Spirit (which must be cultivated through study and prayer) enabling the witness to bring the Word to event effectively and to evoke the crisis of faith in the hearers" ("The New Testament Foundations for Preaching by the Non Ordained," 86).

For women's descriptions of their "call to preach" and their understanding of authority in preaching, see Carol M. Norén, *The Woman in the Pulpit* (Nashville: Abingdon, 1991) 14–29 and 46–61; see also Judith L. Weidman, introduction to *Women Ministers*, 7–11.

A central issue remains: how local communities invite and confirm preachers as well as whether and how charisms are tested in a community. Janet Riggle Huie speaks of women trusting the authority of their imaginations and "gradually earning authority from congregations as members experience [them] as [persons] who can be trusted to tell the truth in word and deed" ("Preaching through Metaphor," in Weidman, *Women Ministers*, 50, 56). Note, in contrast, that womanist theologian Katie Cannon claims that "the preacher must communicate that the authority for the sermon emanates from a guiding force beyond the preacher, in God.... Black preaching concentrates a lot of attention on Jesus, who acts decisively and speaks pointedly" ("Womanist Interpretation and Preaching in the Black Church," 330).

For feminist critiques of traditional notions of the authority to preach and an emphasis instead on the authenticity of what is preached and faith sharing that transforms both speaker and listeners, see Christine Smith, *Weaving the Sermon: Preaching in a Feminist Perspective* (Louisville: Westminster/John Knox, 1989) 46–47, and Procter-Smith, *In Her Own Rite* (intro, n. 7, above) 132. See also Letty Russell's discussion of authority exercised in community and "authority of purpose" as opposed to "authority of clerical privilege" in *Church in the Round* (chap. 2, n. 35, above) 46–74; and Schüssler Fiorenza, *Discipleship of Equals.*

59. While the New Testament does ground the legitimacy of the ordering of ministries in the church by competent authorities, Schneiders remarks that "this administrative activity is for the sake of effective proclamation of the Word and is abused when it is used to limit unnecessarily the freedom of Christians to exercise the gifts they have received from the Spirit for the building up of the Church" ("New Testament Foundations for Preaching by the Non-Ordained," 85).

60. See Collins, "The Baptismal Roots of the Preaching Ministry."

61. Schüssler Fiorenza, "Claiming Our Authority and Power: The Ekklesia of Women and Ecclesiastical Patriarchy," in *Discipleship of Equals,* 247. On the question of Jesus' exercise of authority, see also Yves Congar, *Power and Poverty in the Church,* trans. Jennifer Nicholson (Baltimore: Helicon, 1964).

62. O'Meara, *Theology of Ministry,* 187. Both Power and Komonchak also argue against a false dichotomy of charismatic versus ordained ministries (see Power, *Gifts That Differ,* 113–32; Komonchak, " 'Non-ordained' and 'Ordained' Ministers," 48–49).

63. O'Meara, *Theology of Ministry,* 185. Komonchak also points out that according to the basic principles of ecclesiology of Vatican II, the hierarchy's role is "more discernment and coordination than delegation and subordination" (" 'Non-ordained' and 'Ordained' Ministers in the Local Church," 44). See n. 43.

64. For description of both patriarchy and clericalism in terms of "group bias," see Mary Collins, "The Refusal of Women in Clerical Circles," in *Women in the Church,* vol. 1, ed. Madonna Kolbenschlag (Washington, D.C.: Pastoral Press, 1987) 51–63; and Johnson, *SHE WHO IS* (chap. 2, n. 30, above) 13–16, 22–33.

65. *The Church History of Eusebius* 6.19.18.

66. See Maureen Carroll and Kathleen Cannon, "Enfleshing the Word: The Case for Lay Preachers," *Liturgy* 24 (1979) 31–34; Sarah Ann Fairbanks, "Liturgical Preaching by Women: A New Sign Language of Salvation," *The Way Supplement* 83 (1995) 131–40; Barbara Brown Zikmund, "Women as Preachers: Adding New Dimensions to Worship," *Journal of Women and Religion* 3 (1984) 12–16, 56; and Norén, *Woman in the Pulpit.*

Chapter 10 / The Good News in Different Voices

1. Carol Gilligan later nuanced the thesis of her influential book *In a Different Voice: Psychological Theory and Women's Development* (Cambridge, Mass.: Harvard University Press, 1982), which challenged Kohlberg's theory of moral development and claimed that women resolve moral dilemmas more on the basis of a relational "ethic of care" than on universal principles of justice. In more recent writings Gilligan admits that women as well as men do draw on an ethic of justice and that the two systems of ethical evaluation are not polar opposites. See Gilligan, "Moral Orientation and Moral Development," in *Women and Moral Theory*, ed. Eva Feder Kittay and Diana Meyers (Totowa, N.J.: Rowman and Littlefield, 1987) 19–33. See also Carol Gilligan et al., eds., *Mapping the Moral Domain: A Contribution of Women's Thinking to Psychological Theory and Education* (Cambridge, Mass.: Harvard University Press, 1988), and Carol Gilligan, Nona P. Lyons, and Trudy J. Hanmer, eds., *Making Connections: The Relational World of Adolescent Girls at Emma Willard School* (Cambridge, Mass.: Harvard University Press, 1990). For a helpful review of the literature related to Gilligan's work, see Cynthia Crysdale, "Gilligan and the Ethics of Care: An Update," *Religious Studies Review* 20 (1994) 21–28. See also Cynthia Crysdale, "Gilligan's Epistemological Challenge: Implications for Method in Ethics," *Irish Theological Quarterly* 56 (1990) 31–48; idem, "Horizons That Differ: Women and Men and the Flight from Understanding," *Cross Currents* (1994) 345–61; and Linda K. Kerber et al., "On *In a Different Voice*: An Interdisciplinary Forum," *Signs: Journal of Women in Culture and Society* 11 (1986) 304–33.

2. See the next section of this chapter.

3. Aimee Semple McPherson, "Live Wire — Beware! A Divine Healing Sermon," in *And Blessed Is She* (chap. 9, n. 5, above) 50–51.

4. Mark A. Matthews, "Virility in the Ministry," *Western Recorder* 94, no. 38 (June 26, 1919) 2, as quoted in Betty A. DeBerg, *Ungodly Women: The First Wave of American Fundamentalism* (Minneapolis: Fortress, 1990) 87–88.

5. Norén, *The Woman in the Pulpit* (chap. 9, n. 58, above) 9.

6. Smith, *Weaving the Sermon* (chap. 9, n. 58, above) 11–13. See also Edwina Hunter, "Weaving Life's Experiences into Women's Preaching," *Christian Ministry* (1987) 14–17.

7. Smith, *Weaving the Sermon*, 25. Smith's survey of women's psychology included Carol Tavris and Carole Wade, *The Longest War: Sex Differences in Perspective* (San Diego: Harcourt Brace Jovanovich, 1977; Ann Bedford Ulanov, *Receiving Woman: Studies in the Psychology and Theology of the Feminine* (Philadelphia: Westminster, 1981); Gilligan, *In a Different Voice*; Nancy Chodorow, *The Reproduction of Mothering: The Psychoanalysis and the Sociology of Gender* (Berkeley: University of California Press, 1978); Jean Baker Miller, *Toward a New Psychology of Women* (Boston: Beacon, 1976); and Luise Eichenbaum and Susie Orbach, *Understanding Women: A Feminist Psychoanalytic Approach* (New York: Basic Books, 1983). For more recent discussion of feminist psychology and potential connections with theological anthropology, see Ann O'Hara Graff, "Strategies for Life: Learning from Feminist Psychology,"

in *In the Embrace of God* (chap. 2, n. 28, above) 122–37. A number of other essays in that volume also draw on resources from feminist psychology.

8. See note 1.

9. Smith, *Weaving the Sermon*, 40. For further discussion of women's experience from an ethical perspective, see Susan L. Secker, "Human Experience and Women's Experience: Resources for Catholic Ethics," in *Readings in Moral Theology*, vol. 8: *Dialogue about Catholic Sexual Teaching*, ed. Charles E. Curran and Richard A. McCormick (New York: Paulist, 1993) 577–99. Secker asserts that the work of Gilligan, Belenky, and their colleagues "has confirmed that relationality and connected knowing are characteristic for many women of our moral development process and hence, of our way of arriving at moral truth" (592).

10. Janice Riggle Huie, "Preaching through Metaphor," in *Women Ministers: How Women Are Redefining Traditional Roles* (chap. 9, n. 34) 51–52.

11. Ibid., 52.

12. Kelly, "Preaching in the Black Tradition" (chap. 9, n. 34, above) 72.

13. Cheryl J. Sanders, "The Woman as Preacher," in *African-American Religious Studies* (chap. 2, n. 39, above) 372–91.

14. Katie G. Cannon,"Womanist Interpretation and Preaching in the Black Church," in *Searching the Scriptures* (chap. 2, n. 38, above) 326–37.

15. Smith, *Weaving the Sermon*, 10, 26–27.

16. The term "feminist theology" is problematic in itself both because such great diversity exists within approaches to the field (hence, feminist theolog*ies*) and because the term "feminist" is often associated primarily or exclusively with white, middle-class, highly educated women. For brief discussion and bibliography, see Susan A. Ross and Mary Catherine Hilkert, "Feminist Theology: A Review of Literature," *Theological Studies* 56 (1995) 327–30; and Mary Aquin O'Neill, "The Nature of Women and the Method of Theology," *Theological Studies* 56 (1995) 730–42. For more developed analysis, see Maria Riley, *Transforming Feminism* (New York: Sheed and Ward, 1989); Schneiders, *Beyond Patching* (chap. 5, n. 3, above); and Chopp, *The Power to Speak* (chap. 2, n. 31, above) 107–28. For overviews of feminist theory, see Chopp, *The Power to Speak*; Mary Ann Zimmer, "Stepping Stones in Feminist Theory," in *In the Embrace of God* (chap. 2, n. 28, above) 7–21; and Rosemarie Tong, *Feminist Thought: A Comprehensive Introduction* (Boulder, Colo.: Westview, 1989). On the question of diversity within women's experience, see Ann O'Hara Graff, "The Struggle to Name Women's Experience," in *In the Embrace of God*, 71–89; Mary Ann Hinsdale, "Heeding the Voices," in *In the Embrace of God*, 22–48; María Pilar Aquino, "Including Women's Experience," in *In the Embrace of God*, 51–70; Shawn Copeland, "The Interaction of Racism, Sexism, and Classism in Women's Exploitation," in *Women, Work, and Poverty*, vol. 194 of *Concilium*, ed. Elisabeth Schüssler Fiorenza and Anne E. Carr (Edinburgh: T. & T. Clark, 1987) 19–27; Grant, *White Women's Christ and Black Women's Jesus* (chap. 7, n. 13, above) 195–230; Hayes, *Hagar's Daughters* (chap. 2, n. 39, above); Susan Secker, "Women's Experience in Feminist Theology: The 'Problem' or 'Truth' of Difference," *Journal of Hispanic/Latino*

Theology 1 (1993) 56–67; and Jeanette Rodriguez, "Experience as a Resource for Feminist Thought," *Journal of Hispanic/Latino Theology* 1 (1993) 68–76.

17. Elizabeth Johnson attributes the image to Rosemary Radford Ruether (see *SHE WHO IS*, 32).

18. For further discussion of the notion of gender, including challenges to the notion that gender is socially constructed but sex is a biological category, see the bibliography in note 35.

19. Huie, "Preaching through Metaphor," 52.

20. Edwina Hunter, introduction to *And Blessed Is She*, 91.

21. A phrase used by Rebecca Chopp in the lecture "Naming God and the Poetics of Desire" (Eden Theological Seminary, St. Louis, Missouri, March 7, 1990). See Chopp, "Feminism's Theological Pragmatics: A Social Naturalism of Women's Experience," *Journal of Religion* 67 (1987) 239–56; and idem, *The Power to Speak*.

22. See Ruether, *New Woman, New Earth* (chap. 2, n. 28, above) 137–61; idem, "The Female Nature of God: A Problem in Contemporary Religious Life," in *God as Father?*, vol. 143 of *Concilium*, ed. J. B. Metz and E. Schillebeeckx (New York: Seabury, 1981) 61–66. For critique of the Jungian approach to the binary distinctions masculine/feminine, see Naomi Goldenberg, "A Feminist Critique of Jung," *Signs* (1976) 443–49. Note also Conn, *Women's Spirituality* (chap. 7, n. 6, above) 1–2; Mary Grey, *Feminism, Redemption, and the Christian Tradition* (Mystic, Conn.: Twenty-Third, 1990) 25–30.

23. See Sandra M. Schneiders, "The Effects of Women's Experience on Their Spirituality," *Spirituality Today* 35 (1983) 100–116. Note also Thomas Hoyt Jr.'s assertion: "It is almost axiomatic that in interpreting Scripture those who are marginalized and those who have more of a stake in the status quo would bring a different set of questions to the text" ("Interpreting Biblical Scholarship for the Black Church Tradition," in *Stony the Road We Trod* [chap. 5, n. 10, above] 29).

24. See P. Frostin, "The Hermeneutics of the Poor — The Epistemological 'Break' in Third World Theologies," *Studia Theologica* 39 (1985) 127–50; Lee Cormie, "The Hermeneutical Privilege of the Oppressed: Liberation Theologies, Biblical Faith, and Marxist Sociology of Knowledge," *Proceedings of the Catholic Theological Society of America* 33 (1978) 155–81; and Ivone Gebara, "Option for the Poor as an Option for the Poor Woman," in *Women, Work, and Poverty*, 110–17.

25. Moltmann with Meeks, "The Liberation of Oppressors" (chap. 7, n. 4, above) 316. See also Norbert Greinacher, "Liberation Theology in the 'First World'?" in vol. 187 of *Concilium* (1986) 81–90. Robert McAfee Brown calls for a similar conversion: "Our starting point should involve a new attempt to see ourselves and our world through eyes other than our own, and to move from that new angle of vision to the beginning of acts of identification with the oppressed, putting bodies where words alone were once put" (*Is Faith Obsolete?* [Philadelphia: Westminster, 1974] 135–36).

26. See chapter 7 for discussion of the theology of the cross and specifically the critical issues raised by feminist theologians regarding the traditional models of atonement and sacrifice. While the symbol of the cross can be, and has

been, misused, the proclamation of the death and resurrection of Jesus is at the heart of the Christian faith and of all Christian preaching. Thus it is essential for preachers to consider critically the theology of the cross from which they preach. For feminists who are in many ways the dominants in social systems, this involves reflection on the meaning of the cross not only in terms of the suffering and abuse of women as women but also in terms of the call to *kenosis* as regards power, privilege, and status. I am grateful to Shawn Copeland for her insights on this.

27. Procter-Smith, *In Her Own Rite* (intro, n. 7, above) 129.

28. For the distinctions that follow, see Pamela Dickey Young, *Feminist Theology/Christian Theology: In Search of Method* (Minneapolis: Fortress, 1990) 49–69; and Anne E. Carr, "The New Vision of Feminist Theology," in *Freeing Theology* (chap. 2, n. 30, above) 24–25. In "Feminist Theology: A Review of the Literature" (see n. 16, above), the authors distinguish between women's "bodily, socialized, psychological, historical, religious, political, cultural, racial, class, and economic experience" (328). Another frequent reference in feminist literature is to women's experiences of friendship. See Elisabeth Schüssler Fiorenza, "Why Not the Category Friend/Friendship?" *Horizons* 2, no. 1 (1975) 117–18; Carr, *Transforming Grace* (chap. 2, n. 30, above) 201–14; Mary Hunt, *Fierce Tenderness: A Feminist Theology of Friendship* (New York: Crossroad, 1991) esp. 80–84; Johnson, *SHE WHO IS* (chap. 5, n. 13, above) esp. 144–46; McFague, *Models of God* (chap. 2, n. 28, above) esp. 157–80.

For discussion of the real differences in women's experiences, see the bibliography in note 16. Note also Elizabeth Johnson's discussion of human experience in terms of "the interdependence of multiple differences" in "The Maleness of Christ," in *The Special Nature of Women?* vol. 1991/6 of *Concilium,* ed. Anne Carr and Elisabeth Schüssler Fiorenza (Philadelphia: Trinity Press International, 1991) 108–16. For critique of the universal term "women's experience," see Sheila Greeve Davaney, "The Limits of the Appeal to Women's Experience," in *Shaping New Vision: Gender and Values in American Culture,* ed. Clarissa W. Atkinson, Constance H. Buchanan, and Margaret Miles (Ann Arbor, Mich.: UMI Research Press, 1987) 31–49.

29. See Johnson, "The Incomprehensibility of God and the Image of God Male and Female" (chap. 2, n. 34, above) 441–80; and *SHE WHO IS* for specific references to God as female in the Bible and classic Christian writers as well as for further bibliography.

30. Note, for example, that one of the seven biblical readings selected by the Roman Catholic lectionary for use at the Easter Vigil liturgy refers to "the defilement of a menstruous woman" as a parallel for Israel's defilement (Ez 36:16–28, at verse 17). See also Trible, *Texts of Terror* (chap. 5, note 8, above).

31. See, for example, Margaret Moers Wenig, "God Is a Woman and She Is Growing Older," *Reform Judaism* 21, no. 1 (1992) 26–28, 44–45.

32. Carr, "The New Vision of Feminist Theology," 23.

33. See chapter 5.

34. See, for example, FitzGerald, "Impasse and Dark Night" (chap. 7, n. 6, above); Conn, *Women's Spirituality;* and the references to Christian feminist spirituality in chapter 9, n. 3.

35. Recent work on gender analysis by sociologists and anthropologists focuses not on the uniqueness of women's experience but on the difference gender makes in social organization and interaction. The literature challenges the traditional twofold distinction of sex as biologically determined and gender as socially constructed. Some have proposed a threefold distinction of "sex" (socially agreed upon biological criteria for classifications of male and female), "sex category" (socially constructed categories for understanding masculinity and femininity in a given society), and "gender" (a term that is constantly being redefined in social interaction). To "do gender" is not always to correspond with normative categories of masculinity and femininity. See Candace West and Don H. Zimmerman, "Doing Gender," in *The Social Construction of Gender,* ed. Judith Lorber and Susan A. Farrell (Newbury Park, Calif.: Sage, 1991) 33, as quoted by Catherine Vincie in "Gender Analysis and Christian Initiation," *Worship* 69 (1995) 507. Vincie's article offers a helpful overview of recent sociological and anthropological literature on sex and gender as well as an exploration of the connection between ritual and gender. Consult Vincie's article for further bibliography. See also Teresa del Valle, *Gendered Anthropology* (London: Routledge, 1993); Sue Rosenberg Zalk and Janice Gordon-Kelter, *Revolutions in Knowledge: Feminism in the Social Sciences* (Boulder, Colo.: Westview, 1992); Suzanne G. Frayse, *Varieties of Sexual Experience: An Anthropological Perspective on Human Sexuality* (New Haven: HRAF, 1985); Pamela R. Frese and John M. Coggeshall, eds., *Transcending Boundaries: Multidisciplinary Approaches to the Study of Gender* (New York: Bergin and Garvey, 1991); Lorber and Farrell, *The Social Construction of Gender;* Barbara Diane Miller, ed., *Sex and Gender Hierarchies* (Cambridge: Cambridge University Press, 1993); Henrietta A. Moore, *Feminism and Anthropology* (Minneapolis: University of Minnesota Press, 1988); and Sandra Morgan, ed., *Gender and Anthropology: Critical Reviews for Research and Teaching* (Washington, D.C.: American Anthropological Association, 1989).

36. See Copeland, "The Interaction of Racism, Sexism, and Classism in Women's Exploitation"; Irene Monroe, ed., "The Intersection of Racism and Sexism: Theological Perspectives of African American Women," *Journal of Women and Religion* 9–10 (1990–91) 7–101; Susan Brooks Thistlethwaite, *Sex, Race, and God: Christian Feminism in Black and White* (New York: Crossroad, 1989); T. Cordova et al., *Chicana Voices: Intersections of Class, Race, and Gender* (Austin, Tex.: Center for Mexican American Studies, 1986); b. hooks, *Talking Back: Thinking Feminist, Thinking Black* (Boston: South End, 1989); E. Ngan-Ling Chow, "The Feminist Movement: Where Are All the Asian American Women?" in *Making Waves: An Anthology of Writings by and about Asian American Women,* ed. Asian Women United of California (Boston: Beacon, 1989); Secker, "Women's Experience in Feminist Theology"; and Rodriguez, "Experience as a Resource for Feminist Thought."

37. "Lift Every Voice" is the title of the Negro national anthem written by James Weldon and J. Rosamund Johnson and adopted as the title of the book *Lift Every Voice: Constructing Christian Theologies from the Underside* (chap. 2, n. 38, above). The title of the volume *Stony the Road We Trod* is taken

from the second verse of the same hymn. The full text of the hymn is available in *Lead Me, Guide Me* (chap. 2, n. 39, above) no. 291.

38. See Copeland, "The Interaction of Racism, Sexism, and Classism in Women's Exploitation."

39. See Barbara Hilkert Andolsen, *Daughters of Jefferson, Daughters of Bookblacks: Racism and American Feminism* (Macon, Ga.: Mercer University Press, 1986); Thistlethwaite, *Sex, Race, and God;* Grant, *White Women's Christ and Black Women's Jesus;* Moltmann and Meeks, "Liberation of Oppressors"; Robert McAfee Brown, *Is Faith Obsolete?;* idem, *Creative Dislocation* (Nashville: Abingdon, 1980).

40. Justo L. González and Catherine G. González, *Liberation Preaching: The Pulpit and the Oppressed* (Nashville: Abingdon, 1980).

41. Boff, *When Theology Listens to the Poor* (see chap. 2, n. 21, above) ix.

42. See Schüssler Fiorenza, *Bread Not Stone* (chap. 5, n. 7, above) 1–22; Weems, "Reading *Her Way* through the Struggle" (chap. 5, n. 10, above) 55–77; Sheilah Briggs, "Can an Enslaved God Liberate? Hermeneutical Reflections on Philippians 2:6–11," *Semeia* 47 (1989) 137–53; Alison M. Cheek, "Shifting the Paradigm: Feminist Bible Study," in *Searching the Scriptures* (chap. 2, n. 38, above) 338–50; Lieve Troch, "A Method of Conscientization: Feminist Bible Study in the Netherlands," in *Searching the Scriptures,* 351–66; and Carol J. Schlueter, "Feminist Homilies: Strategies for Empowerment," in *Women's Visions: Theological Reflection, Celebration, Action,* ed. Ofelia Ortega (Geneva: WCC Publications, 1995) 138–51.

43. Copeland, "The Interaction of Racism, Sexism, and Classism in Women's Exploitation," 26. See also idem, "Toward a Critical Christian Feminist Theology of Solidarity," in *Women and Theology,* ed. Mary Ann Hinsdale and Phyllis H. Kaminski (Maryknoll, N.Y.: Orbis Books, 1995) 3–38; and Jon Sobrino, "Bearing with One Another in Faith: A Theological Analysis of Christian Solidarity," in *The Principle of Mercy: Taking the Crucified People from the Cross* (Maryknoll, N.Y.: Orbis Books, 1995) 144–72.

44. See Joe Holland and Peter Henriot, *Social Analysis: Linking Faith and Justice,* rev. ed. (Maryknoll, N.Y.: Orbis Books, 1985); Maria Riley, *Transforming Feminism,* chap. 3; and T. Howland Sanks and John A. Coleman, eds., *Reading the Signs of the Times* (Mahwah, N.J.: Paulist, 1993).

45. Michael Scanlon, "Language and Praxis: Recent Theological Trends," *Proceedings of the Catholic Theological Society of America* 43 (1988) 83.

46. See Paolo Freire, *Pedagogy of the Oppressed,* anniversary edition, trans. Myra Bergman Ramos (New York: Continuum, 1993) esp. 75–118.

47. Daly, *Beyond God the Father* (chap. 9, n. 3, above) 8.

48. Belenky et al., *Women's Ways of Knowing* (chap. 5, n. 45, above). See also Sölle, *Suffering* (chap. 7, n. 4, above) 61–86.

49. Belenky et al., *Women's Ways of Knowing,* 15.

50. On the importance for women to "name [their] own experience" and to "create the stories of [their] own becoming," see Rebecca Chopp, *The Power to Speak,* esp. chap. 4; and Carolyn Heilbrun, *Writing a Woman's Life* (New York: Norton, 1988).

51. Audre Lorde, "The Transformation of Silence into Language and Action," *Sister Outsider* (Freedom, Calif.: The Crossing Press, 1984) 43.

52. The title is taken from the poem "The Hidden Sun" by the Japanese woman Hiratsuka Raicho. "In her poem, she claims that 'originally woman was the sun. She was an authentic person. But now woman is the moon.' That means once Asian women were self-defining women but now they have become dependent women defined by men in their lives. Therefore she perceives Asian women's struggle for liberation as 'Struggle to Be the Sun Again' " (Chung Hyun Kyung, *Struggle to Be the Sun Again* [Maryknoll, N.Y.: Orbis Books, 1993] frontispiece).

53. Isasi-Díaz and Tarango, *Hispanic Women* (chap. 2, n. 35, above) 98. See also Isasi-Díaz, *En La Lucha/In the Struggle* (chap. 2, n. 38, above).

54. Molari continues: "Numerous episodes in recent years provide us with much food for thought, but for me they all converge upon this fact: the people of God are asking to speak the Word. It would be a tragic error not to let them do so. An underground church would be born instead, or worse still, a church in the piazza to which the priest would no longer have access. A new division in the Church would arise and through our own fault. A division which yet again would find in the Eucharist its own pain and its own condemnation" (Carlo Molari, *La Fede e il suo liguaggio* [Assisi: Cittadella Editrice, 1972] 280–84). I am grateful to John Dunn for the translation and for calling this text to my attention.

55. See chap. 2, nn. 28 and 36.

56. On this point, see especially Johnson, *SHE WHO IS;* Sandra M. Schneiders, *Women and the Word* (New York: Paulist, 1986); McFague, *Models of God* (chap. 2, n. 28, above); Mary Collins, "Naming God in Public Prayer," *Worship: Renewal to Practice* (chap. 2, n. 36, above) 215–29; Gail Ramshaw, *God beyond Gender: Feminist Christian God-Language* (Minneapolis: Fortress, 1995); idem, *"De Divinis Nominibus:* The Gender of God," *Worship* 56 (1982) 117–31; idem, "Naming the Trinity: Orthodoxy and Inclusivity," *Worship* 60 (1986) 491–98; Ruth Duck, *Gender and the Name of God: The Trinitarian Baptismal Formula* (New York: Pilgrim, 1991); Rebecca Oxford-Carpenter, "Gender and the Trinity," *Theology Today* 41 (1984) 7–25; Marjorie Suchocki, "The Unmale God: Reconsidering the Trinity," *Quarterly Review* 3, no. 1 (1983) 34–49; and LaCugna, "God in Communion with Us," in *Freeing Theology* (chap. 2, n. 30, above).

57. See, for example, anonymous, "God as Food for the Hungry," in *Feminist Theology from the Third World: A Reader,* ed. Ursula King (Maryknoll, N.Y.: Orbis Books, 1994) 259–60; Chung Hyun Kyung, *Struggle to Be the Sun Again,* 48–52, 72–73; Gustavo Gutiérrez, "Reflections from a Latin American Perspective: Finding Our Way to Talk about God," in *Irruption of the Third World: Challenge to Theology,* (chap. 2, n. 38, above) 222–34; Cone, *God of the Oppressed* (chap. 2, n. 39, above); and Isasi-Díaz and Tarango, *Hispanic Women,* esp. 12–59.

58. Nelle Morton, "A Word We Cannot Yet Speak," *The Journey Is Home* (Boston: Beacon, 1985) 87. The phrase comes originally from Sally Gearhart.

59. Ibid.

60. On this point, see Isasi-Díaz and Tarango, *Hispanic Women,* 107, and Procter-Smith, *In Her Own Rite,* 133.

Conclusion

1. Larry Kaufmann, "Hunting for the Treasure," *Challenge: Church and People* 24 (1994) 5.

2. Thomas Long uses this metaphor in *The Witness of Preaching* (Louisville: Westminster, 1989) 20–21. See also Mary Catherine Hilkert, "Bearing Wisdom: The Vocation of the Preacher," *Spirituality Today* 44 (1992) 143–60. For development of the metaphor with emphasis on the preacher as "facilitator of liberation," and with an accompanying homiletic methodology, see Theresa A. Rickard, "The Preacher as Midwife" (M.Div. thesis, Union Theological Seminary, 1993). For rich development of the birthing imagery in relation to preaching, see Joan Delaplane, "Birthing the Sunday Sermon," *Pulpit Digest* 72 (1991) 94–96.

3. Rickard, "The Preacher as Midwife," 3.

4. Exod 1:15–22 and Gen 38:27–30. See Rickard, "The Preacher as Midwife," 3–5; and Drorah O'Donnell Setel, "Exodus," in *The Women's Bible Commentary,* ed. Carol A. Newsome and Sharon H. Ringe (Louisville: John Knox, 1992) 30–31.

5. See Phyllis Trible, *God and the Rhetoric of Sexuality* (Philadelphia: Fortress, 1978).

6. Taken from Gerard Manley Hopkins, "God's Grandeur," in *Poems and Prose of Gerard Manley Hopkins* (Baltimore: Penguin Books, 1953) 27. The entire poem is a marvelous poetic expression of the sacramental imagination.

7. The activity of the Spirit both within and beyond the boundaries of the church is the theological foundation that grounds an approach to preaching as "naming the grace" in the community's human and/or religious experience. Such an approach applies to the context of evangelization or preaching among those who are not baptized as well as to preaching within the Christian community. A survey of recent works in pneumatology and the theology of grace is beyond the scope of this study, but the following resources suggest several diverse foundational works in this area: Karl Rahner, "Observations on the Problem of the Anonymous Christian," *Theological Investigations,* vol. 14, trans. David Bourke (London: Darton, Longman, and Todd, 1976) 280–94; idem, "Atheism and Implicit Christianity," *Theological Investigations,* vol. 9, trans. Graham Harrison (London: Darton, Longman, and Todd, 1972) 145–64; idem, "Anonymous Christianity and the Missionary Task of the Church," *Theological Investigations,* vol. 12, trans. David Bourke (London: Darton, Longman, and Todd, 1974) 161–78; idem, "Anonymous Christians," *Theological Investigations,* vol. 6, trans. Karl-H. and Boniface Kruger (Baltimore: Helicon Press, 1969) 390–97; Jürgen Moltmann, *The Spirit of Life: A Universal Affirmation,* trans. Margaret Kohl (Minneapolis: Fortress, 1992); Kilian McDonnell, "A Trinitarian Theology of the Holy Spirit?" *Theological Studies* 46 (1985) 191–227; idem, "The Determinative Doctrine of the Holy Spirit, *Theology Today* 39

(1982) 142–61; C. M. LaCugna and K. McDonnell, "Returning from 'The Far Country': Theses for a Contemporary Trinitarian Theology," *Scottish Journal of Theology* 41 (1988) 191–215; and Yves Congar, *The Word and the Spirit* (San Francisco: Harper and Row, 1986).

8. Mary Collins, "Eucharist and Justice," in *Worship: Renewal to Practice* (chap. 3, n. 19, above) 259. Here Collins is drawing on the insights of Clifford Geertz. See Geertz, *The Interpretation of Cultures* (New York: Basic Books, 1973) 89–100, 127.

9. Cooke, *Ministry to Word and Sacraments* (chap. 8, n. 9, above) 222.

10. Ibid., 220.

11. Oscar Romero, cited in James R. Brockman, *The Church Is All of You* (Minneapolis: Winston, 1984) 14.

12. The phrase is taken from the African-American spiritual "Wade in the Water"; text available in *Lead Me, Guide Me* (chap. 2, n. 39, above) 107. Cain Hope Felder notes that the verses of the spiritual combine the Old Testament Exodus motif of liberation with a provocative understanding of baptism as the New Testament parallel (see Felder, *Troubling Biblical Waters* [chap. 5, n. 19, above] xiii–xiv).

13. See Edward Yarnold, *The Awe-Inspiring Rites of Initiation: The Origins of the R.C.I.A.*, 2d ed. (Collegeville, Minn.: Liturgical Press, 1994).

14. For theological development of the claim that authentic human life is participation in the life of the Trinity, see Catherine Mowry LaCugna, *God for Us* (San Francisco: HarperCollins, 1991) esp. chaps. 8–10.

15. Paul Ricoeur, "The Language of Faith," in *The Philosophy of Paul Ricoeur* (chap. 6, n. 21, above) 237. For more theoretical discussion of this approach to imagination, consult Ricoeur's discussion of the semantic theory of imagination. See Ricoeur, "Imagination in Discourse and Action," in *Analecta Husserliana* 7, nos. 3–22 (ed. Tymieniecka); idem, "Metaphor and the Main Problem of Hermeneutics," and "The Language of Faith," in *The Philosophy of Paul Ricoeur*, 134–48, 223–38; idem, *The Rule of Metaphor* (chap. 6, n. 21, above); Brueggemann, *Finally Comes the Poet* (chap. 5, n. 5, above); idem, *The Prophetic Imagination* (intro., n. 8, above); Power, *Unsearchable Riches* (chap. 6, n. 28) esp. 190–92.

This notion of imagination has rich roots in the Jewish tradition. See Jacob Neusner, "Enchantment through Words," in *The Enchantments of Judaism: Rites of Transformation from Birth through Death* (New York: Basic Books, 1987) 3–12.

16. Georges Bernanos, *The Diary of a Country Priest*, trans. Pamela Morris (New York: Macmillan, 1962 [1937]) 255.

17. The phrase is taken from Wolfhart Pannenberg's writings on the resurrection.

18. Emily Dickinson, "This World Is Not Conclusion," in *Selected Poems and Letters of Emily Dickinson*, ed. Robert N. Linscott, (New York: Doubleday/ Anchor Books, 1959) 135.

19. McFague, *Metaphorical Theology* (chap. 2, n. 20, above) esp. preface and chap. 1. Note June O'Connor's response that both feminist religious thought

and process theology offer possibilities for a "new theology of sacramentality" ("Sensuality, Spirituality, Sacramentality," [chap. 2, n. 32, above]).

20. See David N. Power, *The Eucharistic Mystery: Revitalizing the Tradition* (New York: Crossroad, 1992) 304–27; Peter Hodgson, *God in History: Shapes of Freedom* (Nashville: Abingdon, 1989); Johnson, "Jesus and Salvation" (chap. 7, n. 10, above); Schillebeeckx, *Church* (chap. 2, n. 12, above) chaps. 1 and 2; and David Tracy, *Plurality and Ambiguity: Hermeneutics, Religion, Hope* (San Francisco: Harper and Row, 1987); idem, "Evil, Suffering and Hope: The Search for New Forms of Contemporary Theodicy," in *Proceedings of the Catholic Theological Society of America* 50 (1995) 15–36.

21. Mary Collins, "The Refusal of Women in Clerical Circles," in *Women in the Church,* ed. Madonna Kolbenschlag (Washington D.C.: Pastoral Press, 1987) 60.

22. See, for example, Schillebeeckx, *Christ* (chap. 2, n. 12, above) pt. 4; idem, "Resistance, Engagement and Celebration" (typewritten translation by Robert Schreiter of the original text, "Verzet, engagement en viering," which appeared in *Nieuwsbrief Stichting Edward Schillebeeckx* 5 [October 1992] 1–3); David Power, *The Eucharistic Mystery,* 304–49; further references in chapter 4, n. 11; and Mary Collins, "Critical Questions for Liturgical Theology" and "Eucharist and Justice," in *Worship: Renewal to Practice* (chap. 2, n. 35, above) esp. 115–32, and 247–63.

23. This language is borrowed from Nathan D. Mitchell (see "Who Is at the Table? Reclaiming Real Presence," *Commonweal* 122 [January 27, 1995] 14–15).

24. Ibid.

25. Mitchell, "Who Is at the Table?" 14, quoting Rahner, "Considerations on the Active Role of the Person in the Sacramental Event" (chap. 2, n. 10, above).

26. See David Tracy, "On Naming the Present," in *On Naming the Present: Reflections on God, Hermeneutics, and Church* (Maryknoll, N.Y.: Orbis Books, 1994) 3–24.

Index